Louis Dumont and Hierarchical Opposition

Methodology and History in Anthropology

General Editor: David Parkin, Director of the Institute of Social and Cultural Anthropology, University of Oxford

LOUIS DUMONT AND HIERARCHICAL OPPOSITION

Robert Parkin

Berghahn Books
New York • Oxford

First published in 2002 by

Berghahn Books

www.BerghahnBooks.com

©2002, 2009 Robert Parkin
First paperback edition published in 2009

Library of Congress Cataloging-in-Publication Data

Parkin, Robert.
    Louis Dumont and hierarchical opposition / Robert Parkin.
        p. cm. -- (Methodology and history in anthropology ; v.9)
    Includes bibliographical references and index.
    ISBN 978-1-57181-578-3 (hbk) -- ISBN 978-1-84545-647-4 (pbk)
        1. Structural anthropology. 2. Ethnology--India. 3. Kinship--India. 4. Dumont, Louis,
    1911-   5. Hertz, Robert, 1881-1915. I. Title. II. Series.

GN362 .P39 2002
305.8--dc21   2002025599

British Library Cataloguing in Publication Data

A catalogue record for this book is available from the British Library

Printed in the United States on acid-free paper

ISBN 978-1-57181-578-1 hardback
ISBN 978-1-84545-647-4 paperback

CONTENTS

PREFACE

The genesis of this book lies many years back. In 1983, a conference was held in Oxford to discuss the ethnographic usefulness of Dumont's ideas of encompassment, value and hierarchical opposition. Although I did not take a direct part in the conference myself, a quirk of fate led me to act as both publisher and co-editor, in a very junior capacity, of the conference proceedings (see Barnes et al. 1985). This experience stimulated me to delve further into the matters then raised, and, as time allowed over the next few years, I began reading around the topic as widely as possible. This led to me writing extensively on it in the late 1980s and early 1990s while at the Free University of Berlin, where I also lectured on it on occasion.

As a result, a history began to emerge of the genesis of Dumont's ideas, especially in so far as they represented a reaction to the approaches to the notion of binary opposition propagated by Robert Hertz early in the twentieth century and continued by Rodney Needham some fifty years later. This led ultimately to a study of Hertz himself, drawing partly on archival materials in Paris that I had an opportunity to examine in the early 1990s. This was progressively developed as a single manuscript that included much of the present work. For reasons of size, however, I was eventually compelled to divide the work. One part concentrated on Hertz's life and career and the intellectual response to his work (now published as Parkin 1995a). The other was to focus on the subsequent development of one of his articles, that on the symbolism of the right hand (Hertz 1909), by Needham and more especially by Dumont and his some of followers and fellow travellers. It is this latter part, further revised at intervals in an even busier period of my life from the mid-1990s, that forms the present work.

One result of this history is that most of this book was written before Dumont's death in 1998. In general, in revising the text for publication subsequently I have retained the present tense as much as possible, not least in the belief that Dumont's ideas are still relevant, even urgent. This is not, however, an intellectual biography of Dumont himself, nor an assessment of his work as a whole—which is perhaps still premature—but an attempt to evaluate the inspirations and ramifications of a key aspect of his thought which has been both influential and contested. I hope to show that, although in most respects a structuralist, Dumont was far from being a slavish imitator of Lévi-Strauss, even though this equally great figure was an early influence on Dumont's work on both kinship and India; and that his conversion of the latter's binary asymmetries into hierarchical oppositions in which one pole ordinarily encompasses the other has deservedly created its own intellectual legacy. But also, however structuralist and ideologically focused his anthropology may have been, Dumont kept a place for the empirical as well as the ideological: indeed, his model of hierarchical opposition can be seen as a means of relating the two. A significant part of Dumont's achievement has therefore been to retain and develop structuralism by incorporating rather than excluding the empirical, as Lévi-Strauss often does quite explicitly. This is one of the reasons Dumont continues to claim our attention.

The desire to give adequate coverage to Hertz's article on right and left in both halves of the original work has occasioned the duplication of some pages (principally in Chapter 1 of the present work), and I am grateful to the publishers of the earlier volume, Harwood Academic Publishers, for permission to do this. Other parts of the present work have also previously appeared in print (see Parkin 1992a, 1994); I am grateful to the editors of *Recherches Sociologiques* and my co-editors on the *Journal of the Anthropological Society of Oxford* for allowing material then published to be incorporated here. In the course of writing this book, Maurice Godelier and Serge Tcherkézoff gave me invaluable help and support in arranging two research trips to Paris, in spring 1992 and early summer 1993, for which they are duly thanked here. These were funded by the Centre National de la Recherche Scientifique (CNRS), and I also acknowledge the help of Hinnerck Bruhns of CNRS in this regard. Serge Tcherkézoff was also kind enough to read parts of the manuscript at a relatively early stage. This not only reassured me in respect of certain intellectual issues, but also helped me through the organizational thicket of Parisian anthropology. I have also benefited over the years from discussions of these topics with N.J. Allen, Cécile Barraud, Daniel de Coppet, André Iteanu, Josep Llobera and Chris McDonaugh.

In citing passages from works originally published in French, I have used published translations where these exist, except in the case of Dumont 1991, which was only published in translation after the bulk of this work had been written. Passages from this work and from texts for which there is no published translation have been translated by myself.

R.J.P.
Oxford
May 2002

Chapter 1

INTRODUCTION

The long career of Louis Dumont, spanning over half a century till his death in 1998, simultaneously represented forward-looking innovation, continuity with the past, and parallelism with the work of his contemporaries. In his analyses of Indian and later European ideologies, he developed and exploited the notion of hierarchical opposition as a clear departure from the essentially neo-Aristotelian and neo-Kantian tradition of dichotomy pursued by his Durkheimian forebears (most explicitly Robert Hertz) and his near contemporary Rodney Needham. However, continuity was also present in the form of an interest in the phenomenon of opposition. Also, Dumont's comparisons between India and the west were at the same time comparisons between what he called non-modern and modern societies, thus continuing that aspect of the Durkheimian tradition which opposed the two in broad terms in a manner that could also be, and was, set in an evolutionary sequence.

The present book is not an intellectual biography (unlike my earlier work on Hertz, to some extent; Parkin 1995a) and it therefore does not aim to cover all aspects of Dumont's work or career. However, it does focus on what is arguably his most innovative and productive idea: the notion of hierarchical opposition. What I therefore discuss is its nature and where it differs from other, more conventional notions of opposition (Chapter 3); its genesis in Dumont's work on India, and how he used it to say something about the contradictions in the (at first sight) anti-hierarchical ideology of the west (Chapter 4); its initial reception by the rest of the academic community, which has not always restricted itself to matters scholarly but has occasionally gone so far as to question Dumont's moral commitments (Chapter 5); the work of some of Dumont's colleagues and followers, especially Daniel de Coppet, Serge Tcherkézoff, Cécile Barraud and André Iteanu, in developing

---

Notes for this section can be found on page 14.

his ideas, which they have applied in particular to the analysis of ritual (Chapter 6); and the further shift in focus made by certain members of this original group to the interpretation of whole cosmologies (in which a consideration of ritual nonetheless remains important), though the group as a whole began to differ among themselves on certain matters of interpretation (Chapter 7). This chapter also considers the relevance of hierarchical opposition to the relationship between ritual activities based on cosmological ideas and the economic activities that support such activities.

It will also be shown how hierarchical opposition might clarify the interpretation of many quite varied bodies of ethnographic data, even where the authors of existing interpretations have either been explicitly reluctant to go down that path or have simply ignored, or been innocent of, Dumont's model. This leads directly into a discussion of the applicability of hierarchical opposition in the study of ethnicity, where it has hardly featured thus far (Chapter 8).

The first two chapters are not so much exegetical, as designed to set the scene in respect of the proximate intellectual history of hierarchical opposition. The remaining sections of the present chapter concentrate on Dumont's roots in the Durkheimian school, which is based chiefly on his discovery of Mauss, whose courses he followed and who seems to have inspired him more than anyone else in Parisian intellectual circles at that time. Mauss clearly played a major part in Dumont's long-term conversion from menial museum employee in the 1930s into major structuralist voice in the 1950s and after (see Allen 1998). In fact, Dumont's career was an unusual one in many other respects, such as his relatively late start in taking up intellectual pursuits; his original interest in culture-history projects—his original reason for going to India in 1948; his learning Sanskrit in a German POW camp from a German Sanskritist; the confirmation of his conversion to structuralism while in India, simply because he felt it was the best way of interpreting his Indian material; and his sojourn at Oxford from 1951 to 1955, which gave him a better insight into British anthropology than most of his French contemporaries (see Dumont 1984; Allen 1998).

One of the major representatives of this British anthropology in the 1960s and 1970s (that is, after Dumont's departure from Oxford) was Rodney Needham, who was himself greatly inspired by the Durkheimian tradition, including its partial continuation under Lévi-Strauss. This interest was reflected not only in his own work but in his many translating activities. As is well known, Needham's explicit admiration of Lévi-Strauss was rewarded by the latter having the effrontery to contradict him in the preface he wrote for Needham's own translation of *Les structures élémentaires de la parenté* (1949; translated 1969). What is less well known is that this history broadly repeated itself with respect to Dumont, to whom Needham dedicated a major early double article on kinship (1966, 1967, at 1966: 141 n. 1). Despite this encomium, Dumont did not hesitate to criticize Needham as typifying the sort of approach to binary opposition (or, in Needham's terms, 'dual symbolic classification') that he regarded as fundamentally mistaken and advocated replacing. On this occasion, Needham himself launched an extended reply to both Dumont and Tcherkézoff, another critic coming from the same direction (1987). Chapter 2 therefore concentrates not only on attempting to establish Needham's ideas on this issue, but also on matching them to the criticisms of others (discussion of Dumont's own critique is deferred to Chapter 3). Chapter 9, finally, attempts to sum up the legacies of both Hertz and Dumont in this area, and to draw lessons from the foregoing chapters.

The informed reader will no doubt notice the relative lack of any discussion of Lévi-Strauss in these pages, despite the importance of binary opposition in his own work. In fact he is not totally absent, and I have sought on occasion to show where some of his examples actually indicate the existence of a hierarchical opposition, despite his reluctance to develop the point. But present-day anthropology requires yet another exegesis of his ideas far less than it needs a clear demonstration of Dumont's approach and of its centrality to what has developed into a distinctive, though related, intellectual lineage. This lineage has the same roots as Lévi-Strauss's in so far as links with Durkheim and Mauss are concerned; but it also notices Hertz more, as well as Needham, in the very act of criticizing them, as well as incorporating not only Dumont himself, but a significant collection of followers and fellow-travellers.

The work of the latter also represents a partial return to Durkheim in being more interested in ritual and what it can do than in belief and myth in the manner of Lévi-Strauss. However, the main difference is in what we mean by opposition and distinction: in the Dumontian school, Lévi-Strauss's binary opposition and Needham's dual symbolic classification have been replaced by a model which stresses value instead of asymmetry, ideological levels instead of contexts, and the encompassment of levels instead of the equivalence of contexts. This model is hierarchical opposition.

Even the none-too-attentive reader will also quickly realize that, in general, I have a great deal of sympathy for Dumont's project, and a great deal less for the attacks of his detractors, which often appear misdirected, if not naïve, and in any case based on a more or less total lack of understanding of Dumont's position. I ought to make some attempt to justify this specifically here, though as I cannot be terribly original I shall endeavour to be straightforward instead. I have tried particularly hard to be fair to those Dumont has criticized, especially

Hertz and Needham, since the latter has perhaps been exposed to Dumont's criticisms (and others from this direction, especially from Tcherkézoff) more than anyone else. But ultimately I find Dumont's approach convincing overall, and I would agree with him that many of his colleagues have neglected at least some aspects of difference that Dumont calls hierarchical. As far as the latter point is concerned, this is confirmed by the relative ease with which hierarchical oppositions can be demonstrated to exist even where authors have been reluctant to recognize them themselves, whether through opposition to the idea or uncertainty as to whether they really are involved (see especially below, Chapters 7 and 8).

Part of the problem here may be, as Dumont says, the egalitarian and individualistic ethos in which most of the practitioners in what is still institutionally a very Eurocentric subject have been conditioned. But Dumont himself has also contributed to the misunderstandings of his own model through his ambiguous use of certain key terms (especially 'hierarchy', but also 'levels', 'encompassment' etc.). Social scientists have a long history of appropriating words in the everyday language, altering their meanings in that language and applying them to their own, often quite different ends; Dumont is no exception in this respect. If the present book can clear up some of these difficulties, it will have served one of its major purposes.

In part too, my sympathy with Dumont stems from a basic if unseasonal readiness to continue to find value in Durkheimian sociology, to which Dumont adhered firmly, despite his attempts to develop it. While no anthropologist at the present day can be unaware of the entirely valid shift to process, action and agency in the subject in recent decades, not to say the postmodern turn, there is no convincing proof that these approaches on their own are capable of providing satisfactory accounts of human social life. No action that is not purely instinctive is completely unreflective: as Dumont himself remarked, 'actual men do not behave, they act with an idea in their heads' (1980: 6, emphases removed). Not even Weber himself, from whom action-based approaches ultimately derive, ignored the impact of social ideologies and representations. An anthropology that neglects these aspects is as lopsided as one that concentrates solely on it. [1]

The irony is that Dumont managed to bridge this divide himself better than most of his contemporaries (Bourdieu is one notable exception). This is due precisely to the model of hierarchical opposition that so many have found problematic. Although he was indubitably part of the Durkheim school through Mauss's teaching, Dumont was well aware, as Allen reminds us (1998), of the ideas of Weber and Parsons, to which I would add certain American anthropologists of the German tradition like Kluckhohn. Although privileging ideology over practice in the Durkheimian manner, hierarchical opposition still allows the latter a clear place as the level of the encompassed. This will, I hope, become clear later, but for the moment let us simply note that one way in which Dumont and others have explained hierarchical opposition is precisely by saying that it relates, as well as separates, the ideal and the actual, or ideology and action.

For example, societies often have a view of economic activity as lacking the value or prestige that attach to ritual activities that are designed to communicate with the divine and express transcendent ideas (see further below, Chapter 7). Economic activity may also be seen as actions by individuals that are predominantly self-seeking, selfish and even illicit (in respect of overcharging, etc.), but which, *ipso facto*, have agency. Yet these actions are still necessary to earthly existence, and actually also to the maintenance of ritual activities, through their conversion into offerings etc. For Dumont, these actions have their place, but are located, and therefore only made manifest, on a lower level of the ideology. They are also encompassed by the transcendent, which does not recognize them on its own level (for example, in carrying out ritual activities).

One result of this accommodation of both pragmatics and ideology is that Dumont's ideas continue to receive more attention from anthropologists at the present day than those of his main contemporary among the structuralists, Lévi-Strauss. But it can also be argued, I believe, that Dumont's ideas have a clear relevance for current human dilemmas generally. For example, in accepting the reality of hierarchy and the difficulties of attaining any true equality, the model of hierarchical opposition seems better placed than many anthropological approaches to provide a genuine understanding of inequality and intolerance, which are not just academic notions but the everyday experiences of countless individuals for whom any sort of education is a mirage. Whether or not the model is political in itself, as is sometimes alleged, it is certainly capable of throwing a more focused light on certain aspects of the political. For those brought up in a western, egalitarian, individualistic social environment, it helps reveal the true nature of that environment by penetrating received wisdom about it in a manner that is entirely in keeping with the best traditions of social science. These traditions are an intrinsic part of the Durkheimian project that formed Dumont himself.

Origins in the *Année sociologique*

Although Dumont acknowledged many influences in his work (see Chapter 4 below), as Mauss's student he was made fully aware of the

Année sociologique (i.e. Durkheimian) tradition. Although a number of its aspects might be identified in his work, in this chapter I want to focus on two in particular, which are also perhaps the most and least obvious respectively. The notion of simple opposition—which for Durkheim and Mauss was enshrined in the distinction between sacred and profane, and which Hertz generalized in modifying it, using right and left merely as emblems—is discussed in the next section. Here, we deal with what is probably less immediately obvious, namely the peculiarly Durkheimian approach to evolutionism, which basically consisted of setting a broad dichotomy between non-modern and modern societies in an evolutionary sequence. It thus differed from the nineteenth-century English school, which not only sometimes envisaged three basic stages instead of two (for example, Frazer's magic, religion and science), but also confined its interest for the most part to modes of thought, being less interested in forms of social solidarity or in the development of institutions. Dumont's comparisons between India and the west were essentially a later application of the Durkheimian dichotomy. [2]

Any dichotomy entails differentiation. What is the essence of this differentiation in the Durkheimian tradition? In brief, it is that, in respect of a number of concepts, modern societies separate out aspects that a non-modern society will combine in intimate if not inseparable relation. An early example is Durkheim's distinction between mechanical and organic types of solidarity. This is also one between segmentary social systems (for example, clan systems), where each segment is essentially identical to any other and can disappear without detriment to the whole, and the interdependence of social groups produced by the division of labour, such that the disappearance of one group impairs the whole (Durkheim 1984). This means, *inter alia*, that each segment will perform for itself all or most of the functions that are distributed among several interdependent groups where the division of labour obtains. [3] Durkheim also saw this conflation of functions as separating out in the course of history. Other examples are especially prominent in some of Mauss's work, for example *The Gift* (1954), in which early society merges the notions of disinterested gift-giving and economic exchange, which in course of time become separated as gift and commercial transaction. Here, Mauss's well-known concept of holism is explicitly linked to the non-modern situation (ibid.: 1). Similarly, his essay on the concept of the person (1938) opposes the form it initially takes in history, involving roles and the occupation of a series of bodies by a series of reincarnations, to the modern notion of the autonomous individual personality, which is distinct both from other such personalities and from society. While the non-modern concept of the person is thus one of an entity embedded in society and with little ideological individuality but enjoying a constant supply of lives, the modern version sees an autonomous individual of limited life-span. [4] The early joint article with Durkheim (Durkheim and Mauss 1963 [1903]) on primitive classification sees the classification of nature as originally rooted in the classification of humans in society, from which it subsequently frees itself progressively to become a value-free and socially neutral scientific classification, leaving social classifications separate. Hubert's essay on time (1905) presented a similar evolutionary dichotomy between an initial stage, when calendrical points and periods were each infused with ritual significance, to the present day, when calendars have separated from ritual to become simply vehicles of time-reckoning in a rationalist world (see Parkin 2002: Chapter 13).

Lévy-Bruhl's notion of mystical participation is also relevant here. There are really two elements to this concept: the mystical and the participation. For Lévy-Bruhl, the mystical fuses perception with representation. Evans-Pritchard's commentary (1965: 84) makes this clear, at the same time showing how Lévy-Bruhl saw the two as separating later in human evolution:

> The mystical perception is immediate. Primitive man does not, for example, perceive a shadow and apply to it the doctrine of his society, according to which it is one of his souls. When he is conscious of his shadow he is aware of his soul. We can best understand Lévy-Bruhl's view if we say that, in his way of looking at the matter, beliefs only arise late in the development of human thought, when representation and perception have already fallen apart. We can then say that a person perceives his shadow and believes it to be his soul. The question of belief does not arise among primitive peoples. The belief is contained in the shadow. The shadow is the belief.

Mousalimas, in his commentary on Lévy-Bruhl's work (1990: 43), uses a similar formulation, save that he talks not of belief but of 'affective perception' as opposed to sensory perception. In non-modern thought in Lévy-Bruhl's view, the two perceptions are experienced simultaneously. This interaction is one example of participation. More widely, however, participation can be described as any mode of thought in which categories subsume or invade one another: thus the person participates in his or her family, clan (including totem), society etc. In Mousalimas's words (ibid.: 38):

> Indifferent to the rule of non-contradiction, participation allow[s] multinumeration, consubstantiality and multilocation. In other words, it allow[s] something to be both singular and plural, both itself and something else, both here and elsewhere at the same time.

The projection of a power or influence out of something while it remains in the same place is clearly another instance (ibid., quoting Lévy-Bruhl 1985 [1910]: 76-7). Further, mystical participation is pre-logical and pre-cognitive, perceptual but not reflective. It is therefore absent from modern thought, which not only separates reflection, belief and logic from perception, but also regards categories as discrete: 'By definition, this mentality exclude[s] the theologies of consubstantiality, consubstantiation, and omnipresence' (Mousalimas 1990: 35).

The overlapping categories of a polythetic classification have also been regarded as characteristic of non-modern thought and as opposed to the monothetic classification of modern thought. In the latter, each category is defined with reference to a single criterion or set of criteria, which are invariably present; in the former, each category consists of a variable combination of several criteria in overlapping configurations, no single criterion necessarily being present (see Needham 1975; also 1971: 8-13, for an application of polythetic classification to a scholarly topic, namely descent).

Although Robert Hertz is mainly of importance to this account for refining the Durkheimian view of opposition in his article on the right hand of 1909, it is notable that he also partook of the Durkheimian approach to evolutionism without ever constructing his articles around it the way that Mauss sometimes did. The article on sin recognized the separation of church and state, and of sin and crime, in modern (or at least 'non-primitive') societies (e.g. 1994: 108-10). In the article on death can be found passages suggesting that historical changes have led to the decoupling of the parallel fates of the corpse, soul and mourners that Hertz had identified for non-modern societies, through, for example, conflation of the initially separate first and second burials, or the tokenization of the latter (1960: 40-1, 75-6). The article on right and left, finally, acknowledged that in modern society the two notions have a mostly spatial meaning, devoid of the different values with which non-modern societies invariably infuse them (1973: 11-12).

This kind of evolutionary thought is also discernible in the work of later declared adherents of the *Année sociologique* tradition. An example is Needham's analyses of symbolic systems, carried out under the direct inspiration of Hertz's article. This was linked with his views on the evolutionary development of kinship systems. His conclusion was that the conformity between the symbolic order and the social order is greater in those societies with terminological prescription and positive marriage rules, which had an evolutionary priority over those lacking such features (see further, Chapter 2). Allen's tetradic theory similarly envisages a progressive evolutionary separation of the sociological and terminological aspects of kinship as one moves away from the earliest stage (to which he gives the name tetradic society), when the two were exactly co-ordinate (see 1986, also 1982; both articles owe much to Mauss). Another example is Lévi-Strauss's distinction between hot and cold societies, essentially, that is, between societies that recognize their histories as something apart from themselves (though as still determining the present) and those that do not (1966: 233-42), which again can be seen as a dichotomy between essentially modern and non-modern societies. Finally, the notion of cosmomorphic societies has been introduced by some of Dumont's supporters (Barraud et al. 1994: 118) to distinguish societies that have no name for their values and therefore regard themselves as 'co-extensive with the universe' from 'a society which "speaks" its values [and therefore] implicitly accepts a universe wider [and therefore separate] than itself' (see further below, Chapter 7).

In identifying non-modern societies as those which fuse fact and value and modern ones as those which separate the two (below, Chapter 3), Dumont was clearly following this Durkheimian trend. Dumont's dichotomy differs, however, in that it is ultimately resolved as another hierarchical opposition, because even modern societies, though thinking of themselves as egalitarian, are ultimately compelled to recognize the hierarchies that are inevitably contained within them (see further Chapter 5, below). This is partly because modern societies are themselves not entirely free from all manifestations of non-modern thought. This is also one respect in which Dumont recognizes the empirical as distinct from, though valued less than, the ideological.

What Dumont and earlier writers call modern thought is essentially the thought of science and of similarly analytical, critical and intellectual environments and situations. The idea that modern humans uniformly and consistently think rationally and logically is at root a fiction. It is also true that no more than actors in non-modern societies do they always identify the contradictions in modern life but instead find ways of accommodating them. Given that this is so and that such contradictions are resolvable precisely through hierarchical oppositions, the latter are bound to figure in modern societies as well as non-modern ones.

Though developed in reaction to Hertz's influential article of 1909, the notion of hierarchical opposition is nonetheless traceable historically to it, and as we shall see (below, Chapter 6), even discernible in it. It is to this key text that we now turn.

Right and Left in Hertz

Mauss tells us (1969 II: 156) that one of the first texts to impress Hertz with the problem of right and left was White's *Ancient History of the*

Maori (1887-90), especially in showing the division of Maori gods into gods of the right and gods of the left, gods of war and gods of peace, gods of dreams and gods of magic, etc. Durkheim, as Hertz's doctoral supervisor, can also be expected to have had some influence over him as regards the problem of right and left, but he himself was not entirely consistent, even the course of the same work. In some passages in *Elementary Forms of the Religious Life*, for instance, he concedes that the individual can distinguish right and left before he is socialized (Durkheim 1915: 145; Durkheim and Mauss 1963: 7). Elsewhere, however, when citing Hertz in the context of the social determination of spatial distinctions (which had already been argued by Durkheim and Mauss in 1903), he says:

> Thus the social organization has been the model for the spatial organization and a reproduction of it. It is thus even up to the distinction between right and left which, far from being inherent in the nature of man in general, is very probably the product of representations which are religious and *therefore social*. (1915: 12, my emphasis)

Hertz's first task in 'La prééminence de la main droite' (1909) is to examine the possibility that the apparently physiological asymmetry between the right and left hands is in fact of social, not physical or organic origin. He starts by observing how all societies avert internal opposition by claiming to be grounded in 'the nature of things', an example being right-handedness. But right-handedness is not so axiomatic as is generally supposed. Not that there has been no scientific examination of the problem. The greater power of the right hand is known, he says, to be connected with the greater development of the left hemisphere of the brain, which controls speech and voluntary movement. The question is, *how* are the two connected? Biologists claim that the brain is the fundamental and controlling factor, that is, that 'we are right-handed because we are left-brained'. But man is unique among primates in not being ambidextrous, suggesting that the reason for his handedness might lie outside the organism. Hertz therefore counters with the proposition that 'we are left-brained because we are right-handed', and that it is outside, cultural factors that have determined the preference for the right hand in both ritual and mundane tasks. This has led in its turn to the development of the left hemisphere being greater than that of the right.

This, left as it stands, would have been one of the more extreme examples of the Durkheimian sociological method and of the doctrine of the tyranny of society over the individual in the *Année sociologique* tradition. In fact, Hertz retreats just enough to accept an underlying organic asymmetry, his real concern being how and why this asymmetry is exploited by society in its collective representations. This asymmetry is real but slight, and can be overcome physically with training (for example, by a violinist)—it is society that gives it value. Hertz clearly prefers the evidence of those who point to variations in natural handedness and who stress the importance of socialization in promoting right-handedness as a norm: 'it is not because the left hand is weak and powerless that it is neglected: the contrary is true' (1973: 6). In other words, society takes this slight biological asymmetry and reinforces it through training, endowing the two hands with contrasted attributes that are always opposed in any ritual or social context that refers to them. The right usually but not invariably has the more positive connotations, the left the more negative ones (see further below). As Mauss was to say of this text years later, when discussing the use of the left and right hands by a Moslem (1950 [1936]: 375): 'In order to know why he makes this gesture and not another, neither the physiology nor the psychology of motor dissymmetry in man are sufficient; it is necessary to know the traditions that impose it.'

But why does society elaborate the organic asymmetry so tremendously and endow it with such deep cultural relevance? Given such an insignificant degree of biological asymmetry, reason would lead one to expect that the hand that has been less favoured by nature would be trained up by society to parity with the more favoured. To answer this, Hertz invokes the human mind's 'innate capacity to differentiate', by which he means to dichotomize. This would have existed regardless of the organic basis of the asymmetry: 'If organic asymmetry had not existed, it would have had to be invented'. It would be over-generous to regard this as an explanation, however: the evidence for it—the 'innate capacity'—arises directly out of the phenomenon that is supposed to be explained. Rather, it is simply an acknowledgement of an aspect of that dualism that the Durkheimians dogmatically assert to exist as the basis of all human thought and of which Hertz gives a number of examples (his Section III). It is only by drastically minimizing the significance of the organic asymmetry between the two hands that he himself is able to avoid a naturalistic or intellectualist explanation for this dichotomizing.

The most famous expression of this dualism among the Durkheimians is, of course, the dichotomy between sacred and profane (on Hertz's revision of this, see Tcherkézoff 1994–5). Hertz accepts both this and Durkheim's further division of the sacred into pure and impure, which, put together, can be represented thus: sacred (pure + impure) / profane; or, pure sacred > profane < impure sacred, in which the profane is threatened by both the pure sacred and the impure sacred (the arrows represent ritual danger). Hertz wants to relativize this, because he regards it as representing the perspective of the profane only. For the *pure* sacred, he argues, not only the profane but also the impure sacred is dangerous and must be kept at arm's length. However, he regards the impure sacred and the profane as virtually identical. In this way dichotomy is restored, but refocused: we do not end up with a triple distinction between pure sacred, impure sacred and profane. As Isambert remarks (1982: 243 n.87), this makes the profane ambiguous, not the sacred, as with Robertson Smith, Durkheim, Hubert and Mauss. As Das says (1977a: 26 n.2), 'Hertz did not use the term "profane" in the sense of mundane. He used "profane" and "impure" as interchangeable categories.' His modification therefore takes the form: pure sacred / impure sacred + profane. He also indicates that he will return to the question elsewhere in order to justify this change properly (his note 14), but never did so.

Henceforward, Hertz applies the symbolic values of right and left etc. to the dichotomy between pure and impure, for despite continuing to use the words 'sacred' and 'profane' frequently, he seems to have regarded this as 'more essential' (Granet 1973: 43). In doing so, however, he reverts to seeing them as emblems of or metaphors for sociocentric factors no longer dependent on particular perspectives. On the whole, most of those who have subsequently applied his ideas ethnographically have followed him in these respects, and the actual notion of a distinction between pure and impure, though apt to be modified into one between auspicious and inauspicious, or positive and negative, has not come under fire like that between sacred and profane. Nor are there the same conceptual uncertainties over the definition of the less valued pole. Both of Hertz's poles are decidedly within the ritual-cum-social: once he has disposed of the purely physical basis of the right/left asymmetry in collective representations and modified the dichotomy between sacred and profane, he recognizes nothing like the mundane as of significance. Following Durkheim, Hertz regards the social as being grounded in the religious (see his discussion of dual organization), thus implying that every human activity, eating with the right hand as well as right/left symbolism at a wedding or funeral, has a social or cultural basis. In other words, the only distinction between normal and ritual activities is that made by the society itself. This too has normally been perpetuated by those who follow him, apart from occasional allusions to the right-handedness of 'everyday' (i.e. ritually or ideologically neutral) practices and situations (e.g. Granet 1973; Matsunaga 1986), a debatable conception in itself. Hertz talks, moreover, of 'a single category of things, a common nature, the same orientation towards one of the two poles of the mystical world' (Hertz ibid.: 14). This was to become a bitter source of controversy in respect of the use Needham was to make of Hertz's ideas decades later.

Hertz continues his article by giving a broader idea of the range of values associated by society with right and left, the former being positive, sacred, pure, good, auspicious, legitimate, homely, the latter negative or ambiguous, profane, impure, evil, inauspicious, disorderly, hostile etc. (Hertz himself does not use all these words). It is not, however, a matter of strength and weakness, or of ability and inability; both poles have an equal but opposite effect. Right and left are associated respectively with life and death, as well as being emblematic of a whole range of asymmetric oppositions, but they are not their basis. He mentions especially the connection of right and left with the cardinal points, though the associations of north and west with left, and of south and east with right, are not so consistent worldwide as he suggests. But he realizes that what counts as right may differ, citing as an instance the appearance of animals in omens: it may be a good omen if the animal appears on the right of the person concerned, or alternatively if it appears on his left in such a way as to present its right side to him (see Leeuwen-Turnovcova 1990: 6 ff.). In the penultimate section he gives some ethnographic examples of the use of the two hands in ritual activities and gestures. His closing remarks address the trend even then under way in his own society towards accepting left-handedness as natural and unproblematic. He clearly approves of this, looking forward to the full 'development of the [human] organism', and dismissing any thought that it would impair either aesthetic clarity or our ability to distinguish good from evil.

For Hertz, the problem of the asymmetry of right and left is a special case, and for the modern age a rather irrational one, in so far as society has exaggerated it beyond its organic basis. Here, Hertz allows his own values to intrude in a way that seems out of place in modern (if not always postmodern) anthropology. Yet in proposing equal treatment for the two hands, he was fully in accord with key modern, progressive trends in the west. Thus he served as a fitting starting point for Dumont, who clearly admired his work in general, when, many decades later, he set out to show the anthropological community at large how their devotion to notions of equality had blinded them to its absence in the very 'non-modern' societies they were most likely to be dealing with. First, however, the applicability of the theme of opposition which was at the root of Hertz's article was to be extended considerably (though without it being radically altered in its essentials) in the work of Rodney Needham.

Notes

1. There is also a certain tendency to dismiss Durkheim (1858-1917) simply for his historical remoteness from the present day. We should not forget that Weber (1864-1920) was his almost exact contemporary.
2. It is not, of course, the only such dichotomy: Tönnies' distinction between *Gemeinschaft* and *Gesellschaft* (literally, 'community' and 'society'), and perhaps Redfield's between Great and Little Traditions, might also be mentioned here, as too can Maine's distinction between status and contract. See Cahnman (1977).
3. Any functions it does not perform for itself (such as, for example, the provision of women in marriage or certain ritual services), it will perform for other groups on a reciprocal basis.
4. At the outset of this article, Mauss recognizes explicitly actual self-awareness as something different from the ideological representation of the person. While the former appears as universal, it is not relevant to Mauss's thesis on the different culturally determined varieties of the latter.

Chapter 2

NEEDHAM'S DEVELOPMENT OF HERTZ

From the Right Hand to Dual Symbolic Classification

Although there was considerable reaction to Hertz's text in France, especially during Mauss's dominance of French anthropology in the 1920s and 1930s, fifty years were to pass before it had a similar impact in English-speaking anthropology. It was Needham's translation of it (aided by his wife Claudia) in 1960, and his later reissue of this translation, slightly revised, as the banner article of a collection of subsequent papers by other authors on this same theme (Needham 1973d), that really brought it worldwide attention. Another important stimulus was Needham's own development of Hertz's basic insights in what he called 'total' structural analyses of a number of Southeast Asian and African societies.

In making his analyses, Needham shifted the focus away from the Durkheimian reduction of classification to society and instead saw dichotomy as more basic, in the sense of it being a global feature of human thought. Hertz had concentrated on a rather narrow selection of oppositions in his article and had regularly associated them with right and left, though he regarded this opposition as only one aspect of the more general Durkheimian dualism. Needham's studies went further in establishing a whole series of oppositions in particular societies, oppositions which need not be directly connected with right and left at all: although this opposition would normally feature, it was 'not a determinant of the other oppositions' (1981: 45). Needham recognized that dual symbolic classification did not necessarily pervade the symbolic representations of any particular culture: classifications

---

Notes for this section can be found on page 40.

based on other numbers than two might also figure (1979a: 9ff., 12ff.). Nevertheless, he was especially keen to incorporate analyses of dualistic classifications into his studies of societies with prescriptive systems of affinal alliance, since he felt that 'the structural concordance between ... the social and symbolic order' was particularly impressive in such cases (1960a: 108). Indeed, 'social organization and symbolic forms in such societies are aspects of one conceptual order, only arbitrarily to be separated for our purposes of description and analysis' (ibid.: 108-9; see also 1960b: 105; 1959: 134).

Thus in the case of the Lamet of northern Laos (1960a), we are first shown how asymmetric dualism obtains in respect of the opposition between wife-givers and wife-takers, both in the kinship terminology and in respect of actual alliances, wife-givers being superior. The analysis then proceeds to show the same dualism in respect of the layout of the house, prestations between affinal alliance groups (of goods and services as well as women), the village layout (though this could only be speculative on the data available to Needham, which was basically Izikowitz's monograph of 1951), and the different sorts of spiritual being. The demonstration culminates in a double-column list in which 'the oppositions are listed seriatim as they have been elicited or inferred in the exposition of the relevant facts' (1960a: 115). It is not claimed that the analysis is exhaustive, nor is this necessary:

> in making this analysis we are discerning a *mode of thought*; and further oppositions would not be of value in "completing" the classification, but in illustrating in other contexts how exactly this mode of thought has been apprehended and in extending the social and natural range of its recorded application. (ibid., original emphasis)

Indeed, so much are they reflections of a common mode of thought that in making demonstrations of this kind it hardly matters where one starts (Needham 1973c: 330). Among the means of identifying oppositions is reversal, for example, aspects of movement between the world of the living and the world of the dead, or between the realms of religion and secular authority (e.g. Needham ibid.: 306ff.).

Needham carried out similar analyses around the same time of similar groups living in the Indo-Burmese borderlands, such as the Kom (1959), Aimol (1960b) and Purum (1962a; also 1958), as well as the Wikmunkan of Australia (1962b). The inspiration of Mauss's 'total social fact' is very evident. However, there were doubts whether this method of analysis could be applied to all types of society. Needham attempts to correlate the type of descent system and the degree of concordance with the symbolic order:

in societies based on descent such symbolic representations may be expected
to correlate with the type of descent system. Roughly, in cognatic societies
the relation of symbolic to social order may be indefinite or minimal; in lineal systems the relationship may be discernible in a limited range of partic-
ulars but not commonly in a comprehensive manner; and in lineal systems
with prescriptive affinal alliance there is usually a correspondence of structure between the two orders such that one may speak of a single scheme of
classification under which both are subsumed. (1973b [1960]: 111)

And further: 'In lineal descent systems without prescriptive regulation
of marriage a total structural analysis is generally far less feasible, and
in cognatic societies it is even less possible' (1960a: 117-18). This was
strikingly shown subsequently by Howell, one of Needham's students,
in her work among the Chewong of West Malaysia, a group with cognatic descent and no positive marriage rules: she was not able to identify many oppositions that were ordinarily considered asymmetric
(1985; see below, Chapter 5). Nonetheless, such oppositions can still
be discerned in societies not regulated by prescriptive affinal alliance
systems, as Needham himself endeavoured to show with respect to
two African ones (1973b, 1973c). This made Durkheim and Mauss's
specific reduction of symbolic classifications to social ones unsuitable
as a model. Although Needham applauded Mauss's holism, he
declined to follow his and Durkheim's evolutionism here, taking the
view that a lack of concordance between the two sorts of classification
could be explained synchronically if both were referred to underlying
principles of order, like opposition (Needham 1972:154ff.). [1]

However, the configurations of the symbolic order also led Needham to reject Lévi-Strauss's notion of exchange as a fundamental feature of the human mind in favour of opposition, of which exchange,
like reciprocity, was merely one manifestation (e.g. 1960b: 105ff.).
One can exchange wives, after all, but hardly symbols or values linked
by dualistic classification. In the case of dual symbolic classification,
this focus on abstract principles of order extends to analogy and
homology as well as to opposition. In this respect, Needham drew
inspiration explicitly from Hertz's essay, which he saw as a disquisition
on opposition and polarity as principles of order, though he also modified, to the point of denying it, Hertz's assumption that a homology
necessarily existed between the terms in any system of dual symbolic
classification (Needham 1972: 154-5, 210; 1979b: 296-7).

Needham and his Critics

Needham's analyses have frequently been criticized, partly because of
suspicions as to their cogency as ethnographic facts. The idea of an

extended, coherent classification seems too neat for many, and the suspicion has also been voiced that it is often really the analyst who is imposing his sense of order on data drawn from indigenous statements that are less rigorous. The outcome often seems to be a degree of interference of the Aristotelian categories and/or Kantian dichotomies of western thought with the representation of the indigenous view (see Goody 1977: Ch. 4; Beattie 1968, 1976). Yet however ambitious such analyses may seem, few would deny the faculties of opposing and dichotomizing to very many if not all the peoples of the non-western world too. The question is, rather, what forms such oppositions take (see further, Parkin 1995a: Ch. 4).

More relevant in this connection are the criticisms revolving around the use, by Needham and others, of two-column lists or tables to record the oppositions established in any particular society. These tables place the respective poles of each opposition in one of the columns, for example, right in one column and left in the other. This normally means that the column including right is listed before that including left, thus reversing the spatial arrangement of the hands in representing them on the page itself—a further reminder of the disjunction between symbolism and reality in these matters. As Leeuwen-Turnovcova points out (1990: 15-16), this is in fact precisely what one would expect, that is, the more auspicious poles of each opposition being listed before the less auspicious ones. Her further claim, that it is also usual to mention right before left in speech and writing, is contradicted, *inter alia*, by the title of Osbert Sitwell's autobiography, *Left Hand, Right Hand* (1945, 1946).

These tables may not have been suggested to Needham by Chapter XX of Hocart's *Kings and Councillors*, which he was to edit and reissue in 1970, but Hocart's use of them may at least have satisfied him that they had a respectable precedent. There is a further example in Hocart's *Social Origins* (1954: 89, 90), concerning Aristotle's discussion of the Pythagoreans (*Metaphysics*, I, 5, 986; the table is Hocart's, not Aristotle's). They are, of course, a fairly obvious means of representation, also used by Lévi-Strauss on occasion. Needham's efforts in keeping Hocart's name, as well as many others', including Hertz's, before the anthropological public are well known, and in one of his earliest ventures of this kind he cites this chapter of Hocart's specifically alongside Hertz's essay (1958: 97; cf. too 1960b: 103).

But although these tables have regularly been used by Needham and many of his own followers, those less under his influence have openly expressed their doubts as to their usefulness. In accordance with his thesis that the invention of literacy and writing altered the way man saw and thought about his world, Goody charges that the very act of constructing these columns has encouraged the formation of a rigid dichotomous structure which is insensitive to the different contexts in which particular oppositions might be evinced: black is not always evil in Africa, for example (where, after all, 'black' more readily signifies 'us'), nor white always good (1977: 66). These oppositions are often entered into the tables without any clear evidence that they are indigenous conceptions rather than the analyst's constructions of those conceptions.

For example, even as a western notion the nature/culture divide is, for Goody, only traceable back to the eighteenth century, no further, and may not have meaning at all in many societies (ibid.: 64). [2] In short, for Goody, such tables tend to remove all contextualization and add extraneous matter out of the anthropologist's own mind, or rather, out of his own cultural tradition. This dichotomizing tendency has come to pervade post-Durkheimian sociology and seems to stem directly from Greek (especially Aristotelian) thought; yet, 'the reason for the Greek concern with opposites lies not so much in their debt to an earlier oral culture as in their relationship to a contemporary literate one' (ibid.: 70). In other words, the Greeks' own literacy encouraged them to formulate oppositions specifically; the western intellectual tradition has been steeping itself in the resulting classification ever since; and anthropologists, who are themselves ultimately a part of that tradition, have been attributing it to the rest of humanity with abandon. Goody thus sees the structuring if not consciousness of the fact of opposition as a historical and therefore contingent event. In reply to Goody's scepticism, the question that has to be asked is whether a sense of opposition really relies on there being a means of recording it in the culture.

The fact that Needham, in most of his published work, was analyzing material collected and published by others made it almost inevitable that, sooner or later, he would be challenged on purely ethnographic grounds. A major early critique concerned the Banyoro of Uganda, whose supposed system of dual symbolic classification Needham had examined partly but not wholly on the basis of Beattie's then still quite recent ethnography. This resulted in an extraordinary exchange of papers, mainly in the journal *Africa* and spanning some eleven years from start to finish (Needham 1973c [originally 1967]; Beattie 1968; Needham 1973a; Beattie 1976, overlapping with Needham 1976; Beattie 1978), in which an increasingly exasperated Beattie and an increasingly icy Needham battled it out not only over the merits of the theoretical approach chosen by the latter, but also over the finer points of Banyoro ethnography, of which only Beattie had direct experience.

In fact, much of Beattie's critique was based on Needham's alleged misrepresentations of the evidence and on the supposedly dubious assumptions that he made in interpreting it. Needham's argument is cast in the form of a puzzle. Banyoro diviners are auspicious, since their actions are beneficial to their clients; but in casting shells to divine, they use the left hand, which conflicts with the fact that left-handed people are normally 'hated' (Needham 1973c: 300, after Roscoe). They also, he claims, throw either nine cowrie shells or three leather counters when divining, although odd numbers are normally inauspicious, and use animals that are the equally inauspicious colour of black for sacrifice. His solution, essentially, is that, since the left hand, the colour black and odd numbers are also associated with females, the diviner, though biologically male, 'is symbolically associated with the feminine' (ibid.: 309).

The sense of identity between the poles of the various oppositions being discussed becomes progressively stronger as the article proceeds. On p. 315 we read: 'The left connects the diviner not only with the feminine but also with other values which themselves are connected, either by direct association or by analogy, with the feminine', and with 'black, evil, danger, the inauspicious, and death ... '. And, with reference to a parallel discussion of the maleness of Banyoro princesses, on p. 316 we read: 'In their several associations, the princess *becomes* a man, and the diviner *becomes* a woman' (my emphases; this page and half of the next continue in a similar vein).

Beattie starts his reply by questioning the evidence for this argument (1968: 414-22). There is no evidence that the diviner is inauspicious or associated with the feminine, nor that odd numbers are inauspicious—the number nine, at least, is fully auspicious. Nor are there data showing that left-handed people are hated, although use of the left hand is certainly disapproved of, and the left is generally inferior to the right. Women are certainly inferior, but not necessarily inauspicious, nor linked especially with the left, nor with odd numbers, nor with black: they must ordinarily use the right hand too, just like men. It is not only black animals that are sacrificed during rituals but white animals too, since the dichotomy between white and black is used not to mark a transition *into* a ritual event but to mark the stages of liminality and completion *within* it. There is a similar neutrality regarding divination itself, since auspiciousness or inauspiciousness are not intrinsic to it but depend on the outcome: 'the primary purpose of divination is diagnosis' (ibid.: 416). Reference to the left, conversely, appears to be used to mark entry into a ritual state rather than inauspiciousness (ibid.: 417). Beattie's own preferred explanation for the diviner's use of his left hand is that it enhances his mystical power, that is, it has an instrumental, not a symbolic function (ibid.: 440). In short, there are no absolute values here in terms of what is auspicious and inauspicious.

Thus, concludes Beattie, dual symbolic classification among the Banyoro, although 'significant', occurs 'a good deal less extensively and pervasively than Needham supposes' (ibid.: 424-5). But it is not only the evidence as such that Beattie queries. In constructing his tables, Needham must depend either on direct evidence in respect of the entry of each opposition into it, or on deductions from one piece of evidence to another. The latter would entail either that the values female, left, odd and inauspicious can be linked by something they have in common, or else that, taking the oppositions involved, male : female :: right : left :: even : odd :: auspicious : inauspicious, or both. [3] Beattie's charge here is essentially that the necessary evidence for the first approach is lacking, the implication being that Needham's case *must* therefore rest on the deductions, which themselves suffer from these same defects in evidence. Indeed, he questions Needham's attribution to the Banyoro of 'an ideological and symbolic scheme which is defined in its entirety by opposition and made unitary by analogy' (Needham 1973c: 327). Many of Needham's 'oppositions' are in fact mere distinctions as far as the Banyoro are concerned, such as that between cooking and brewing. Others in Needham's table are either doubtful in the Nyoro context (e.g. gift exchange/sexual intercourse; sheep/cattle) or else may be described as 'true but unremarkable', since they are either logical, or cross-culturally very general, or both. In Beattie's view, accepting them into the scheme simply impoverishes the analysis by extending it indefinitely and making it insignificant. Here, Beattie touches on one of the greatest dangers of such analyses, namely that they may simply become facile in stating the obvious, for example that, yes, this or that group too opposes right to left, or male to female, or black to white. What are needed are genuine 'complementary opposites' that 'relate to a single universe of discourse' (Beattie 1968: 434-5).

Beattie's other main charge as regards the theoretical aspects of Needham's analysis relates to the solidity of the latter's tables, which Beattie infers from the way the analysis has been carried out. He does not accept Needham's statement that the scheme of dual symbolic classification is 'made unitary by analogy', because he regards that unity as actually deriving from associations made between the terms in each of the columns of the table taken separately (see especially Beattie 1976: 225-7). In his later work Needham applies the term 'homology' to this aspect of the tables, 'analogy' referring instead to the oppositions themselves, that is, to the relations between the relations—something in which he has always been consistent (see further below).

Yet whatever one calls the relationship between the terms in each column, Needham's arguments often seem to depend heavily on transitivity between such terms or on their having at least the quality of auspiciousness or inauspiciousness in common (see Hallpike 1979: 232). 'Of course, it does not necessarily follow that because Banyoro associate women with the left hand, and because Nyoro diviners throw their cowries with the left hand, therefore Banyoro think that diviners are like women, or possess a feminine quality' (Beattie 1968: 417-18). As for a common quality, on the one hand many of the oppositions in Needham's table 'could hardly be opposed otherwise than as auspicious and inauspicious respectively in any culture in which these concepts are framed, since they assert rather than symbolize the distinction between favourable and unfavourable aspects of human existence' (ibid.: 435). On the other hand, others are either not defined as auspicious or inauspicious at all by Banyoro, or not regularly, and therefore cannot be linked together by even this degree of common quality. This Needham would accept if his more explicit statements are anything to go by, but for Beattie these 'unlinked' terms pose a particular problem in the construction of the tables, since there is no reason to put them 'in one column rather than the other' (ibid.: 434 n.2). Thus, Beattie concludes (ibid.: 437), 'the quality of Nyoro symbolic thought would be gravely misrepresented if it were suggested ... that it exhibits a "total" character, based on a division of all the things and qualities listed into two opposed and mutually exclusive spheres.'

Here we are faced with the chief source of both dispute and confusion in respect of the way Needham conducts analyses of this sort. As noted above, his evident reliance on the connectedness of many actual terms in his Banyoro paper contradicts his more general statements. For example, in the Wikmunkan article (Needham 1962b: 255ff.), we find this general statement: 'The most common expressions of symbolic values throughout the world are those associated with right and left' (ibid.: 255). Associations between terms enter freely into the construction of the table here, not least because in this case the ethnography is rather sparse. The associations generally seem plausible, even when they are not actually recorded. There is one contradiction, mentioned by Needham himself. Most myths associated male with south and female with north, which can also be read to mean with east and west respectively, assuming that east, like south, is taken as a generally auspicious direction. It can also be read to signal an association with right and left respectively, since 'it is well known that the right is typically associated with the south, in the southern as well as in the northern hemispheres' (ibid.: 257; cf. Hertz 1973: 27 n.86). However, a different myth associates women with east, men with west. It is not clear whether there is some ideological reason for this or whether it simply reflects differences between informants. Whatever the case, 'this single exception cannot seriously challenge the cumulative and consistent tenor of the numerous other reports' (Needham ibid.: 258).

The association of female with left also enables Needham to suggest an opposition between affines in the left column and agnates in the right column, this being 'a reasonable inference' because 'maternal relatives' can be seen as the affines of the previous generation (ibid.). There are a number of remarks indicating that this is as far as the ethnography will go, but no admission that the reasoning might, in certain circumstances, be problematic.

An earlier paper, on the Kom of Manipur, India (Needham 1959: 133), also recognizes some confusion in the associations for the term 'right' that one might expect. If the priest faces the auspicious east, the south will be to his right, leading one to suppose that the south too will be auspicious. In fact, it is inauspicious, being the direction of death, 'which is inconsistent with the associations of "right"'.

That the discussion of connectedness, or what would eventually be termed 'homology', was not simply a response to the criticisms of Beattie and others is shown in another article dating originally from 1960 and therefore predating these criticisms (1973b: 117). This article is perhaps the most important in terms of the various debates centring around Needham's development of Hertz's ideas, and we discuss it here at some length. Needham's preemptive disclaimer runs as follows:

> it has to be kept in mind that the ascription of terms to one series in the scheme [i.e. to one side of the table] does not entail that they all share the particular attributes of any one term. The association of these terms rests on analogy, and is derived from a mode of categorization which orders the scheme, not from the possession of a specific property by means of which the character or presence of other terms may be deduced. One does not, therefore, say that the Mugwe *is* feminine [original emphasis], any more than one would say that night or south or the subordinate age-division is feminine.

The table itself 'represents a symbolic classification in which pairs of opposite terms are analogically related by the principle of complementary dualism' (ibid.: 116). But this article too contains ambiguities, for a few pages later Needham talks of the the Mugwe being 'symbolically assigned to the category of the left' and says that he 'belongs symbolically to the category which includes the left' (ibid.: 119), while the right side of the 'scheme' is said to denote 'what is socially and mythically dominant and superior' (ibid.: 120). In this, he was evidently following Hertz very closely (cf. Hertz 1973: 14; Beattie 1976: 223). Indeed, only if this is assumed is the famous statement that the Mugwe's left hand is symbolically his right at all understandable. In building his table of Meru oppositions (1973b: 116), Needham freely associates various values with one another as they occur, especially in relation to the Mugwe. He also talks of 'the equation north = right' (ibid.: 118), and of 'south = left' (ibid.: 121, parentheses removed). Because of these associations, he is led to put the Mugwe himself in the left-hand column, where his spiritual but dangerous power is opposed to the secular power of the elders in the right-hand column; or, in Needham's terms, where spiritual authority is opposed to political power. It is clear that it is mainly because his left hand is the significant one that the Mugwe finds himself in the column that is headed with the value 'left'.

In his introduction to this key article, Needham makes it plain that it is the very significance of the left hand that has occasioned his surprise, hinting too that normally (i.e. worldwide) one would expect religious authority to be superior to secular and therefore to be associated with the right: 'in every quarter of the world it is the right hand, and not the left, which is predominant' (ibid.: 110). Thus in this case the puzzle arose out of a conflict with the lessons of cross-cultural comparison rather than evidence from within the culture itself, as was the case with the Banyoro. Needham also assumes (ibid.: 114; there seems to be no direct evidence) that since the Mugwe's left hand 'is reserved for his sacred function', his right hand must be his profane hand. By all the conventions of such analyses, profaneness belongs in the left-hand column, as, normally, does secular as opposed to religious authority; sacredness, or mystical power as well as religious authority, are characteristically 'right'. Yet here we have a left hand with all these attributes (this is true of the Imenti sub-tribe but not, apparently, of the other Meru sub-tribes, where it is the right hand that is normally dominant). Needham's solution (ibid.: 120-1) is to propose that, although the Mugwe himself may be a left-category figure, his left hand 'must be assigned to the right-hand series in the scheme'; similarly, 'as far as symbolic attributes are concerned his right hand is his left'.

There are ethnographic precedents, within Africa, for this apparently contradictory statement, as for example the Nuer opinion that a left-handed person's left hand is really his right (Evans-Pritchard 1973: 97). The problem comes in representing this diagrammatically. In terms of the table of Meru oppositions, we obtain the analogical series left : right :: Mugwe : elders :: religious authority : political power; but when it comes to the Mugwe's two hands, what Needham in effect proposes is the series right : left :: sacred : profane ('as on the most universal grounds we should anticipate', p. 120) :: left : right (because of the sacredness of the left hand). Needham does not actually place the opposition between the hands themselves in his table, presumably because to put the Mugwe's left hand in the right column of the table as it stands would not only be illogical, it would actually separate it from the religious authority which it, no less than the Mugwe himself, represents. In effect, there is a choice between putting the Mugwe and religious authority all in the column containing the left precisely because of the association of the latter two with the left, but ignoring the circumstance that religious authority is usually associated with the right; or putting the Mugwe and religious authority in the column containing the right precisely because of this association, but ignoring the circumstance that the left hand is the significant one in divination. The first solution accords better with the ethnography, the second with cross-cultural precedents.

Yet in addition to the contradictions they represent, both choices make assumptions about the sort of qualities that are to be put in each of the two columns, in the first case the allegedly normal inauspiciousness of the left, and in the second case the allegedly normal superiority of religious over secular authority. The problem is not solved by severing the Mugwe's left hand from his body: the choice is now either to leave it in the left column although it represents religious authority, or to place it in the right column although it is a left hand. Despite Needham's frequent assertions to the contrary and his clear statements (1973a: xxv; 1979a: 8) that individual terms might belong in opposite columns in different contexts, his problems here arise from the apparent assumption that the columns of his tables must have at least the property of auspiciousness or inauspiciousness, an assumption which is absolutely basic to the ways these analyses are actually conducted. Here, in effect, Needham discovers for himself the main problem with his tables that Beattie, Dumont and Tcherkézoff, among others, were to complain about (see also below, this chapter; on the Mugwe, below, Chapter 4).

Makarius and Makarius reiterate these objections and make others in a chapter dedicated to this analysis, in a book which in general regards all aspects of the structuralist message as being based on a comprehensive disregard of the facts (1973: 195-233). There is the by now familiar complaint about two-column tables, in which some of the entries are based on occasional, not regular occurrences of what they are supposed to represent. They are also frequently placed arbitrarily in the columns; for example, on the basis of an alternative myth to that cited by Needham, children might be listed with the old rather than with women. Similarly, first wives might just as well be listed with predecessors as with successors, since they have obviously preceded all subsequent wives into the marriage. Nor is the presence of an opposition between the terms as listed by Needham always apparent. There is not any obvious opposition between age grades, for example, only alternation: one is concerned with affairs in a certain period; the other has been previously and will be subsequently. This is found critically to affect Needham's main thesis, for the writers also see no reason for opposing the Mugwe to the elders, nor even religious or mystical power to secular power.

In fact, the Mugwe represents both types of authority (a point taken direct from the original ethnographer, Bernardi 1959: 140), and, moreover, he too is an elder, though superior. Both he and other elders are associated with the colour black, which is, significantly, the only term for which Needham does not provide an opposite in his table (cf. Tcherkézoff on this point, 1994). Although the Mugwe is superior, a sort of 'father', Needham places him with inferiors and with women. Most surprisingly of all, religious authority, though superior, finds itself in the inferior column. The problem for Needham is that, if he accepts the Mugwe as an elder, he would be depriving himself of an example of one of his favourite ideas, dual sovereignty (e.g. 1980a). For these authors, portraying the relationship between the Mugwe and the elders as one of complementarity simply covers up the fact that there is no genuine opposition between them that would justify placing them in separate columns. This is to go too far. The elders and the Mugwe are clearly opposed to one another, even though the Mugwe has many of the formers' attributes.

But it is again the nexus between the Mugwe, the left hand, the feminine and the mystical that is the main focus of the Makarius' criticism, because of the dilemma in which it places the analyst. Whether one chooses to put the Mugwe in the left column because of his left hand, though he is superior, or in the right column because of his superiority, though this mixes up right and left, an exceptional solution has to be found for what is the 'centre of the problem' (Makarius and Makarius 1973: 209). Needham gets round this by separating symbol from fact and saying that the Mugwe's left hand is really his right, in contradiction to his treating the terms as facts in the rest of the analysis. It can hardly be said, though, that Needham disregards the symbolic dimension of these 'terms-as-facts'—indeed, this is the whole point of the exercise. It would seem that here the critics are opposing fact to symbol in an epistemological sense. More generally, their criticism of Needham is that he relies less on the facts (i.e. 'ethnographic facts', which include symbolization) than on inference, analogy—in a word, structure—in making these analyses. And it is the idea of structure that the authors are most opposed to.

They do not stop at mere criticism but attempt an explanation of their own for the association of the left with the mystical (ibid.: 214-32). They begin by noting, with Hertz, the frequent association of right with male, and of left with female, and also the common male fear of feminine impurity in the form of menstrual blood. The next step in the argument, namely that left and right 'lend themselves admirably to becoming a symbolized expression of the distinction between the two sexes' (ibid.: 218), is not always applicable ethnographically. Nonetheless, their view of the multivalent nature of the left is certainly one

possible solution to the dilemma. As Hertz had noted, the left and associated values (e.g. blood), though linked to the impure, can themselves
be beneficial because they can be effective against malevolent forces in
a way that the right etc., being linked to the pure, cannot. This necessitates ritual action, because the spilling of blood in a sacrifice itself
entails breaking a taboo. In this sense, the Mugwe is a violator of
taboos—which is why he is surrounded with them.

This multivalence is also offered as a reason for the lability of terms
for left as compared to those for right (cf. Hertz 1973: 11, after Meillet).
Most particularly, however, it means that no reversal is involved when
switching between auspicious and inauspicious because they are both
aspects of the Mugwe's authority—they exist, that is, in the same
domain. The authors therefore claim that no opposition and therefore
no structuralism is involved, and further, that the dichotomy right/left
cannot be taken as the model of elementary logical oppositions, as an
essential aspect of human thought etc., as Needham has so often
claimed. [4] What makes them think that the different aspects of the
Mugwe's authority cannot themselves be dichotomized in a perfectly
standard structuralist fashion is not entirely clear. Although empha-
sising other aspects of Hertz's article in making their criticisms of
Needham, their own reliance on the quasi-naturalistic explanation of
menstrual blood constitutes a step backwards beyond Hertz himself,
who had decisively rejected such explanations in his article of 1909.

In his own attempts to justify the Mugwe anomaly, Needham introduces similar data from the Fulani of the Sudan and the Purum of
northeast India (1973b: 121-2). In the Fulani case, the consistent
transitivity between pairs is compromised by the fact that the apparently normal series north : south :: junior : senior is reversed in the
female context of where the beds of the various wives—who are
ranked according to seniority—are placed in the homestead. Of
course, Needham's table can only show one order, otherwise confusion would result through some terms being on both sides of the table.
But this means that it cannot show that the normal series female :
male :: junior : senior does not obtain in this context, since the male
category is absent and the female category itself split between junior
and senior.

In the Purum case, auguries at name-giving ceremonies for boys
are auspicious if the right leg of the fowl falls over its left leg after it has
been sacrificed, while for girls the reverse is the case. Thus the transitivity of the sets right : left :: male : female and right : left :: auspicious
: inauspicious does not obtain in contexts where left : right :: auspicious : inauspicious. In both examples, one might speak of reversals,
but what is really happening is that a person (a female) that one would
conventionally place in the inauspicious column is symbolized as

important or auspicious through an attribute which is normally also considered inauspicious. Thus the Fulani senior wife sleeps to the north because north is a female-connected category, and a Purum girl receives a good augury when the bird's left leg is uppermost because left is a female-connected category. In neither case, moreover, are the contexts involved intrinsically negative. Thus these connections are context-specific and do not necessarily, or even probably, shape the whole symbolic system. A form of representation which can be read as if they do is almost bound to invite criticism.

Homology and Analogy

As already noted (and cf. Makarius and Makarius 1973: 211-12), Needham's statements concerning the coherence of the tables and their constituent columns are less contradictory when they are heuristic in intent and do not form part of an actual analysis, though they are still not free from all problems. One is the question of the 'limited circumstantial predictability' (Needham 1985: 139) involved in conducting analyses, which is only possible because of the cross-cultural constancy in the values accorded to many frequently occurring terms. A supposedly globally occurring structure like lateral symbolism 'can be a reliable instrument in the interpretation of further ethnographical cases' (ibid.: 187), and it seems to have been used as such in most of Needham's analyses (the Wikmunkan case, discussed above, is a particularly bold example). But his most frequent general statements concern what the tables are intended to mean, and they revolve more particularly around the difference between analogy and homology, the former but much more problematically the latter being involved in their constitution. One can say that statements of the type 'right : left :: white : black' suggest analogy, that is, a similarity of relation, whereas statements of the type 'right : white :: left : black' suggest homology, that is, the direct association of terms. It is noticeable that most of these statements date from a later period, when Needham had largely set aside ethnographic analyses of this sort in favour of comparative and at times programmatic studies.

    In his first reply to Beattie's criticism (Needham 1973a: xviii ff.), Needham denied that there was any common substance, saying that these tables have 'no more than an expository convenience' (ibid.: xxv). The most he was prepared to concede here is that there *may* be a relation of homology between certain of the terms in each column, but only if this can be established ethnographically: there is no guarantee that this will be the case, though there are apparently exceptions, such as the dualistic division of all things between Yin and Yang in China.

In his textbook *Symbolic Classification*, published six years later, Needham's attitude towards the existence of a homology between the terms appears to have become more positive. Now we are told (1979a: 66) that the terms in a single column 'need not be connected by qualitative resemblances between individual terms, but instead they are connected as homologues (*a:c* and *b:d*) in a classification by analogy'. Further elaboration came a year later (1980a: Ch. 2) in the course of a demonstration, using dual symbolic classification as an example (and following Maurice Leenhardt), that classification need not be hierarchical, as Durkheim and Lévy-Bruhl had both supposed, but could be analogical instead. More specifically, the relations between the dyadic oppositions listed in the typical table are said to be ones of analogy, and those between the constituent terms in each column ones of homology. Here, analogy is defined initially in its Kantian sense to mean 'a perfect similarity of two *relations* between quite dissimilar things' (Needham ibid.: 46, my emphasis; also 1970: xlv-xlvi), and not in its everyday sense of a rough similiarity between two things *in themselves*. Its importance is that it 'constitutes a distinct mode of classification which is independent of hierarchical division' (1980a: 47; cf. 1973a: xxix).

In another essay in the same volume (1980a: 76), Needham talks of 'the indirect (analogical) connection of the Mugwe with the feminine' among the Meru. This use of 'analogical' is not new in Needham's writings: Purum 'polarities' are said to be analogically linked, 'since they are related to each other in the form a : b :: c : d' (1958: 97); the Lamet example is described as 'a dualistic scheme of analogical classification' (1960a: 115); the concept is briefly introduced theoretically in the Aimol article (1960b: 104); in the Mugwe article it is said that 'the association of these terms rests on analogy' (1973b: 117); and two key Banyoro oppositions, right/left and male/female, are said to be linked by analogy (1973c: 327, 331). At least Needham has been consistent on this score. In principle, the analogy could be thought to rest on the circumstance that one term in each pair is auspicious and the other inauspicious, as Beattie clearly thinks, since he argues that 'lacking this ethnographically based information, there is no "analogy"' (1976: 234 n.20). Such a procedure would clearly be deductive rather than inductive (cf. Lloyd 1966: 421, 440). However, Needham never makes any explicit link with auspiciousness or its opposite. Although his analyses often appear as if this is what is in his mind, in his more general statements the analogy is clearly thought to rest in the fact of opposition, not in the linkage of the terms, which if anything are a matter of homology (see below). It is clear that what Needham is seeking is not a matter of substance but of relation, and of a basically non-hierarchical relation, despite the asymmetry, which is merely relative (i.e. the values of the terms change according to context; see 1979a: 8, 67). This is of some importance in respect of his later dispute with Dumont.

As for Needham's use of homology, again this, ethnographically contingent in 1973, later appears as a necessary factor in or implication of the construction of his tables (Needham 1980a: 46; cf. Barnes 1985b: 14-15). Yet there is still, Needham says, no question of a common substance (1980a: 56-7): homology is, after all, merely an abstract relation, a common dictionary definition of homologous being 'corresponding', in the sense of 'having the same relative position'. The most Needham concedes here is that the terms in a single column may constitute a polythetic class (ibid.: 46, 56). In that this tends to increase the connectedness of those terms, Barnes was to hint later (1985b: 15) that this also tends to increase the solidity of his columns that Needham was at such pains to deny. Perhaps a source of Dumont's apparent misunderstanding of Needham's method was precisely this notion of homology, since in discussing that method (Dumont 1979: 807-8) it was the relations between the oppositions that Dumont calls homologous, not those between the terms (cf. Needham 1987: 114).

There is no retreat in Needham's more recent statements on the matter, though those of 1980 seem cursory by comparison. In 1985, the principles involved are again said to be opposition, analogy and homology, 'by which terms that are analogically alike ... are more sporadically related to one another. It is these principles that constitute the system, assure its constancy, and permit prediction' (1985: 141). And two years later we read that 'a relation of homology [indicated as ≡, R. P.] ... can be posited of individual terms' (1987: 114). But again, he states plainly that the three principles of dyadic opposition, analogy and homology 'do not necessarily consolidate the columns and their respective terms into a unitary structure' (ibid.: 150), and that neither the tables themselves nor the way they are constructed constitute a method. The intention is much more modest: 'what the tables actually sum up is the fact that each of the constituent dyads is asymmetric, in the sense that they are unequally valued in each of the definitive contexts' (ibid.: 151). We are left in no doubt here that the homology between the terms is not to be regarded as in any sense solidary, since this is dependent on the other two factors in the construction of the table. All three factors 'stand in an order of logical priority: first opposition, then analogy, and subsequently homology' (ibid.: 222; also 1983: 94).

But the analogy between the relations themselves would seem not to be a simple matter, given the varieties of opposition that may be encountered (1987: 227-8). Of course, this very variability accounts for the attractiveness of analogical classification in the sophisticated and economical expression of social values (Needham 1980a: 56). It also means, however, that the analyst is not entitled to add other oppositions by inference from what is already given ethnographically, but only as they appear as social facts (ibid.: 58-9; 1987: 151-2). It is also a further reason why the tables cannot be seen as a solidary structure. Unmentioned is the likelihood that this would also undermine their predictability, something that is offered as an advantage of this method, however limited, at around the same time (1985: 139, 141, 187).

At all events, the Kantian formulation of analogy can only be accepted if it is seen as an abstraction in which the faculty of opposing, or at least distinguishing, is consistently present, but in which the form the opposition takes is not constant (Needham 1980a: 55). Because of this latter circumstance, Hallpike (1979: 224-35) challenges the idea that even analogy is involved in the structure of these tables. He is mainly concerned to establish, as a development of Piaget, the existence, character and basis of a distinct form of thought to which he provocatively gives the term 'primitive'. Binary opposition is an obvious candidate for discussion here, given structuralism's explicit reliance on it. This is especially the case for Lévi-Strauss, for whom duality is axiomatic, there being no special need to explain it, though Needham too routinely sees the faculty of opposing as a basic faculty of the human mind.

For Hallpike, however, dualism can and should be explained as arising simply out of the ability to differentiate, out of the 'awareness of discontinuity' (1979: 224). The problem is that there are many different sorts of opposition, as Aristotle pointed out long ago, and as Needham too has argued more recently (1987). Hallpike lists the main possibilities, basing himself immediately on Ogden (1932), though the Aristotelian tradition is of course its ultimate source. Contradictories (e.g. edible/inedible) exhaust their universe of discourse. Contraries (e.g. black/white) do not, basically because there are other possibilities (e.g. red, green) rather than because they allow intermediaries (e.g. grey; cf. Needham's definition, 1980a: 51). For Hallpike, the poles of a complementary identify themselves by being in a part-whole relationship 'distinguished by a break rather than a boundary' (1979: 227). Needham suggests (1987: 199) that these belong rather to the Aristotelian category of correlative. Hallpike says that some complementaries are functional (lock/key), while yet others may involve similarity rather than dissimilarity (brother/brother; in practice, though, same-sex siblings are very often distinguished through relative age). Yet other oppositions in his inventory are empirical rather than either logical or functional, and they may be either associates (sun/moon) or dissociates (village/bush). Here, we begin to meet cultural variation, since the opposition sun/moon might equally be regarded as dissociative in some societies. Finally, Hallpike distinguishes symmetries from asymmetries, an example of the first being the two sides of the body, an example of the second being head/feet.

Thus for Hallpike, a table of pairs such as that which Needham presents for the Banyoro is actually very heterogeneous in terms of the sorts of opposition presented, though many of them refer implicitly to auspicious and inauspicious. Lloyd too has noted that such tables 'depend on recognizing an *analogy* between the relationships between pairs of opposites of various sorts [whereas] the *distinctions* between different modes of opposition tend ... to be ignored ...' (1966: 103, original emphasis; also pp. 89-90). However, this is a logical rather than an ethnographic circumstance, given that on the level of everyday discourse these niceties are routinely ignored: contraries, for instance, normally seem to be treated as contradictories in most contexts. Fox argues (1988: 26), with reference to dualism in Indonesia, that there may also be differences in the rigour with which the dualistic idea is applied. In Indonesia, for example, dual symbolic classification, when compared with the lability of the terms that are paired in ritual languages, is both more limited and more ordered:

> The systems of social and cosmological dualism described for eastern Indonesia do not consist of a simple pairing of elements but rather of an analogical concordance of elements within pairs according to some criterion that establishes an asymmetry between them. In other words, one term of a pair has to be 'marked' or designated as somehow different from the other. To create even the simplest of dualistic systems, a consistent relationship is required among sets of dual categories. 'Right', for example, might be distinguished as superior to 'left'; 'wife-giver' as superior to 'wife-taker'; 'elder' as superior to 'younger', and so on. In short, dual systems must consist of ordered pairs. By contrast, the pairing of terms in ritual languages is unordered.

For Fox, therefore, not only are systems of dual symbolic classification based on analogy, the analysis itself reflects something quite definite, namely the regular superiority of one pole over the other. Fox is, in fact, just one of a number of authors who have been less cautious in assuming a unity between the terms in a column, and even in postulating a whole structure, than Needham. Another is Willis, who found among the Fipa of Tanzania that 'two dominant and analogical symbolic polarities, Settler/Stranger and Head/Loins, define a cognitive and semantic space that includes the lesser polarities of male and female, sky and earth, village and wilderness, senior and junior, centre and periphery, intellect and energy, etc.' (1985: 212). Another is Hicks, in his ethnography of the Tetum of Timor, where the dyads are said to form a 'meaningful whole' which 'cohere into a set' shaped by an all-embracing dichotomy between sacred and profane (1976: 108; see also above). This unity is made even more explicitly by Middleton in his paper in *Right & Left*, which ends with a whole page of oppositions grouped under a general and all-embracing polarity between order and disorder (1973: 386-7), though earlier he had told us that 'essentially these categories refer to the distinction between good and evil' (ibid.: 370).

Beidelman, similarly, talks of the Kaguru having 'a dualistic symbolic classification which is best considered under the categories of either "male" and "female" or "right" and "left"' (1973: 132); the information, though scanty, 'forms a consistent whole' (ibid.: 152). De Josselin de Jong, in his review of Needham's handbook (Needham 1973d; de Josselin de Jong 1976), finds other instances of explicit links being made between the terms in a single column, and he points out that studies of dual organization, whose origin predates Hertz's work, are also examples of all-embracing dualistic systems. Here, at least, is someone wishing Needham well in his debates with Beattie, for he is clearly keen to establish such systems wherever possible. Dual symbolic classification was, of course, one of the four key traits identified by his uncle as characteristic of the Field of Ethnological Study that the latter had defined Indonesia to be (J.P.B. de Josselin de Jong 1935).

Another sympathizer, King, has sought to develop the possible significance of homology in a different way, relating it directly to sociological factors (1977, 1980). He starts by taking up Needham's argument that the factors that permit a total structural analysis involving systems of dual symbolic classification are, on the whole, best developed in societies with prescriptive alliance, less so in societies with lineal descent systems, and least so in societies with cognatic descent. King seeks to modify this with respect to two societies with cognatic descent in Borneo, the Iban and the Ngaju (data on the latter are taken mostly from Schärer 1963). He accepts Needham's statements that no linkage between the terms of a column in a table of pairs is to be expected and also makes the observation that the poles of a simple opposition may carry different values according to occasion: a term may be placed on one side of the table in one context, on the other in another. His further argument is that, although tables of dual symbolic classification can be drawn up for both societies, the degree of linkage between the terms in a column is greater in the Ngaju case, while the Iban allow a greater degree of contextualization. This he correlates with the fact that the Iban have a basically egalitarian society, whereas the Ngaju have a rank system similar to the dichotomy between wife-givers and wife-takers in an asymmetric prescriptive alliance system, in the sense (and only in the sense) that there is a status difference between them. Thus Ngaju society and symbolism are both more 'structured' (1977: 85), though there is no single direction of causality. 'The point of the exercise is merely to isolate logical principles of order which underlie the two systems' (1980: 16)—words which might have been uttered by Needham himself.

King accepts that not all aspects of Ngaju thought as described by Schärer are dyadic: the numbers 3, 4, 5 and 7 are also significant (King 1980: 13ff.). Nonetheless, dualism is central. His own data on the Maloh, another Borneo society with a rank system, support his basic hypothesis:

> ... I would maintain that the majority of Maloh make explicit connections between items in a given column, and that there is a clear relationship between social rank and a host of complementary pairs arranged in relationships of superiority and inferiority. ... there is a more marked sense of inequality between opposites, and the series of dual oppositions are more clearly discerned and more consistently and comprehensively connected. (1980: 26)

How far such examples involve the analyst's reductionism rather than indigenous representations is not always clear, though Beidelman avers that the 'Kaguru themselves do go surprisingly far in such interpretation and synthesis' (1973: 153). Hicks, Middleton and Beidelman, at least, all show the influence of Needham in their work, Hicks very generally and the other two at any rate in their two articles in *Right & Left*, and in this respect even appear to want to outbid him. They and King have clearly followed the view, originating really with Hertz, that the poles of each side of the tables which they have all used must be linked by some common quality—at least of auspiciousness and inauspiciousness—in order to give definition to the asymmetry. An earlier article by van der Kroef is even more explicit: 'the Javanese do not say "South is connected with red" but "South *is* red, Pahing *is* money"' etc.' (1954: 854-5, original emphasis; also Needham 1979a: 11, after Duyvendak). According to van der Kroef, this principle is reflected in divination: if something black is found at the scene of a theft, it signifies that the thief came from the north (cf. Needham 1979a: 22-3). Whether this necessarily involves identity rather than mere association is another question.

Lienhardt has given us one of the clearest warnings of the perils of mistaking relational analogy for an identity of terms, in a passage which ends with a clear allusion to Evans-Pritchard's earlier discussions of the nature of belief:

> it is in the apprehension of analogies that much non-scientific thought seems to lie—analogies such as, for example, sky is to earth as God is to

man, as rain is to crops, as high is to low, and so on. Such systems of analogy vary from society to society, and they are accessible to anthropological study. It is only when we take them to be other than they are—to assert the identity of rain and God, for example, and not an analogical relationship between them—that we begin to wonder how reasonable beings could come to `believe' them. (Lienhardt 1954: 106-7)

Du Boulay (1982: 220) presents a similar thought in a more general form:

> Emphasis [in such analyses] has been on bringing together symbolic correspondences observed in widely divergent contexts, thus making possible an interpretation of specific institutions by revealing in them the operation of a unified system of meaning. Thereafter the coherence of these meanings may give rise to a variety of consequences of which solidarity may or may not be one, and it is the meanings themselves which hold the clue to understanding the part they play within the social order.

As for Needham himself, what he probably intends minimally by his more theoretical statements is that his tables simply list oppositions in accordance with what the ethnography says, and that the choice as to which way round they are to go in the table is dictated by the associations between particular terms that can also be evinced from the ethnography. In practice, as we have seen, some of the terms seem to find themselves being listed according to a general cross-cultural tendency to distinguish auspiciousness from inauspiciousness, especially when standing in opposition to one another. It is this that seems to have led Terence Turner to accuse Needham of 'confusing a formal principle (binary opposition) with a substantive content (i.e., a basis for homology between specific oppositions)' (1984: 369; cf. Howell 1985: 175-6). But even a table formed from mere associations can present seeming contradictions if the associations differ according to ethnographic context within the same culture, as they are very likely to, as Needham himself has conceded (1979a: 8).

In other words, contradictions may arise either through conflicts between contexts within the culture, or through conflicts between specific ethnographic data and the general cross-cultural findings that help form the methodology whereby such analyses are carried out. Conversely, without some sense of connectedness, the tables tend to lose all meaning, and certainly much of their predictability. If they have coherence simply analogically, that is, as regards the simple fact that each pair forms an opposition, this simply means that one can postulate, for example, right : left :: female : male as readily as right : left :: male : female, and list the pairs whichever way round one pleases. One is then free from the difficulties of contextualization and

still has a record of the oppositions in their basic form. But if this is
unacceptable, then one needs some criterion for listing the terms in
one column or the other, thus inevitably bringing some sense of connectedness to each column.

In Needham's actual analyses, therefore, there is a clear conflict
between his general statements as to what the tables are supposed to
represent and the assumptions he often follows in constructing them
from the data. These assumptions derive from Hertz's conceptualiza-
tion of all dichotomies under the general banner of right and left,
which was itself a continuation, though also a modification, of
Durkheim's equally all-embracing and much more problematic
dichotomy between sacred and profane.

There is another, more general consideration. Needham's analyses
of dual symbolic classification certainly have value as legitimate scholarly exercises in themselves. The very ubiquity claimed for such features, however, if such it is, means that their ability to distinguish
societies from one another is severely limited. In that sense, and more
generally because of his endless search for what he frequently calls
the primary factors of human experience or some other such term,
Needham is one of the subject's great systematizers, despite his decon-
structing efforts in other directions. But this also means that studies of
a common theme with the purpose of showing how differences
between distinct societies or types of society are articulated (one could
cite many examples, but Lévi-Strauss's article 'The Bear and the Barber', 1963, is as convenient and as well known as any) are denied
Needham as regards dual symbolic classification. This conformity
means that there must be many societies for which it would be difficult
to say anything that was not simply facile as regards dual symbolic
classification. Needham himself anticipated and answered this point
in the Mugwe article (1973b: 123-4; see also Fox 1989: 44), and was
later to concede that 'binary oppositions are of course commonplace'
(1985: 184). Nonetheless, this may have been one reason why
advances began to be sought in other directions, though it was not
what mainly prompted the dissatisfaction of some of his colleagues.

The Transition from Needham to Dumont

Despite Needham's qualifications, the original problem has not gone
away but continues to centre on the use of two-column tables to represent the incidence of dual symbolic classification in particular societies. These tables are still apt to be interpreted as a structure in which
the terms in either column have a common quality or compose a common category. As we have seen, this is partly because of a distinct

temptation to place terms which are normally valued as auspicious together in one column and those which are normally valued as inauspicious in the other. This in itself, of course, is tantamount to giving them a common quality or entering them in a common category. However, anything else would be untidy and would invite condemnation for that reason.

The problem really lies in the very resort to a diagrammatic device, though not in the way Goody and other critics meant. Diagrams simplify data, but in simplifying they sweep away all qualifications, which the reader is commonly expected to have understood or taken for granted. In short, they often inhibit understanding instead of improving it.

Another notorious example is the use of a matrix diagram instead of a diagram consisting of genealogical symbols to depict a kinship terminology. This apparently originated with Hocart (1937: 549) in an attempt to wean us from inappropriate genealogical thinking in our cogitations concerning kinship systems, and it was subsequently taken up by Leach, Dumont and Needham especially. Yet as Needham himself has pointed out (1960a: 105), it too can be read as a genealogy: father still appears above male ego, for example (assuming a terminology diagrammed by patrilineal descent), and son below. This, of course, is especially the argument of those who are wedded to a genealogical way of thinking anyway. Conversely, as Dumont, hardly a proponent of genealogical thinking, also makes clear (1983: 74), the symbols on a genealogical diagram can perfectly well stand for whole groups or categories as for individuals. This simply shows the extent to which diagrams have to be interpreted and not merely read.

Needham himself has remarked (1980b: 78), 'a matrix ... does not depict a structure: it permits a structure to be conceived'. This is not to say that it will actually be conceived in the way the author intends. It is the same with the tabular representation of dual symbolic classification. Barnes remarks (1985b: 15), 'presumably ... if Needham had never drawn up the table of Meru oppositions, no one would have suggested that the north was feminine', nor claimed, whatever Needham's text had to say, that his tables ignore the fact that the asymmetry of particular dyads might be reversed in particular contexts. For this very reason, this same student of Needham's has declared, of his own work on Kédang in eastern Indonesia: 'I have not even found it possible, or at least useful, to put all Kédang oppositions into a single table' (ibid.: 14).

One can readily see why from his earlier monograph (1974). The village in which he worked is oriented towards the mountain, with right and left, up and down, and the centre all marked. Only enemies may be buried within the village, their bodies being divided according to these different directions. However, if it is not possible to bring back the whole body, the head and the right hand should be secured. Thus one can say that above (= head) : right :: below : left. This is confirmed by the way a corpse is laid out across the slope, with the head to the right and the feet to the left. Furthermore, the left is associated with death, since the bindings tying the corpse are twisted to the left; thus the right must be associated with life. But here contradictions begin to be encountered, since death can also be associated with above, for when the dead return they first emerge uphill. Life, or rather the progression of life, is, conversely, associated with downhill, which is also the direction of descent. Thus the statement that right : above :: right : life is not transitive as far as the relation between above and life is concerned.

Similarly, Rigby remarks (1973: 280), concerning the Gogo scheme, that 'the ascription of certain terms to one or other of the series [i.e. columns] is surrounded by ambiguity in some contexts', though he does not develop the point. Tcherkézoff had similar problems when analyzing data on the Nyamwezi (1985a, 1987). Here, in certain contexts (selection of the king, initiation), black stands for rain and is therefore auspicious, white for drought, which is therefore inauspicious. But in other contexts (the divination of illness or of death), white stands for ancestors, black for witches and (in royal sacrifices) for night. In yet other contexts (family sacrifices, initiation) the ancestors are divided between paternal and maternal, and white stands for the former, black for the latter. Finally, white is a positive sign in family (death) divination, but a negative one in royal divination. Thus black and white have no intrinsic qualities applicable in all contexts. To put black in one column and white in the other would be to confuse the contexts in which either was auspicious or inauspicious, and vice versa. Strathern (1988: 187-8) makes a similar objection to Tcherkézoff's, basically because, in New Guinea at least, oppositions like male and female 'are expansions and contractions of one another, tropes in a general sense of the term, not sub-categories of a category or the species of a genus or components of any overarching classificatory system'.

Iteanu (1990a) makes the same basic point about the subject/ object distinction among the Orokaiva, in contradistinction to the normal neat distinction in the west. Forth points out (1985: 110ff.) that on Rindi, right/left signals male/female and living/dead contrasts, but clearly these two themselves cannot be fitted together so readily, since women have life as well as men, and men die as well as women. The two oppositions belong to different contexts, though the people themselves prefer to ignore the difference, or use a tendentious argument to explain away the 'classificatory dilemma' (ibid:. 109) they nonetheless feel. Thus the winding of men's clothes around the body and the arranging of women's hair in a spiral, which go in opposite directions when seen from the same observation point, are both represented on Rindi as movement to the right—in one case when seen from above, in the other when seen from below (ibid.: 108). This example shows that, while anthropologists are sometimes accused of neglecting different contexts, some of the peoples they study seek positively to elide them. Finally, Hallpike (1979: 232), in examining Needham's Nyoro oppositions, points out that the terms 'evil eye' and 'blessing', though themselves opposed, both belong with the mystical and are therefore entered on just one side of the table; conversely, the pair ruler/subject both belong with order, not disorder, despite their being placed in different columns.

In short, dual symbolic classification is subject to contextual variation, in that the values of particular dyads are sometimes reversed. Put another way, not only do the contexts in which particular oppositions occur differ, so also do the other oppositions they occur with, and their relationship to them. For Needham, this is not an objection to a tabular representation, since the table is merely a list: it does not 'depict a structure', and so the reversibility of particular dyads does not create any contradiction. However, it *is* an objection for those who like to think of each column as denoting at least the quality of auspiciousness or inauspiciousness, since particular terms suddenly change their quality in particular situations. In other words, any assumption that the terms in the column do share such a quality is bound to conflict with the fact that they do not share it all the time, that is, when all the relevant contexts are taken into account. Needham may think he has justified this form of representation by setting out exact stipulations as to its use and significance: but for others, the very likelihood of misunderstanding makes it unacceptable.

Notes

1. The theoretical and methodological objections Needham makes in his introduction to his translation of Durkheim and Mauss 1903 (Needham 1963) have themselves been subjected to critical scrutiny by Allen (1994).
2. The distinction between nature and culture has been extensively discussed more recently, of course, as part of the general deconstruction, and rejection, of Lévi-Straussian structuralism.
3. This formula is to be read 'male is to female as right is to left' etc.; similar ones will appear frequently below.
4. See Makarius and Makarius (1973: 211). Needham himself regards right : left :: male : female as an exception to the variability of associations between terms in being 'world wide' (1978: 14-15).

Chapter 3

THE DUMONTIAN REACTION
UNDERSTANDING HIERARCHICAL OPPOSITION

Dumont on Hierarchy

One solution to the problem of different contexts is simply to have a separate table for each (e.g. Middleton 1973). This, however, amounts to no more than an attempt to refine the diagrammatic representation of what remains the same theoretical approach. For Dumont and his followers, the problem is more than the simple neglect of contexts (or 'situations') that a tabular representation implies: their relation to the ideology as a whole is also ignored. The prime reason for this is that the relation of opposition necessarily involves hierarchy. In fact, Dumont grounds this neglect in the very egalitarianism and individualism of western or modern society, of which most anthropologists are themselves a product (1971a, 1979, 1982). This is what has led them to disregard the presence of both hierarchy and totality in what he calls 'non-modern' societies.

At first sight, this seems implausible. Certainly there have been explicit attempts to dismiss or minimize the existence of hierarchy in non-modern societies. For example, Hallpike's view is that, 'while some hierarchical classification exists in most primitive societies, it is not well formed or of particular utility. More significant are categories based on realms of experience, which need not be hierarchically organized' (1979: 235). On the other hand, anthropologists routinely recognize status differences between individuals, groups and concepts in their work, wherever they feel this to be appropriate. It is clear, however, that Dumont is not talking about hierarchy in the usually accepted sense of the term (Barnes and de Coppet 1985: 1; Needham

---

1987: 127-9): that is, he is not referring to social stratification, nor to any other sort of ranking system, nor to the hierarchy of a scientific taxonomy, nor to mere inequality of status, though these may be expressions of it. It concerns rather the attribution of value that accompanies or occurs in any differentiation. Indeed, value is the same as hierarchy in Dumont's sense, and he relates how he only started to use the former term in a final attempt to get round the anthropological profession's distaste for the latter (1982: 208). Of course, value affects social morphology like anything else, but the two are really distinct. In any case, in his own use of the idea Dumont has largely restricted himself to classifications of various sorts, including those relating to social morphology, and it has been left to his followers to extend it to other spheres, above all ritual.

Hierarchy thus refers to the articulation of the fundamental values of a society's ideology, not to their expression in social forms *per se*, though this also occurs. In non-modern societies, ideology is the unity of fact and value. Modern man, conversely, habitually separates them (Dumont 1979: 809; 1980: 244) and thus 'equates ideology with "false consciousness"' (1971a: 61-2). Morality is divorced from fact, which is scientific and universal and is made the concern of the individual conscience, while modern science takes its character from the exclusion of the moral. It is the *sein–sollen* dichotomy, the Comtean perspective, the positivism of science. Modern society can only reunite fact and value by suppressing one of them. Suppressing value leads to amorality and/or pragmatism (*sollen* gives way to *sein*). Suppressing fact leads to totalitarianism or ideological monopolies generally (*sein* gives way to *sollen*), in which only one ideology is allowed; all others are suppressed, though in suppressing them one implicitly recognizes them (cf. Needham 1980a: 101, on religion being suppressed rather than absent in totalitarian states). Neither process leads to the totality of non-modern societies, in which there *is* only one ideology, uniting fact and value into one 'simultaneity' (cf. Ardener 1982: 6; below, note 2). In Dumont's own words:

> I call ideology a system of ideas and values current in a given social milieu. [...] What is a predominant ideology? It is not exactly the ideology of a majority of the people nor something stable that would be seen to under-line historical changes. It is rather something that comes spontaneously to the mind [*sic*] of people living in the cultural milieu considered, something in terms of which those people speak and think, and which is best revealed by comparison with other cultures. (1992: 259)

This recalls Durkheim's dictum that collective representations are not to be found in individual minds, but in something like the 'ethos' of the society. The Maussian influence is, of course, also as evident here as with Needham with regard to the necessity of taking a total, or in Dumont's terms holistic perspective, though the interpretation which Dumont gives to it is radically different.

This idea of the totality of non-modern ideology, in the sense of a closed system of thought for which the only alternative is scepticism, is also found elsewhere in anthropology, quite explicitly in Lévy-Bruhl and Horton, and more implicitly in Evans-Pritchard's work on the Azande. At the same time, both Evans-Pritchard and Horton follow Malinowski in distinguishing ideology from an 'empirical' (Evans-Pritchard) or 'common-sense' (Horton) level. The idea of an undifferentiated world view in pre-modern thought is also implicit in the work of such figures as Cassirer, Lévi-Strauss, Mary Douglas and Boas (see Morris 1987). There is a parallel in Bourdieu's notion of *doxa* (1977) as a stage in thought that is prior to the separation of heterodoxy and orthodoxy and is therefore perceived as natural and taken for granted. Some of Dumont's followers have recently introduced the term 'cosmomorphic' (latterly 'socio-cosmic') for such societies, in that they 'consider their societies as co-extensive with the universe, have no words for their values, and do not formulate them abstractly' (Barraud et al. 1994: 118). The authors exclude from their number not only the west but also the Iqar'iyen of the Moroccan Rif, but in general they seem to use the term interchangeably with 'non-modern' in this context. Barraud seems to be referring to this same idea in this passage:

> By 'system of ideas and values' ... we do not have in mind simply the system of representations, but the ordering of all social facts according to the society's hierarchy of values or overall ideology. We argue that these ideas and values are the ultimate values of the society as a whole, comprehended as a 'socio-cosmic' order. (1990a: 37)

Thus non-modern societies accept hierarchy as axiomatic: modern societies, on the other hand, in combining the pursuance of equality with the separation of fact and value, regard hierarchy as unnecessary and relegate it to the undesirable. However, this modern separation of fact and value, which Dumont traces back to Kant (1979: 814), really refers to the scientific or modern intellectual world view rather than that of everyday western discourse (cf. Tcherkézoff 1987: 151 n.1). Indeed, it is clear from earlier studies of value cited by Dumont himself (especially Parsons and Shils 1951; see Dumont 1982: 212ff.) that our discourse is frequently 'non-modern' in character. The difference is that in the west the former has prestige. Dumont certainly feels that this positivist distinction has affected anthropologists, especially the relativists among them, no less than other westerners.

This is significant not only in itself, but also because of the impression created by Dumont's major work on India, *Homo Hierarchicus*

(French original 1966, English translations 1972 and 1980), that only India was hierarchical and that it was essentially in this respect that it differed so radically from the west. This view is encouraged by seeing hierarchy solely as social stratification, whereas for Dumont hierarchy is primarily an objective heuristic, not (or not only) an ideological or cultural peculiarity. A society that values individualism and equality still hierarchizes, in the sense that these values are stressed in opposition to society and hierarchy respectively, which themselves only become manifest secondarily.

If this has caused confusion among anthropologists who stress representations of egalitarianism among the peoples they have studied, it is partly because Dumont's language has tended to produce confusion itself. There are actually two uses of hierarchy in that language, one formal and general, the other pertaining to particular situations. As we have just seen, for Dumont any distinction is hierarchical because of the different values that are given to the respective poles in the very operation of distinguishing. It is this that creates a formal model which is general and which is informed in its entirety by hierarchy, whatever is being distinguished, including such values as right and left, male and female, black and white, north and south, gods and humans, etc. However, on occasion hierarchy itself occurs as a pole, as in India, in which case it is opposed to equality. This is a different situation from hierarchy pervading the formal model, even though it is still present in this sense too. Where the value in this second, particular situation favours hierarchy over equality, this is concealed by the coincidence between valuation and formal model. Where the value favours equality over hierarchy, however, there is a danger of this coincidence being treated instead as a contradiction. In fact, there is none. Representations of equality, or even clear expressions in favour of it, in a particular society do not mean that there is no hierarchy in that society. What the representations or expressions amount to is the declaration of a preference for equality over hierarchy as an ideal. Thus we have equality as a value (the second situation, of those just mentioned), but also hierarchy in terms of the formal model (the first situation) by virtue that a preference is being expressed. There is an additional point to be made with respect to the second situation. The fact that equality is presented as a value does not mean that hierarchy is absent in other, perhaps non- or less ideal aspects of the culture. In fact, it will almost certainly be present somewhere, but (to anticipate what follows a little) on a lower level of the ideology, where it may well occur as a matter of practice. For example, a western society that praises egalitarianism and individualism as core values still has to tolerate hierarchy (for example, in relations between employers and employees) and dependence (through the division of labour) in practical, but less valued everyday matters.

It is thus essential at the outset to distinguish these two uses of the term 'hierarchy' to avoid unnecessary confusion. But hierarchy as Dumont intends it also lends itself to a form of structuralism. In an early work on the theme of hierarchy (1971a: 65), Dumont cites Marriott's transactional approach to the study of the Indian caste system as exemplifying what he is opposing: 'It is once again the old fallacy of producing the whole from the elements, ideas from behaviour ... human order from chance.' This same fallacy has also led anthropologists to treat any dyad in dual symbolic classification as basically symmetrical, an asymmetry being arbitrarily 'super-added' only subsequently and contingently. That is, the basic opposition is factual, the subsequent addition of an asymmetry of value ideological, the implication being that the factual opposition is itself symmetric (1979: 810; 1982: 220).

This can be seen in Hertz, for whom handedness was a problem introduced by society, which had thereby grossly exaggerated the negligible physical asymmetry between the two hands. Society had triumphed over nature, though by the time Hertz was writing modern society was beginning to regard the result as an absurd injustice. Dumont, though he had invoked 'the spirit of his general method' in writing *Homo Hierarchicus*, [1] regards Hertz's point of view as 'wholly mistaken' (1982: 220; also 1980: 243-4). Distinguishing and according a value are not separate activities, nor even two steps in the same process, but another simultaneity: to distinguish *is* to value, and to value is to introduce hierarchy. Thus in a non-modern ideology we should talk of the 'fact-value' or the 'idea-value', which amounts to the same thing: that is, here fact and idea also occupy the same space, since 'actual men do not *behave*, they *act* with an idea in their heads' (1980: 6, original emphases). [2] Conversely, true equality, which the modern world strives for, depends not just on the declaration of equal rights, but on the absolute refusal to recognize difference. Dumont reminds us of the racism inherent in the slogan 'separate but equal' (1982: 238-9), which is obviously for him a contradiction, perhaps the 'logical scandal' (see below) of the moderns.

The idea is not new, and Dumont traces it back to St Thomas Aquinas (1982: 221 n.1). In fact, a remark of Alice Hertz's (1928: x) shows that, despite Dumont's and others' remarks elsewhere (e.g. Willis 1975: 490), it was present in embryo in her husband's understanding of the problem too. Although pedagogically Hertz approved of the modern shift to encouraging ambidexterity, intellectually he had regarded his study as a contribution to the social representation of space, which was always asymmetric for 'primitives', but strictly symmetric for 'geometricians' from Euclid on. This is actually very close to Dumont's distinction between non-modern and modern, since Hertz is comparing value as a part of the notion of opposition with value as something separate from it. What is different is the view of asymmetry not as something unavoidable, but as something to be overcome through education, since symmetry, in the form of equality, is to be preferred. This is made explicit as regards handedness, but the sentiment can also be regarded implicitly as a metaphor for society as a whole.

The Dumontian contrast between egalitarianism and hierarchy is thus clearly also one between substantialist and structuralist approaches to anthropological analysis (see below, and Tcherkézoff 1987: 10, 11). A relational view entails hierarchy and therefore value, because everything takes its definition from its relative place in the whole. A substantialist view, on the other hand, entails equality: everything is defined for its intrinsic qualities, without reference to its relation to anything else. One can turn this round and say that since equality puts everything on the same level, distinctions have to be based on intrinsic qualities—which can ultimately lead to irreconcilable differences (racism etc.). Hierarchy, in not excluding but rather giving everything a different place, defines everything in relation to the whole. This second option starts from a more explicit, conscious level. In addition, in the relational and hierarchical view, the whole pre-exists the parts into which it is divided: it is not a collection formed simply of the parts added together.

Thus Marriott's transactional approach also exemplifies a second consequence of the neglect of hierarchy and totality by western or modern thought for Dumont, namely that it splits up the whole ideology in such a way that its parts are opposed to it. In the typically western taxonomic classification (in biology, for example), although the whole is present, each sub-division of it creates a new stratum, and each successive stratum, right down the hierarchy, excludes the whole. The whole only comes together through the agglomeration of all the strata, and there is no clearly identifiable opposite pole. But this latter circumstance aside, this is also how the dyads in dual symbolic classification are normally seen by the anthropologist: that is, the two poles, whether mutually exclusive or gradable, are regarded as discrete and as forming a whole only by their addition. This is completely wrong according to Dumont, especially for non-modern societies, but also for modern ones to a degree which their stress on equality prevents them from realizing. Instead, the poles are related in a segmented fashion, the inferior pole being a segment of, as well as opposed to, the superior one. In other words, the distinctive opposition should be replaced by a hierarchical opposition. In this case, one pole is not simply superior to the other: in certain situations—or, as Dumont prefers to describe it, on a certain level—it includes or encompasses [3] it and stands for the whole (i.e. for both poles) that is thereby created. The two poles of the opposition are therefore not mutually exclusive (see Dumont 1980: 242, also below, for a diagrammatic representation).

Thus 'the right-left pair is not definable in itself, *but only in relation to a whole*' (1979: 810, original emphasis; also 1971a: 70). This is another way of saying that the opposition 'has a hierarchical aspect' (1979: 810). Dumont admits that this might not be immediately apparent, but he gives an example from Evans-Pritchard's work on the Nuer (also Dumont 1980: 243-4). Here, the spear a man holds in his right hand at the calling out of ox names is an extension of that hand, and as such it represents the whole body, the whole person, and even the clan to which he belongs. Right is also opposed to left, of course, but it is not a simple opposition: right is both part (opposed to left) and whole (including left). It is the reference to a whole that ensures the hierarchy between the two hands, since the reference is different in each case; only the right enjoys identity with the whole. For Dumont, therefore, hierarchy entails encompassment (cf. Tcherkézoff 1987: 9). By contrast, the Needhamite approach refers the pairs not to a conceptual whole but rather to the perceiving (feeling, seeing) ego (see Needham 1987: 125 on this specific point). It is thus reduced to the subject's perception, not conception, of value (Tcherkézoff 1994).

There are many other examples of hierarchical opposition. Allen (1985) has pointed out that language, with its tendency to employ markedness in related pairs, is a good place to find them, and he gives a number of examples. A common one is oppositions between adjectives such as long and short, only one of which is ordinarily nominalized: one usually talks of the length of an object, not its shortness. Brown (1984: 99) adds deep/shallow and sharp/blunt as examples, to which might be added wide/narrow and high/low. He makes the further point that in those examples to do with size it is the greater (i.e. 'more salient') dimension that is 'unmarked' (to use Greenberg's term), that is, ignores its contrasting pole. Other examples of hierarchical opposition in language include a phrase like 'one or more apples', which has plural, not singular concord, i.e. grammatical plurality encompasses the singularity of 'one': a choice has to be made between two opposed values, since there cannot be both [s] and [not s]. It is similar with verbal subjects of mixed gender in French and other Romance languages. These usually require masculine, not feminine plural concord, so that masculine encompasses feminine: one says 'ils donnent', not 'elles donnent', when the grammatical subject is a group of mixed gender, since again the language offers no third choice (cf. Leeuwen-Turnovcova, 1990: 20 n. 67, who offers a similar example from Czech). Even in English, it has been conventional until recently to use masculine pronouns to stand for general categories even where members of these categories may sometimes be female, as in the sentence: 'A doctor should always put his patients' interests first' (cf. Chapter 5).

The opposition man/woman is itself a hierarchical one in the English language (see Dumont 1980: 239-40). It has an element of asymmetry, man being the superior pole in most contexts. But while on one level 'man' stands for one half of humanity only and is strictly gendered, on another it stands for the whole of humanity (cf. the connected word 'mankind'), including 'woman'. In the latter sense it includes or absorbs ('encompasses') its contrary, and, being the superior pole, stands for both: it stands for the unity thus created. In an early statement, Dumont says (1971a: 69) that 'there are two levels: (1) "man" as opposed to animals or to God is male-and-female; (2) "man" as male is opposed to woman as female. In (2), man is superior to woman by virtue of his representing the whole species, including her, in (1)'. This is the view of Genesis, in which woman was created out of man, having originated as one of Adam's ribs: thus man, originally a whole being, produces woman, his opposite, from a part of himself (1986a: 119). [4] This can also be found in other languages, though this is not immediately apparent. While French resembles English here, German can offer the neutral *Mensch* as 'human being' to balance masculine *Mann*, while Greek *anthropos* complements *andros*. On closer examination, these two examples do not, in fact, appear so different from English and French usage. *Anthropos* and *anthros* are clearly linked etymologically, while German *Mensch* is in fact grammatically masculine, not neuter, being the substantivization, in High and Low German, of an originally adjectival form of *Mann*. The German impersonal pronoun *man*, though gender neutral in its present-day use, is also derived from *Mann*, something which brings it fully in line with French, the equivalent *on* being linked etymologically with *homme*. [5] However, in French and English it is more obvious that 'the hierarchical relation is precisely expressed in the double meaning of the words' (i.e. of *man* and *homme*).

One is led here to think not only of the purely linguistic categories but also of women as a 'muted group', to use a phrase popularized by Edwin and Shirley Ardener (though it was apparently coined by Charlotte Hardman; see Ardener 1975: 22), that is to say, of women as being more or less invisible or at least unheard, the men's world view alone being represented to outsiders. For Edwin Ardener,

> the real problem is that all world-structures are totalitarian in tendency. The Gypsy world-structure, for example, englobes that of the sedentary community just as avidly as that of the sedentary community englobes that of the Gypsies. The englobed structure is totally 'muted' in terms of the

englobing one. There is then an absolute equality of world-structures in this principle, for we are talking of their self-defining and reality-reducing features. (1975: 25)

Despite his use of the world 'englobe' here, Ardener is not following Dumont: the equality, autonomy and mutual exclusivity of his world-structures stand in complete contrast to the hierarchy of Dumont's model. This is a concrete objection for some authors, for example, Müller (see below, Chapter 6). Other explicit examples of the encompassment of female by male categories, but also vice versa, are to be found in a brief comparison of two Pueblo (southwest United States) societies, the Keres and the Tewa (Miller 1972; also below, Chapter 7): 'A Tewa man is considered to possess both male and female qualities, while a Tewa woman has only femininity. A Keres man is manly, but a Keres woman is both manly and womanly.' The moiety organization of the Cashinahua of Peru is also of interest here:

All Cashinahua are members of two moieties, *inubakebu* and *duabakebu*, each of which is subdivided by sex. The female counterparts are *inanibakebu* and *banubakebu* respectively. [...] The male term is used to designate the male and female members of a moiety as a group. (Kensinger 1984: 231)

A further example concerns the dominance of one moiety over the other in a system of dual organization. Recognition of this is nothing new, but it has not explicitly been interpreted as a hierarchical opposition. Hocart (1954: 95) noted that on Fiji, the chief of the noble moiety is chief of the whole tribe, including the commoner moiety (for a discussion of Toren's more modern work on Fiji, see below, Chapter 7). He also draws attention (ibid.: 96) to the 'moral' dimension associated with dichotomies (which Dumont might rather term 'value'), though characteristically he does not suggest this development as a primary human characteristic but gives it a place in world history. Lévi-Strauss also noticed the phenomenon early in his career, in a note on Bororo moieties (1944: 267-8; see further below), at the same time adducing other examples from elsewhere in lowland South America and from as far away as Assam.

A further and I think (*pace* Needham 1987: 133ff.) equally good example is the dichotomy between good and evil (which is also utilized by Dumont), at least as found in certain schools of Christianity. Here, one has opposition and asymmetry, and also a situation in which good encompasses evil, for evil only exists because of Satan's rebellion against the authority of God: Satan is no less an angel for having fallen from God's grace. Needham's charge that this example is not ideologically grounded can thus be answered. Yet at the same time good needs evil. In other words evil, though subordinate, is still essential in composing the whole: 'good must contain evil while still being its contrary. That is, real perfection is not the absence of evil but its perfect subordination. A world without evil could not possibly be good', for good would have nothing to oppose to itself, nothing against which to define itself (1982: 224). [6] Possibly the duality is more extreme in other ideologies, for example pre-Islamic Iran, where in some sects of Zoroastrianism evil was not subordinated to good but almost as powerful (cf. Duff-Cooper's 'Manichean differences', ms.: 27). The word 'almost' should impose a caution even here, however: other sects, like Hinduism and Buddhism, seem to encompass evil more completely than Christianity, Islam or Judaism (see David Parkin 1985: 8-9; Zaehner 1961).

Dumont calls this co-occurrence of identity *and* opposition in what amounts to a part–whole relationship a 'logical scandal', and it is among the reasons he cites for the anthropological profession's aversion to the very idea of hierarchy. In some ways it may be compared with synecdoche, basically a figure of speech (though it is capable of wider application) in which a part stands for the whole (e.g. 'head' for 'cattle', in enumeration; 'crown' or 'throne' for 'sovereign, royal'; the journalistic designation of countries by their capital cities). There is not necessarily any opposition, however. Only if opposition were also present could one begin to talk of hierarchy in the Dumontian sense. Similar remarks apply to the closely allied notion of metonymy.

Encompassment and Reversals

This model of opposition is not static, however, but has a dynamic aspect that is quite different from the Hertz–Needham alternative. In certain contexts, which are reversals of and therefore subordinate to the overall ideology, the normally inferior pole itself becomes superior. An example is the Berber house discussed by Bourdieu (1977): crossing the threshold, the boundary between outside and inside, not only reverses the direction of the cardinal points, it also changes the nature of the space one is in. While Bourdieu treats the interior of the house as a continuation of the external space, for Dumont it is both the same and different, the difference only being apparent from the inside, not the outside (cf. Dumont 1979: 812). For Bourdieu too the division of the Kabyle house itself into male and female space is thus merely a different context from the female nature of the entire house when compared to the maleness of the world outside (1977: 90-1); neither is superordinate, neither is subordinate, as it is for Dumont. The Chinese division between Yin and Yang also clearly belongs here: 'while the left is generally Yang and superior, and the right Yin and inferior, ... in the sphere of what is itself common or inferior, the right ... has precedence over the left' (Lloyd 1966: 39 n.3, after Granet 1973: 57; also Tcherkézoff 1987: 68, 95, 97).

Whereas for Bourdieu the threshold of the house is simply the site of a distinctive or complementary opposition, Dumont refers to such a reversal as a change of level in the ideology, which is identified as such through the reversal itself. For Dumont, therefore, reversal does more than merely announce a new stage in the rite, as in the traditional view (see Barnes 1985b: 17). 'Reversal is ... no longer a contradiction but the sign of a movement. It indicates that there has been a change of level and that *a*, which was superior, is now inferior' (Tcherkézoff 1987: 68). There is therefore 'not a contradiction within a single level, but a circulation of values between two levels of the ideology' (Tcherkézoff 1985a: 65).

Reversal is not the only possible indication that levels have been changed: the very partition of the whole into parts (see Iteanu 1985: 101, on different levels of exchange among the Orokaiva of New Guinea), and conversely the subsuming of the parts into a whole (see Allen 1985: 24, on final *d* and *t* in German, in which position they become identical), denote the same. In their joint comparative paper on four different societies (1994: 120-1), Barraud et al. remark that reversal is more marked among the Iqar'iyen of the Rif and Tanebar-Evav (Indonesia), the division of the whole into parts more marked among the Orokaiva and 'Are'are of Melanesia, though both are present in all four cases. Tcherkézoff has suggested that passing the high point of any ritual, what he calls the 'hierarchical threshold', is another example (1986b: 92, 104-5; see Chapter 6). Thus although it may be true that, in Dumont's own writings, 'no criteria are specified by which one level can be distinguished from another' (Needham 1987: 138-9), one has plenty of indications from elsewhere of what form a transition between levels might take.

There are, as so often, certain obscurities in the language Dumont chooses to use: we have already seen this of his use of the term 'hierarchy'. The possibility of reversal means that Dumont's use of 'encompassment' signifies more than just the absorption of one thing by another, as in the encompassment of minorities by a state structure. The notion of reversal is significant with respect to the question as to whether there is encompassment on the second level signalled by that reversal. A close reading of his explanation of the difference between complementary and hierarchical opposition clearly rules this possibility out. Writing of the latter, he says: 'At the superior level there is unity [i.e. the unity of encompassment]; at the inferior level there is distinction, there is, *as in the first case*, complementariness or contradiction' (1980: 241-2, my emphasis; there is a very similarly worded passage at 1971a: 70). The words emphasised in this passage clearly refer to the simple or distinctive opposition that Dumont attributes to Needham and his followers. This property is also mentioned slightly earlier in the same work: 'In the hierarchical case ... one category (the superior) includes the other (the inferior), which in turn excludes the first' (1980: 241). In other words, there is no encompassment on the second level.

Tcherkézoff has contributed to this question in an attempt to clear up certain ambiguities (1994). Reversal produces not encompassment, but at most merely an asymmetry or inequality (i.e. one should not even exclude the possibility of symmetry or equality at this level). The point is made clearer by returning to the dichotomy 'man/woman' in English as an example. The word 'woman' is regularly used in contexts (or at levels) proper to itself, of course, but it never stands for all humanity even on these occasions (except perhaps among the more robust feminist circles, which might, therefore, be considered as having a different value; see below, Chapter 5). In other words, the second term can never represent the whole. Logically, of course, this tends to strengthen the sense of hierarchy overall, if only one pole has the ability to encompass its contrary and thus to stand for the whole ideology. The other has to content itself with temporary assertions of superiority without encompassment, that is, without being able to represent the whole. This also makes it easier to identify subordinate domains and detect reversals.

The first level therefore integrates or elides distinction and represents only the main or ultimate value, the whole and not the part. The part only emerges when moving between levels, through reversal, when it not only reveals itself but enters into a distinctive opposition with the encompassing pole. Being encompassed is thus synonymous with being distinguishable, and encompassment implies a second level by virtue of the part. Reversal still signals a change of level, and the second level is still dependent ideologically on the first.

Partly on the basis of the lack of dependence of superiors over inferiors (see further below, Chapter 5). Parry has suggested (1994: 267) that the association of the superior pole with a whole indicates that it is linked with substance rather than relation. If the notion of Brahman as 'Absolute Being' (not, here, the different but related notion of a *varna*) contains within himself all creation, then this is divinity 'substantialized'. However, as with the medieval Great Chain of Being discussed in the next chapter, which Dumont himself uses as an example, there would not appear to be any identifiable opposite pole making this a true hierarchical opposition.

In any case, it is not how Dumontians see things. Indeed, inferiority is characterized precisely by the appearance of the *subordinated* pole taking substantial form: 'Hierarchy is always, at its most general, an encompassment between relation and substance' (Tcherkézoff 1994–95, emphasis removed; also 1995). In other words, the second level can only be one of 'substantialist relation ... defined by the intrinsic nature of whatever distinguished the encompassed' (Tcherkézoff 1994, emphases removed). And although the encompasser becomes inferior on the second level, this is qualified through the circumstance that this level is itself inferior: in the opposition between Brahman and Kshatriya, the Brahman, even when subject to the king's authority, is in principle exempt from tax and certain punishments. There is thus no similarity between the two situations: they are quite different. In other words, the reversal in itself produces an asymmetric relation between the two levels. Only if the encompassed term could encompass its opposite on the secondary level could one talk of a symmetric reversal.

The point is important in clarifying Dumont's and Tcherkézoff's otherwise obscure charges that oppositions are always treated by Needham and his followers as symmetric, despite the insistence of the latter themselves that they are quite prepared, when the matter is clear, to regard them as asymmetric. Partly, this is to do with the simultaneity of fact and value, neglect of which, for Dumont, means treating oppositions as symmetric until, and unless, value is added subsequently. Needham himself explicitly supports Hertz on this point: 'There is good reason to agree with Hertz that polarity, or opposition, comes first and that the functional asymmetry of handedness is only subsequently made into a symbol of the conceptual operation' (1981: 45). But the explanation also lies in Dumont's view of what happens on reversal. For Needham, reversing an opposition certainly means reversing the asymmetry between the poles. However, there is still symmetry in the sense that the nature of the relationship between the poles remains the same: it does not change from encompassment to distinctive opposition. This enables Dumont to comment:

> By definition, a symmetrical opposition may be reversed at will: its reversal produces nothing. [On the other hand], the reversal of an asymmetrical [sc. hierarchical] opposition is significant, for the reversed opposition *is not the same as* the initial opposition. (1979: 811, original emphasis)

In this passage, Dumont hijacks the term 'asymmetrical' and applies it without further ado to the notion he elsewhere calls hierarchical opposition. A distinction from the opposite camp is then maintained by insisting that their perspective is merely symmetrical. But what he is really saying here is that with hierarchical opposition the nature of the relation changes. What do not change are the values of the two poles, as is the case in the Needhamite perspective (see further below).

This is obviated by the hierarchy, since although the subordinate pole may become prominent at times, it does so only on an inferior level. Conversely, it may be objected that the term 'reversal' is not really apt here, since it does not produce a mirror image of any sort.

At first sight, there do seem to be circumstances in which the normally encompassed pole does encompass its opposite on reversal. On Rindi, Sumba, life is normally associated with right and male, death with left and female (Forth 1985: 112). Transfer between the two levels, says Forth, does not necessarily produce reversal, since those who were left-handed in life remain so in death. Since left-handedness is an anomaly in life, this example is somewhat problematic. More telling, because it is normative, is the fact that the reception of the deceased in the land of the dead is assimilated to the reception of a bride in her husband's village in life. This is so whether the deceased is male or female, so that the female principle seems to encompass the male in death, just as male encompasses female in life. However, assuming that life ultimately encompasses death, then female encompassment of the male takes place at an inferior level of the ideology. Similarly, Jamous claims that the relation of the segmentary equality of the Iqar'iyen to authority is an encompassing one even at the subordinate level. However, authority, in the form of the peace-making *chorfa*, ultimately encompasses the feuding that is predicated on equality expressed as honour (1981: 187; Jamous drew this directly from the analogy with the opposition between status and power, i.e. Brahman and Kshatriya in India). We may assume that in fact either feuding or peace is actually transcendent.

Mosko denies that the reversal of an opposition produces anything more, like a shift to a different level, with even greater regularity, and has even posited an alternative model, which he variously calls 'double, cross-cutting oppositions', 'recursive bisected dualities' or 'quadripartite structures' (1994a: 48; also 1985; 1994b: 198). Basically these involve the combination of two oppositions to produce four different permutations. Among examples he mentions are pure and impure gods and humans in Hawaii (1994a: 56, after Valeri) and chiefs and sorcerers of war and peace among the Mekeo (1994b: 208ff.). Mosko places the latter in a hierarchical series of peace chief/war sorcerer/war chief + peace sorcerer (with same rank), the first two being swapped in war. Thus we have a double reversal, not only between peace and war, but also between chief and sorcerer, each depending on the other. Again, either war or peace is likely to be transcendent in practice.

There is also some uncertainty concerning the idea of reference to a whole. In essence, the whole is the encompassing pole, and the reference is to it alone, not to anything exterior to it (Tcherkézoff 1994).

In a distinctive opposition, reference *is* to something exterior: with right and left it is to the space they occupy or to the body, with social stratification it is to the society at large, and with a scientific taxonomy it is to the highest stratum. As we have seen, this stratum certainly subsumes (encompasses) all the inferior strata, but it does not stand in obvious opposition to any of them. In any case, a hierarchical opposition is not concerned to push differentiation to the limit but contents itself with just two poles (this is discussed further in the next chapter). Tcherkézoff (e.g. 1994–5) seems to prefer to talk of relation rather than reference to a whole, since it is relations, not terms, that a hierarchical opposition hierarchizes: 'A relation to the whole is a relation in terms of value (which is what distinguishes the "whole" from the "collection") . ...' As we have also seen, relation also ensures the structural character of hierarchical opposition. However, this means denying substantialism, and with it, the ability to distinguish things through their nature, as essences. Hierarchy is therefore necessary in order to show the distinction: if two things have the same relation to the whole, they are indistinguishable.

A related question is whether, with hierarchical opposition, the whole is necessarily present at all on the subordinate level indicated by reversal. The fact that there is distinction on this level would suggest not. Allen hints that it might not be in suggesting priest–medium as a hierarchical opposition among the Thulung Rai of Nepal (1985: 22; of course, it occurs very widely). The problem of Hinduization complicates things here, but at least in pre-contact times the priest will unequivocally have represented the whole as the guardian of tradition. Whether he is actually present in the domain of the medium is a moot point. One may doubt this in the present and similar cases, though in Hinduism in north India rituals of possession ultimately require the intervention of a Brahman, a representative of the Great Tradition (Parry 1994: 247). Along with reversal and the division of the whole, absence of the dominant pole, in denoting absence of the whole, may be another mark of being in the subordinate domain. For Barraud, however, neither of the poles *lor* and *haratut* (both refer to different realizations of 'society') can explain Tanebar-Evav society (in eastern Indonesia) on its own, since both are present at all times (1985: 129).

Another question is whether there is only the one form of hierarchical opposition. Tcherkézoff identified three in relation to the Nyamwezi material (1987: 67), a point he has developed subsequently (1994). The first, which he calls 'unity' or, following Dumont, 'hierarchy in the strict sense', is encompassment as defined above, represented as A / A or B. In the second, called 'conjunction' or 'totalization', the whole appears not as one of the poles, but as both together: A+B / A or B. The question then arises whether this is not an example of a whole by addition. However, Tcherkézoff rejects this, since the conjunction still stands for a unified concept: for example, not the human race composed of two different genders, but a figure or pair representing it androgynously or in some other way, for example, as a bisexual being or an opposite-sex sibling pair (especially if they are twins).

The difference between these two models can be shown by referring to the ways in which Osage moieties are symbolized (a comment on Lévi-Strauss's more conventional analysis, 1966: Ch. 5). One way of doing this is to associate one moiety with the Earth and the other with the Sky, the latter but not the former being linked with the Sun, which stands, however, for both; this is unity. Conjunction, on the other hand, can be seen from the numerical associations of the two moieties: 6 stands for one, 7 for the other, and 13 for the totality. The third model identified by Tcherkézoff is reversal, that is, the figure A>B / B>A. Here, in one situation A is superior, in the other B is superior. One example is the difference in value given to black and white in Nyamwezi royal and family rituals respectively. In the former, black is positive since it signifies rain, while white stands for drought. In the latter white is positive, since it signifies the beneficial influence of the ancestors, while black stands for witchcraft. Although Tcherkézoff claims that this offends our western sense of logic, at first sight it actually resembles the difference of contexts beloved of the Needhamite approach he has been concerned to criticize. What makes it a hierarchical opposition is the fact that royal divination—since it affects the whole community, if not creation itself— occupies the primary level, family divination the secondary level. Thus black is only inferior on an inferior level and, despite the form of the figure, can be said to encompass white.

Dumont has also written about the various figures of opposition that can be logically identified, treating hierarchical opposition as just one of them. There is no reason to think that, in talking of the 'encompassing of the contrary', he means contrary solely in the Aristotelian sense of a gradable opposition (hot/cold or black/white, for example, in contrast to odd/even, which is ungradable; see Lloyd 1966: 86ff.): it is merely the opposite pole to the encompassing term. Indeed, Tcherkézoff is quite explicit (1995) that contraries are redundant where hierarchical opposition is concerned. In an early passage relating to this matter (1971a: 70), Dumont distinguished complementarity from contradictory, the former obtaining when the universe of discourse made up of the two terms is recognized as a thing in itself, the latter when the two terms exclude one another so that 'no third possibility exists'. This is also the difference between a structural and a substantialist approach, since in the latter the relationship between the two poles can only be considered directly, whereas in the former it is rather a matter of their relation through the universe of discourse they share. However, despite this difference, they both seem to be equivalent to Aristotle's contradictory, in the sense that they are ungradable oppositions that exhaust their universe of discourse by admitting no middle term (Barnes 1985b: 13).

Dumont goes on to distinguish them both very briefly from 'contrariness', which does allow a 'third possibility', i.e. is gradable (1971a: 70). The Aristotelian distinction between gradable and ungradable is anyway less significant ethnographically than logically. Logically gradable oppositions are frequently treated as ungradable in speech and symbolism—in Aristotelian terms, that is, as contradictories rather than as contraries (cf. Lloyd 1966: 89-90; Barnes 1985b: 12-13). As for 'contradiction' itself, Dumont uses this term sometimes for the situation in which one pole of a hierarchical opposition may stand for the whole as well as for itself—contradiction as 'logical scandal' (1971a: 70; 1979: 809; see above; also Barnes 1984: 63)—and sometimes for what happens on the second level, where encompassment gives way to it (e.g. 1971a: 70).

We should take it, therefore, that when Dumont talks of complementary opposition he is ignoring Aristotelian niceties and means by it a distinctive or non-hierarchical opposition, treated as ungradable, in which the parts are not related to the whole in segmentary fashion but merely form a whole by addition—the false approach, in his view, of *Right & Left* (Needham 1973d; cf. Barnes 1985b: 13). He certainly would not have agreed with Hallpike (1979: 227), for whom a complementary is defined as a part–whole relationship (see above, Chapter 2). As we saw above, moreover, Dumont specifically regards the complementary opposition as being symmetric or equistatutory (1982: 220; also 1979: 810), which sometimes leads him as a consequence to apply the term 'asymmetrical' to his own notion of hierarchical opposition.

In thus begging the question as to whether earlier writers stretching back to Hertz actually recognized asymmetry or not, the disagreement between many of them and Dumont himself over how this earlier work should be interpreted is understandable. As in other cases of disagreement or misunderstanding, however, this one is resolvable with reference to Dumont's own writings or those of his followers. These writings do not always lend themselves to immediate understanding, but they can generally be made to yield to careful exegesis.

In this regard, Tcherkézoff is somewhat clearer in his criticisms, not only of Needham's supposed tendency towards homology in respect of the terms in each column of his tables, [7] but also of the analogy that the latter has always claimed gives relational coherence to a series of oppositions (see above, Chapter 2; Tcherkézoff 1987 [1983] addresses these matters specifically, both ethnographically and theoretically). For Tcherkézoff, Needham's complementary opposition takes the form 'a > b [being] "analogous" to c > d'. By contrast, hierarchical opposition takes the form '[a > b] subsuming the level [b > a]' (1987: 26; the square brackets are presumably intended to suggest the holism involved in the latter type of opposition when compared with the atomism of the former). Further: 'The analogy does not so much involve the various figures with their various terms as the transformation affecting the terms. It is not the terms that are opposed, nor even dual relations (a > b compared with c > d), but relations between levels ([a > b] encompassing [b > a] compared with [c > d] encompassing [d > c])' (ibid.: 67).

The Dumontian perspective can certainly relate different pairs to one another, since two pairs, [a > b] encompassing [b > a] and [c > d] encompassing [d > c], can themselves enter into a relationship of encompassment. Tcherkézoff gives an example in a much later paper on Samoa (1993a). This concerns the relation between the *alii* or chief and the *tufale* or orator. The former is immobile, silent, closer to the sacred. The latter is mobile, talks, and is remoter from the sacred. Also:

> He eats more 'because he moves' and 'makes things move', but he is less dignified because 'moving' is 'less dignified' than 'sitting still'. However, plenty of food 'makes you stronger' and 'moving' is 'stronger' than 'staying' etc. This talk becomes clearer once one has understood that two relationships are involved, two oppositions, and that the first (1) strong vs. weak :: moving around vs. staying and not moving, is at one level encompassed by the second (2) sitting vs. standing and talking :: sitting in the sacred circle and communicating with the divine (*tapuai*) vs. stepping out of the circle to carry out and do the actions decided in the circle. One would then have to add that the second relation is holistic (all title-holders can be called *alii*, more precisely *tamalii*; if necessary a chief can do the work of an orator), whereas the first is a distinctive opposition. Which is why 'orator' is the term we designate as 'encompassed'. (Ibid.: 78)

The fundamental difference nonetheless seems to be that for Needham the significant thing is the analogy between different oppositions, whereas for Dumont and Tcherkézoff it is clearly the change of levels brought about by the reversal of one and the same opposition. The first formulation would at least grant Needham a recognition of the asymmetry of each opposition. One can also be certain that he would recognize the possibility of reversal, problematic though he has called the conception elsewhere (1983: Ch. 5). What he has missed, according to Tcherkézoff, is the phenomenon of encompassment. In particular, invoking analogy prevents one from constructing a structure in terms of levels. Such an approach allows one to take account of linear gradations between terms, but not of hierarchies between relations. [...] It is clear that only a structure conceived in terms of levels can provide some explanation of the fact that, for a non-modern society, to class things signifies to order the world according to a hierarchy of values, and not to arrange terms according to an order dictated by the nature of each term. (1987: 26)

Contexts and Levels

'Level' is another problematic word. According to Barraud (1985: 111), it differs from context as ideological element differs from actual situation. Yet it is still a distinction that has escaped many. Is not the discrimination of contexts or situations itself ideological? More importantly, just what is meant by 'levels', and how do they differ from contexts?

One of Dumont's charges against the Needhamite approach is that it treats ideology as composed of a series of contexts, all of which are both discrete and equivalent. As with the supposed disregarding of hierarchy by others, his strictures over the neglect of context, especially in *Right & Left* (Needham 1973d), have attracted hostility, not to say sheer disbelief, in their turn (see, for example, Barnes 1984: 62; 1985b: 14; Howell 1985: 168; Needham 1987: 111ff., 123ff.). The contributors to that book regularly deal with asymmetric dyads—that was its point, after all, and of choosing Hertz's essay as its charter—while the significance of different contexts, if not fetishized in the way that levels are for Dumont and his followers, is fully recognized. But it would seem that it is the very treatment of contexts as discrete and equivalent rather than their neglect as such that is the real issue. Although in *Right & Left* each pole is treated as supreme in its own context and, as with hierarchical opposition, as forming a whole together with the opposite pole, there is no sense in which one pole stands for the whole: thanks to complementarity, the inequality between the contexts in which the opposition appears is effaced overall. In other words, the two contexts in which first one pole, then the other, is superior are themselves equivalent in value, even though the polarity is reversed. One source of difficulty is certainly that it is not as clear to everyone as it is to Dumont that the very faculty of opposing things necessarily entails asymmetry or hierarchy. But he clearly sees contexts as being abstracted from the overall ideology in the conventional view.

Dumont's levels, by contrast, are clearly welded together into a whole in a manner that is both segmentary and hierarchical. Although the ideology is unitary, it is divided into levels. Moreover, the relationship between these, and between each level and the whole, is hierarchical. Merely distinctive or complementary oppositions, which can be reversed at will, without encompassment being involved, lack 'orientation', that is, they have no reference to the whole, which is simply left out of account.

At one point (1979: 817 n.22) Dumont refers to levels as sub-systems of the ideology, but in general he prefers to talk of levels, presumably because they too are hierarchical and the very term 'level' suggests this, thus reminding us that one level, in standing for the whole ideology, is superordinate over any others that may be identified. To talk of different contexts is insufficient, for contexts, being equivalent and discrete, are not themselves hierarchical. If a reversal is seen as producing just a difference of context, it means simply that now one pole is superior, now the other: this is the case for the basic symmetric opposition with value, that is, asymmetry, being super-added (see above). In Tcherkézoff's words (1993a: 54), 'in this case, the opposition is distinctive and the difference *symmetrical*, meaning that the relationship of each of these terms is identical with reference to the opposition' (original emphasis, brackets removed). Such oppositions may entail reversal, but they are not distinguished by the fact that there is encompassment on at least one level.

With hierarchical opposition, on the other hand, the values of the poles themselves do not change. Reversal simply means that the subordinate values temporarily manifest themselves in contexts—that is, levels of the ideology—that are subordinate within the ideology as a whole. In manifesting themselves, they also cease to be encompassed. Conversely, the primary, encompassing level is non-segmented (Dumont 1980: 78). Going from the pure to the impure pole of an opposition may, for instance, involve changing hands. For Needham, this is a simple reversal and a change of context; for Tcherkézoff (1987: 9), it signals a change of level within a common whole or ideology. For the latter, moreover, on the secondary level encompassment not only ceases, it is replaced by a simple asymmetry in which the normally encompassed pole, although manifest and temporarily predominant, does not encompass its contrary.

It is because these secondary levels are subordinate that the values of the poles themselves need not change, something which is not true of the Needhamite model that simply reverses a distinctive opposition. According to some of Dumont's followers:

> The existence of different levels of value and the shifts from one level to another do not imply that the values in question vary, but rather that at a given level they are related to one another differently, each in turn assuming a dominant or sub-ordinated position in accordance with the level considered. (Barraud et al. 1994: 84)

And further:

The highest level is distinguished by its capacity to define the overall order of the society, while the lower level or levels, although they incorporate exactly the same values, do so in a different hierarchical arrangement and have, consequently, a reduced scope in relation to the whole. The values of a given society can only be understood by identifying these different levels and determining their respective positions in the hierarchy. (Ibid.: 111)

In other words, the two poles of any opposition are always fixed in value in relation to each other, whatever the level. Even when the lesser pole comes to predominate, it remains subordinate because the level on which it is manifesting itself is subordinate.

This is distinction plus value as simultaneity. As we have seen, it is also a relational view, whereas the earlier, Needhamite view of opposition is substantialist. The latter is itself a manifestation of the stress on equality, since as Needham himself makes clear (1981: 45) each pole is regarded as equal, and therefore as discrete and independent, until its value has been 'super-added'. Explanations for such asymmetries can only be drawn from the culture under examination, that is, they can only be matters of context, not of levels, in other words, of structure (Tcherkézoff 1994). Moreover, the substantialist approach merely atomizes the data, for contexts only make a whole by addition, whereas levels arise out of a whole that is segmented and hierarchical in its relation to those levels: 'the hierarchical distinction unifies the data by welding together two dimensions of distinction—between levels and within a single level' (Dumont 1979: 813). This embeddedness of the polar asymmetry as a fact-value is the hierarchy that others have missed.

There are, of course, also problems with defining 'context'. [8] In respect of dual symbolic classification, a difference in context may be produced simply through the reversal of one dyad, as just mentioned. Alternatively, it may arise through the differential association of one dyad with others, or through its association with another dyad now with one direction of asymmetry, now with that direction reversed. Such differential associations lie at the root of the difficulties that Dumont, Tcherkézoff and others had found with Needham's tables.

As a result, Dumont prefers to link situations hierarchically and through encompassment. In India, value encompasses power to stand for the whole except in situations proper to power itself, when a temporary reversal takes place: the Brahman is only subordinate to the king in temporary situations that are themselves subordinate (that is, at a subordinate level) within the overall ideology. Many have seen ethnographic difficulties in applying this to India, let alone more generally, but there can be little doubt as to what Dumont intends in the theoretical sense. He wants to move away from using dyadic pairs in different contexts that are themselves discrete and equivalent, even where the difference of context is produced simply through reversal. Instead, he wants to use them to form an ideology consisting of levels which are hierarchically ordered, segmented and mutually dependent.

Further understanding of the difference between a genuinely hierarchical opposition and one which allows an overall balance, through reciprocity, even where separate contexts show asymmetry, can be drawn from Lévi-Strauss's short note on Bororo moieties (1944: 267-8; see above). Quite simply, one moiety, Cera, is superior to the other, Tugare, and always supplies the village chiefs. Their opposition is therefore not just asymmetric, it is hierarchical in the sense that one moiety is associated with authority in the society. However, the author tries to salvage something for reciprocity through a dubious argument based on what he had discovered on a field trip in 1936 (and which contradicts another writer, Colbacchini), namely that the word *cera* can also mean weak. This leads, via convoluted and rather specious reasoning involving double unilineal descent, to the conclusion that the Cera are remoter from their ancestors than the Tugare, being of a different generation in relation to them. This constitutes an inferiority for the Cera, which balances their superiority in other respects. Lévi-Strauss sums up his position in these words:

> It is well to remember that the moiety system can express, not only mechanisms of reciprocity but also relations of subordination. But, even in these relations of subordination, the principle of reciprocity is at work; for the subordination itself is reciprocal: the priority which is gained by one moiety on one level is lost to the opposite moiety on the other. Political primacy has to be paid at the price of a subordinate place in the system of generations. (Ibid.)

This is clearly interpreted as being a matter of contexts, despite Lévi-Strauss's use of the word 'level,' which is obviously being used normatively here. No cognizance is taken of the possibility of a hierarchical opposition, nor even of a part–whole relation. The hold of egalitarian thought is especially striking in this example, where the author resorts to an obviously forced argument in order to establish, at the cost of a reduction in plausibility, an overall 'reciprocity' or symmetry of values.

In sum, therefore, differences in context can take many forms and are ethnographically contingent, even fortuitous. Levels, on the other hand, are an intrinsic part of the concept of a hierarchical opposition, and they have only one definition. The suitability claimed for hierarchical opposition as a tool in the comparison of social ideologies comes precisely from its invariant character: its very rigidity gives it analytical force. [9] We can be sure, too, that the followers of this method would not accept King's assertion (1980: 6ff. and n.10) that the contextualization of pairs, such that, for example, left is auspicious in rice-growing but inauspicious in hunting, is intrinsically distinct from reversal as part of a ritual process. Reversal, though not in the sense of a mirror image, is equally an essential factor in the operation of a hierarchical opposition and is what gives it its dynamic as an analytical method. There can be little doubt that this is what Dumont, Tcherkézoff et al., have in mind, even though the former's explanations especially are frequently very compressed, leaving much to the reader's inference. One of these inferences is not so much that context has been misunderstood or neglected as that it is wrong to talk of it at all, rather than of levels (as they define them).

It is interesting that Geirnaert-Martin (1992: xxxi) has nonetheless still been able to find a place for context in the Dumontian model: 'according to the social event or "context" under consideration or, in some cases, even within one and the same "context", different sets of "ideas and values" may be temporarily more highly prized than others'. She goes on to make it clear that she is defining context normatively, as 'particular social activity performed by a specific social group at a particular moment; it describes a situation' (ibid.). Thus a hierarchical opposition that displays different levels through reversal might be a feature of a number of different rituals, each ritual providing a separate context or situation. This does not, of course, mean that hierarchical opposition is only sometimes present, nor that these 'situations' may not themselves be involved in hierarchical oppositions with one another.

Is it nonetheless not contexts rather than levels that the people recognize? Iteanu is quite clear that levels are not analytical abstractions but 'social facts as Durkheim defines them' (1985: 91). The 'contradiction' the anthropologist feels between part and whole does not exist for the people themselves:

> On the contrary, this 'contradiction' seems to be ... the most obvious, or at least the wisest thing in the world. This is because, in the indigenous view ... each fact is perceived in its relation to the society as a whole—a conception which implies the existence, in that society, of a paramount value and a hierarchy, and, within the hierarchy, of levels. For the people, then, things are not contradictory because, belonging to different levels, they are not comparable one to another: they are hierarchically ordered and, in relation to the whole, bear different values. (Ibid.: 100-1)

Diagrams

A final question here—if a relatively minor one, especially in view of what was said about diagrams in the last chapter—relates to how hierarchical opposition might be depicted. [10] Dumont's preference (e.g. 1983: 27) is for one box inside another, as follows:

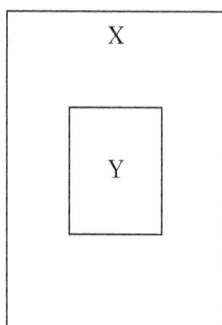

Here, X stands for the whole box, including Y, which it encompasses. A diagram of the distinctive or complementary opposition would consist of a box divided into two halves:

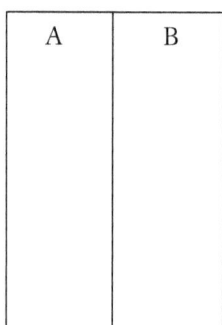

Allen (1985: 26-7) has suggested the following variant for hierarchical opposition:

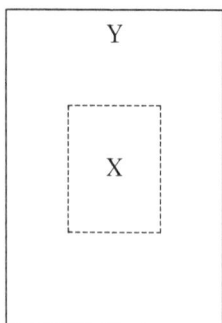

Here, X still stands for the outer, whole box, i.e. the area within the solid lines, Y for the part *outside* the interior box (hence the internal lines are pecked, not solid). This sacrifices the graphic representation of encompassment for an image where the weightiest, ideologically encompassing part occupies the centre, the encompassed part the periphery. Allen gives reasons justifying this ethnographically, such as the opposition insider/outsider and the only slightly less general tendency to distinguish one's own people from others as humans versus non-humans. Certainly one sympathizer of Dumont, Iteanu, sees Orokaiva ideology in that way (1991: 347). Another example is provided by Valeri (1989: 124, 125), where he says that the Hualu village and its communal house represent 'the global society' (see below, Chapter 8). However, there are countervailing examples, such as the Kei Islands, where outside, the source of both life and death, encompasses the inside (Barraud 1985: 126), and Bali, where the caste society, indigenously recognized as an importation from India, encompasses what is regarded as the autochthonous society (Guermonprez 1987: 203).

Allen accepts that 'in thinking about global configurations of idea-values there is room both for the encompassment and centrality representations' (1985: 27). Dumont might well think that the latter sort of representation was exactly what a westerner might be expected to produce (another of the advantages Allen puts forward for it is its 'conforming to much English usage, both everyday and analytical'). For Dumont, in fact, it is just another of our substantialist preconceptions:

> Hierarchically, the superior is that which *encompasses* the inferior. [...] The more general, more encompassing end is superior to the more particular, and the highest group is that in charge of the universal end of the whole society. This is in close agreement with the stress on the whole, or *holism*. With us the stress is on the element, the individual, and correspondingly we are apt to [but should not] equate what is essential with the centre, the core, the nucleus, etc., and to speak of 'peripheral' or 'marginal' in the sense of secondary. For this reason we must make an effort to familiarize ourselves with the idea of the *encompassing* being more important than the *encompassed*. (1966: 19-20, original emphases) [11]

Summing up, therefore, we might say that what is new in Dumont's work is the identification of the part–whole relationship as a method of analyzing non-modern societies especially; the fact that this opposition is inherently hierarchical; and the fact that the phenomenon of its reversal can only be explained through division of the ideology into levels which are themselves hierarchized. Despite the hierarchy of values, 'the whole is not, strictly speaking, preferable to its parts, it is simply superior to them ... apposite in some circumstances' (1982: 221). For example, 'religious duty encompasses progeny, which encompasses pleasure, or similarly the ends of life, *dharma, artha* and *kama*' (Dumont 1971a: 68; also 1960: 40-1). Yet, 'obviously duty includes progeny, as progeny presupposes pleasure. Pleasure is not "less desirable", it is desirable in its subordinate place' (Dumont 1980: 362 n.31c). Consequently, there is not 'subordination', but 'transcendence'—'to call it by its true name'—of the division into parts (1982: 222; cf. Allen 1985: 28).

In Casajus's words too (1985: 76), 'we should be sure that when we speak of "levels" in any given situation, some form of transcendence is involved'. As we shall see later (Chapters 6, 7), this transcendence can be seen as providing contact with the sacred, that is, with whatever embodies the society's supreme values. In this last example here, one can say that the transcendence is provided by *moksha* or salvation, which encompasses the whole *trivarga* (see Malamoud 1982: 38; Parry 1994: 265).

Notes

1. 1972: 28. The full quotation reads: 'less for his theory of "double obsequies" or of the polarity of hands than for the spirit of his general method' (but cf. Hertz's own dichotomizing of pure and impure, used so extensively by Dumont in *Homo Hierarchicus*, 1966, 1972, 1980).

2. Cf. Ardener again (1982: 6), who says that behaviour and category 'cannot be separated. They form a "simultaneity".' The notion can also be found in Durkheim (e.g. 1899: 22). According to Daniel de Coppet (personal communication), facts are not separated from ideas, but linked by value: the 'fact-value' is the result.

3. In French, Dumont uses the word *englober*, which is usually translated into English as 'encompass'. Strictly speaking, this is too weak (Needham 1987: 130), for it frequently means little more than 'surround'. 'Incorporate' or 'absorb' would approach the French meaning more nearly. This not the only use of the term 'encompassment' in recent anthropology: cf. Strathern's discussion of it (1988: 240-60) to mean 'the encapsulation of another's viewpoint, a containment of an anticipated outcome' (ibid.: 259), basically, the realization of what another will expect of oneself in any socially defined relationship. This is drawn especially from data on New Guinea.

4. Genesis 3: 21-2. This rib is often said to have come from Adam's left side, though this is not mentioned as such in Genesis—another example of the hold of the idea of the inauspiciousness of the left. Cf. the metaphor of the superior Brahman being the womb from which the inferior Kshatriya was born (Dumont 1962a: 49).

5. The neuter *das Mensch* is a separate word meaning 'cow, slut', i.e. a depreciating term for a woman (I am grateful to Kirsten Volker for pointing this out to me). On the derivation of *der Mensch*, see the Grimms' *Deutsches Wörterbuch* VI, columns 2021ff.; on the derivation of German *man* and French *on*, ibid., columns 1520ff.

6. The sentiment is traceable to Leibniz. See also Durkheim (1915: 43), on hell being 'indispensable to the Christian religion'; and ibid.: 420: 'Satan is an essential piece of the Christian system; even if he is an impure being, he is not a profane one'; also Needham (1985: 131-2).

7. But cf. Dumont, who quipped (1979: 813-14) that the contributors to *Right & Left* wrote 'as if all the world were Chinese', a reference to the homologous nature of at least the Yin-Yang dichotomy mentioned above, in which Yang encompasses Yin (see Tcherkzoff 1987: 68, 92ff.).

8. For a recent volume dedicated to a discussion of what anthropologists mean by context, see Dilley (1999). Despite its recent date, this volume contains only one contribution that mentions Dumont and his ideas (Prince and Riches 1999: 168-9), although the editor was later to convene a conference on them at St Andrews University in May 2000. Prince and Riches have been led to introduce Dumont because they are mainly concerned to establish the holistic, non-individualistic nature of New Age 'rhetoric', and apparently therefore see some passing parallels with his account of India. Even so, their discussion quickly fizzles out in the familiar criticism that Dumont's model neglects the political aspects that underpin ideology and obscures the actual sources of the latter. Context is seen as determining meaning, but also as 'essentially a political process' (ibid.: 169). The authors also appear to link context to the idea of encompassment in Dumont's model; as we see, this does not actually correspond to Dumont's position.

9. Cf. Llobera (1996: 203), who suggests on the basis of what Dumont himself has written that 'his ideas are not the result of the comparison, but rather the other way round'.

10. Discussion of a further knotty problem, the meaning of 'residue', is deferred to Chapter 7, where it is of more immediate relevance.

11. This is threatening to become a minor academic industry in its own right. More recently, Hage et al. (1995) have sought to interpret hierarchical opposition in terms of graph theory and various types of tree diagram. They also point to antecedents to Dumont's model in what they call 'Austronesian' material.

Chapter 4

THE BACKGROUND
TO DUMONT'S REVISION
IN INDIA AND ELSEWHERE

Theoretical Precursors

There were a number of inputs into the aspects of Dumont's work discussed in the foregoing chapter. He himself acknowledges several precursors in respect of particular aspects of his model: Leibniz, Fichte, Herder, Albert Koestler, and, among sociologists and anthropologists, Parsons, Simmel, Kluckhohn, Bateson and Evans-Pritchard. In a more general sense, he is heir to that aspect of the Durkheimian tradition that sees all social processes as the expression of ideals and values. In addition, Kluckhohn showed him how the distinction between fact and value can be elided even in relation to science: 'When the scientist says, "This is valid," he is making an evaluation in terms of an existential standard, but he is not affectively neutral toward his utterances, for it is made partly in terms of his highest values: truth, validity, correctness' (Kluckhohn 1951: 391). Kluckhohn also recognized that values form a hierarchy and that they are tied to one another 'logically and meaningfully', the most general values having a 'priority' (ibid.: 419-20). [1] As for Evans-Pritchard, his famous demonstration that segmentary lineage systems divide and recombine according to context (1940: 135ff.) showed the possible dynamics of anything that was segmented, including holistic ideology. [2] More generally, in what Dumont calls Evans-Pritchard's 'distinction of situations' (Dumont 1979: 806-7), we find one germ of his later distinction of levels within a hierarchical opposition, while Evans-Pritchard's analysis of Nuer spear symbolism (1973) was a good demonstration of right and left being differentially related to a whole (see above, Chapter 3). Beck's essay in the same volume (1973), on the other hand, is picked out as being 'tendentious' because it lacks such a reference—a criticism which Dumont clearly feels is applicable to all the other contributions too (1979: 810-11).

Dumont acknowledges two more proximate colleagues as having been of significance to him in relation to this theme. One is Raymond Apthorpe, who, as a student at Oxford, identified the various logical types of opposition, including hierarchical opposition (his thesis remains unpublished, but see Apthorpe 1984; also Dumont 1980: xvii, 241). The germ of what Dumont later made explicit can certainly be discerned in what Apthorpe seemed to be groping towards in the 1950s, as can be seen from the foreword he wrote to a publication in the Rhodes-Livingstone series (White 1961; Apthorpe 1961). That publication being about Luvale ritual, Apthorpe was moved to consider van Gennep's classic work on rites of passage (1960 [1909]), pointing out that the changes in personal status that White described did not involve hierarchy:

> he [van Gennep] wrote primarily of rites of passage, not rites of promotion. The analogy he drew constantly was of territorial passage, of *crossing* (not rising) from one condition or position to another, of translation (not elevation) 'from one social or cosmic world to another'. (1961: x, original emphasis)

Apthorpe links the distinction he is making with that between ascribed and achieved statuses. The former are incomparable, unique, and therefore not, as he calls it, 'envied' (ibid.) by others; they appear as part of the order of things. Achieved statuses, by contrast, are comparable and, implicitly, subject to competition, to being challenged, contested and 'envied'.

Much later, Iteanu (1985: 101) was to link the notion of comparability explicitly with the Dumontian version of hierarchy. Apthorpe, however, resisted this development. Although conceding that a series of ascribed statuses *may* involve hierarchy, he invoked what he believed to be their strict incomparability to argue that normally the life-crisis rites that an individual must undergo should all be regarded as autonomous and equivalent:

> For the study of ritual, at least, it would be misleading to view birth, dentition, puberty, marriage and so on as ritual risers in a staircase of life, boyhood and manhood, for example, being as treads, one essentially higher than the other. [Among Luvale] such a world of difference exists between the life of the uncircumcised and the society of men who have been initi-

ated that this cannot be formulated *essentially* in terms of hierarchic difference. (1961: x, original emphasis)

Apthorpe also reads into Durkheim's *The Elementary Forms of the Religious Life* (Durkheim 1915) a denial that the distinction between sacred and profane is sufficiently explained by the concept of hierarchy: 'hierarchical distinction ... is alien ... to the logic of dichotomous difference' (Apthorpe 1961: xii; also 1984: 286-7). This is completely opposed to Dumont's claim that difference necessarily and immediately entails hierarchy (see previous chapter). Indeed, the opposition between sacred and profane has come to be seen by many of his followers as an exemplary hierarchical opposition (see Chapter 6), and the distinction between initiated and uninitiated would certainly be another. For Apthorpe, however, these are still complementary oppositions in the Aristotelian sense of the term. This is because, following Durkheim, he regards sacred and profane as absolutely distinct, so that one must be in one or the other at any one time. There is no overlap, and their relation is one of alienation and hostility.

It is in his concession to the possibility of hierarchy that Apthorpe comes closest to Dumont:

Two adjacent states in an ascribed series may be evaluated one above the other, if evaluation is sought, because every value judgement entails super- and sub-ordination. [...] But such evaluation is possible only in relation to a third context (possibly a third ascribed state) which transcends the two ascribed states in question. (1961: 10)

One is immediately reminded of the example that Dumont drew from Evans-Pritchard, of the Nuer with his spear in his right hand (see previous chapter). Apthorpe's third state would be the whole body to which left and right are, though differently, referred. There is also transcendence. Only the words 'if evaluation is sought' might appear problematic to Dumont: they are redundant, given that distinction and evaluation are a single operation. And by 1984, Apthorpe was more explicitly associating ascription with hierarchy (1984: 291).

Another example of this 'third state' is supposedly the sacred, seen as transcending the dichotomy between pure and impure. More generally, it is found in the idea of a universe of discourse, which Apthorpe regards as essential both in understanding how the various sorts of opposition differ from one another, and in justifying recourse to the usual two-column table of dual symbolic classifications (1984: 286-7):

Provided that the kinds of oppositions between left and right (and men and women, weak and strong, and so on) are all of the same sort, and their universes of discourse or of reference are comparable, those two-column lists of 'pairs of opposites' which are so familiar in some writings in social anthropology can perhaps bear some of the weight they are supposed to carry in various kinds of cultural analysis. But, if these two conditions are not met, they will at best be casuist. (Ibid.: 286)

The other close figure of significance to Dumont is Serge Tcherkzoff, who in Paris examined dual symbolic classification in respect of the Nyamwezi of Tanzania (1977, 1981), a theme subsequently supplemented with a reworking of Needham's study of the Mugwe (Needham 1973b; Tcherkézoff 1987 [1983]). Although his book was to be heavily criticized by Needham (1987: Ch. 8) and Beidelman (1989), especially in respect of his use of other people's ethnography, he showed how the notion of hierarchical opposition could obviate the difficulties in Needham's bicolumnar tables (1985a, 1987). Dumont recognized in him something of a fellow-traveller, and he acknowledged his independent development of these ideas, remarking of him (1979: 817 n.22): 'We see that the spirit of young Robert Hertz is not dead. As Mauss had said somewhere, "another seed will fall and germinate"'. [3]

India: Purity and Power, Individual and Society

Dumont's most important inspiration, however, was his own work on the Indian caste system, especially *Homo Hierarchicus* (1980, originally 1966). This work confirmed his structuralism, which he felt provided the most suitable means of interpreting this system. In a general way he was greatly influenced here by the previous work of one of Durkheim's earliest colleagues, Célestin Bouglé (1908), in which many of Dumont's later ideas can be found in embryonic form. More particularly, by building on previous accounts of the *varna* scheme by Dumézil (1948: 76) and Hocart (1938: 69), and on Evans-Pritchard's demonstration of relative inclusion and exclusion among Nuer descent groups in their acting politically (1940), Dumont showed how the *varna*, the major ideological strata of Indian society, are related to one another in the manner of a set of *matrioshka* dolls or a nest of tables. In other words, the hierarchy is segmented, with the apex ultimately encompassing all the other strata, in which case it also stands for the whole ideological structure (1962a: 48-9; 1972: 106-7; 1982: 225ff.).

Dumont concentrates particularly on the relation between the top two varnas, Brahman and Kshatriya. At one level this is a simple opposition between sovereignty and power, one in which each is competent in his own sphere and controls the other within that sphere. Thus the Brahman, though spiritually superior to the Kshatriya, is still dependent on him in secular matters, and vice versa (1962a: 51-2). So far, this resembles complementary opposition of the sort often dealt with by Needham as regards sovereignty in particular (e.g. 1980a), but rejected as inadequate by Dumont. But the secular domain is actually subordinate to the spiritual overall—the Brahman is the womb from which the Kshatriya is born (Dumont 1962a: 49). At the superordinate level, therefore, the Brahman encompasses the Kshatriya and stands for both. The opposition between Brahman and Kshatriya, and more generally between sovereignty and power in India, is therefore a hierarchical one and not merely complementary. There is also a difference in that, where Needham talks of two forms of sovereignty—secular, and religious or mystical—for Dumont there is only one form, represented by the Brahman. The Kshatriya has only power, which can be seen as an inferior form of authority, but which in the opposite direction also shades into mere force.

Despite their opposition to one another, Brahman and Kshatriya become united in opposing the remainder of society as rulers to the ruled. But the Vaishyas—the third *varna*, and classically creators of wealth—are united with the top two *varna*s as the 'twice-born' in opposition to the rest, that is, to those who are not entitled to the 'second birth' that constitutes initiation. Finally, all four *varnas*—including the lowest, the Shudras or servants—are opposed to the Untouchables, whose occupations are too polluting to allow them to be incorporated into the *varna* scheme. Ultimately, however, it is the Brahman who stands for the whole as the guardian and transmitter of tradition (1962a: 54-5).

Dumont was thus able to go beyond Needham in showing how sovereignty was related to the whole ideology. For Needham, dual sovereignty is a purely complementary opposition, of which the Brahman/Kshatriya relation is but one among many examples. There is certainly asymmetry between priest and king, but this is simply reversed with the opposition itself: each is supreme in his own context and that is all. As Tcherkézoff remarks (1994), 'Needham's reversal in fact expresses symmetry', and indeed the latter prefers to view the relationship as complementary. For Dumont, however, these 'contexts' are actually levels of the ideology that are themselves hierarchized: the level at which the king is dominant is subordinate to the level at which the priest is dominant, because religion is the supreme value. Further, there is no encompassment of priest by king even at the subordinate level (which, as we saw in the last chapter, is one way of telling that it *is* subordinate), but simply asymmetry (see above, Chapter 3). This level is the domain of power, the other level the domain of purity, or of religion (Tcherkézoff 1994).

The contrast between these two approaches can also be demonstrated by returning to the dichotomy between the Mugwe and the elders among the Meru discussed in Chapter 2 (Needham 1973b; Tcherkézoff 1987: 15ff.; 1994). There is no doubt that the encompassing nature of the Mugwe in relation to the elders can frequently be read from Bernardi's ethnography (1959), the main source of Needham's account (cf. Tcherkézoff 1987, 1994). Compared with the elders, the Mugwe is clearly more significant. He is the sole traditional chief of the Meru (Bernardi 1959: viii-ix, 40, 76), their culture hero (63), the 'great parent', father of the country (150), and representative of it as a whole (109, 113, 136). He is identified with his sub-tribe (144, 159), within which his own clan is pre-eminent (148). His authority overcomes all other divisions (76). Members of both Tharaka sub-units, Umotho and Urio, must obey the Mugwe, though he himself is actually a member of the former (ibid.: 10, 42). The ultimate appeal in disputes or other legal matters is to him (119, 139). Unlike the elders, his authority is not affected by the changing nature of the age-class system but is continuously effective (44), and indeed he is the 'guarantor of the orderly continuity of his people' (160). Although not himself divine, his power comes from God, whose representative he is and with whom he is identified (126-7, 136, 159). Although the elders do have ritual and political powers, especially with regard to the ancestor cults, these are mostly restricted to their own clan or lineage (12-13, 159-60): their authority does not match the Mugwe's in its applicability to the whole society. Although like the elders the Mugwe can act as a diviner (i.e. for an individual client; 136), and can also sacrifice (138-9), unlike them he acts for the whole sub-tribe in his invocations to God (125, 159-60). The fact that he can act as an elder—indeed, he is an elder (151)—while the elders cannot act as he can neatly shows his encompassing role. This reminds one of India, where Brahmans could be, and were, kings on occasion, but kings could never fulfil the Brahmanical role (Parry 1994: 268).

The example of the *varna* scheme, with its four categories, may suggest that, through being related to its parts in a segmentary way, the whole can accommodate more than just one other pole. Certainly this is something the simple or complementary opposition cannot easily cope with, since it normally consists of two poles supposedly exhausting their particular universe of discourse. Some passages of Dumont's (e.g. 1971a: 70-1; 1991: 105-6) tend to encourage such a reading without being entirely clear. Moreover, in many of his examples there are more than two terms overall, as with the *varna* scheme, the Hindu *trivarga*, and the different aspects of Hegel's thought (see Chapter 5). Similarly, one of Dumont's followers, Iteanu, distinguishes three levels of exchange in a hierarchical order among the Orokaiva of Papua New Guinea (1985: 99 and passim). It is clear from elsewhere, however, that Dumont really intends us to focus on only one opposition at a time—Brahman versus Kshatriya, rulers versus ruled, twice-born versus those not entitled to a second initiation, etc.—otherwise, a reversal between levels would be impeded. Indeed, he is ultimately quite explicit that hierarchy in itself is necessarily bipolar, saying, for instance, 'I have insisted on the elementary relation between two successive levels' (1982: 222 n.1; also 1980: 244; Tcherkézoff 1994; 1994–5).

This insistence on a fundamentally bipolar hierarchy has enabled Needham to charge (1987: 188) that 'Dumont reduces the significance of hierarchy by defining it as a relation between only two terms'. Yet more terms can be accommodated, so long as the oppositions involved are taken successively and not all at once. This would appear to be necessary because it maintains the coherence of the model. Houseman's dichotomy between initiated and uninitiated (assuming a society with initiation for males but not for females) may be another example with three terms rather than an elaborated variant of hierarchical opposition, as he himself claims (1984:308 ff.). As he rightly points out, the uninitiated can themselves be distinguished between those who will go through initiation one day (boys) and those who never will (girls and women). Here, therefore, one might be tempted to compose a three-stage hierarchy of initiated men, uninitiated boys and all females, and to try and treat the oppositions involved in one go. The problem is that this invites confusion between the oppositions initiated/uninitiated and male/female, which should be kept separate. In this case too, therefore, each opposition has to be taken separately, since each opposition is only relevant separately. For Dumont, it is the modalities of a single opposition that are significant, not the relations of several taken simultaneously.

A corollary of this is that, as one proceeds from opposition to opposition, one is simultaneously moving down the hierarchy, that is, away from the ultimate value: 'the hierarchical disposition entails that the successive distinctions possible are of rapidly decreasing global significance' (Dumont 1979: 808). At the global level of the *varna* scheme there is only the Brahman; the first opposition introduces the Kshatriya, subsequent ones the Vaishya, Shudra and Untouchable (not actually a *varna*, NB) respectively. A substantialist view might see a paradox in the fact that the Brahman is alone on what is supposed to be the most general level, and even that he represents substance, not relation (Parry 1994: 267; cf. previous chapter). This paradox is resolved by realizing that he encompasses the remaining grades of the society on this level and is only distinguished from them on subordinate levels, where the global reference is replaced by particular roles or functions—no longer the supreme spiritual sovereignty of the Brahmans, but successively the lesser secular power and authority of the

Kshatriya, the wealth creation of the Vaishya, the service of the Shudra, and the decontaminating work of the Untouchable.

This question also arises in Das and Uberoi's challenge to Dumont's basic idea of how the hierarchy in India was ordered (1971). As is well known, the integrating medium of the caste system for Dumont is the dichotomy of pure and impure, the Untouchables removing impurity for the higher castes so that the Brahmans in particular can retain the purity necessary to enable them to carry out their sacerdotal functions or—in the case of the superior, non-priestly Brahmans—to maintain Vedic and Hindu traditions through their study of the texts that give them expression. It is interesting to see how Dumont relates this to the dichotomy between sacred and profane. On one occasion, (1972: 87) he compares caste, in which the Brahman is vulnerable from inferiors, to the typical tribal situation (especially in Polynesia), in which the chief endangers his inferiors. Das and Uberoi comment on this (1971: 34): 'We fail to understand how Dumont can conclude that the second position is a "reversal" of the first, unless he introduces a further unwarrantable equation, identifying by analogy the pure with the sacred and the impure with the non-sacred or profane.' What would be 'unwarrantable' here is principally the association of impure and non-sacred, given that Durkheim and Hertz saw the impure as a manifestation of the sacred (see above, Chapter 1).

The problem here lies in the nature of the relationship between the Brahman and the Untouchable. If the Brahman is thought to monopolize the sacred, this may be thought to imply that the Untouchable is non-sacred and purely mundane, despite the threat his impurity represents for the Brahman. Recognizing this, Dumont's solution is as follows: 'We might perhaps say that as modes of relation to the sacred, they [pure/impure] are encompassed within it in hierarchical order: sacred/pure/impure, in which the first two terms can be seen as encompassing the impure ...' (1971a: 75). Thus although at first sight we seem to have three terms, actually there are only two, the sacred being reduced to purity.

How, then, are we to account for the impure? In Polynesia, one can retain the idea of sacred and profane, since active threat and ultimate social value coincide. The profane is simply the Durkheimian world of private interests, which can certainly threaten the sacred by breaking injunctions, but in doing so remains anti-social, outside the ideology. This is the usual Durkheimian encompassment of the individual by society. In India, on the other hand, the active threat is from inferiors, whose power must therefore be brought inside the ideology; this rules out the profane as a candidate. One therefore looks for something which can endow inferiors with sacredness, namely impurity. We need not question Dumont's claim to have found the opposition pure/impure in the ethnography to say that this shift reminds one compellingly of Hertz (see above, Chapter 1).

Das followed up her own involvement in this criticism by using Hertz's work on right and left in an even more direct challenge to the universality of the opposition pure/impure as a value in India (Das 1977b: Ch. 5). This follows on from her interpretation of the place of ritual in the work of Durkheim and van Gennep, in which she takes from the former the view of the sacred as signalling the axiomatic in social life and from the latter the view of life-crisis rites as liminal threats to this order which ritual must overcome. For Das, it is this liminality that is associated with impurity in Hinduism, both arising whenever a life crisis leads the individual subject to perceive his or her social world as separate from the cosmos, instead of as a unity, as in normal times.

For Das, Hindu rituals can be divided according to whether a rightward or leftward direction is chosen in circumambulation, whether the right or left hand is used in ritual tasks etc., the dichotomy also being one respectively between rituals of life and creation (initiation, pregnancy, marriage, the passage of time) and rituals of 'death and destruction' (death, demons, ghosts, serpents, ancestors). So far, this resembles the classic Hertzian dichotomy. However, for Das it is not homologous with the dichotomy between pure and impure. This also exists, but it cross-cuts the dichotomy between right and left. Thus both pregnancy and birth are ritually marked by use of the right hand, but while pregnancy entails purity, birth is impure. Similarly, all death rituals involve use of the left hand, but while cremation involves impurity, propitiating the ancestors is pure. The key lies partly in the fact that birth, and death itself, are liminal events, and partly in the fact that they both entail a rupture of the seamless unity of the universe, to which the human body and society are both assimilated. In birth, the body is divided into two; in death, society loses one of its members. Pregnancy, on the other hand, involves the incorporation of a newly created being in the body, while the propitiation of ancestors goes along with their reincorporation in a new form, back into both cosmos and society; initiation too is a rite of incorporation.

Thus Das explicitly links impurity in Hinduism with liminality, which is, for her, the local version of the idea of marginality generalized in the 1960s and 1970s in the work of Mary Douglas and Victor Turner. Put another way, right and left divide up the whole class of rituals in Hinduism, while pure and impure demarcate stages within each ritual cycle. One might also say that the 'right-hand' ritual cycle, having to do with life rather than death, ultimately encompasses the 'left-hand' cycle, despite having its own internal phase of impurity. In the main 'left-hand' ritual cycle, the cosmos is initially whole and pure; although death disrupts it and makes it impure, this liminal period comes to an end once the deceased has been properly incorporated as an ancestor, making the cosmos whole and pure again. In Das's own words:

> impurity symbolizes liminality; it marks off the events in which man experiences his social world as separate from the cosmic world. The termination of impurity in the case of both birth and death is coterminous with the incorporation of the social into the cosmic world, so that they are again experienced as integrated. We think that this is a much more satisfactory explanation than the one which traces these impurities to the incurring of pollution through bodily processes. (Das 1977b: 126)

This attribution of liminality to the separation of person and society, which is then resolved back into unity through ritual action, foreshadows the later use of hierarchical opposition in the analysis of ritual by some of Dumont's followers (see Chapter 6).

Das also mentions that impurity may itself be divided into auspicious and inauspicious in some parts of India, such as Bengal, where birth impurity and death impurity are so distinguished (ibid.: 128; also Parry 1980: 94). Different yet again is caste impurity, especially as its degree depends on activity and on caste: for example, a Brahman is more vulnerable when eating than when going through a rite of passage, since in the latter case, the higher the caste the less the pollution. Finally, Das argues, although the impure may symbolize liminality, the liminal is not *necessarily* impure in Hinduism. The sinner is both, and permanently, because his sin has removed him from the sacred. The ascetic, however, in achieving the liminality of his indifference to the social world, has transcended it positively and thus approaches the sacred more nearly than ordinary mortals (ibid.: 130).

For Das, therefore, impurity in Hinduism cannot be reduced to any single source, signification, circumstance or definition. In particular, impurity may be auspicious; and although impurity may signal liminality, some liminals are pure. This brings us back to the thought that liminality, while always potentially dangerous, may be creative as well as destructive. In India, it is precisely the marginal figures, the Brahman, king and ascetic, who handle the positive aspects of liminality and ensure, in Das's words, 'that the social order becomes encompassed [by which she presumably means incorporated] in a sacred cosmic order' (ibid.: 131). [4]

Das and Uberoi therefore also challenge the assumption that the opposition between pure and impure actually integrates the hierarchy, much though it may pervade it as a value. For Dumont, this assumption is grounded in the idea of the complete reciprocity of ritual services, not by direct exchange (as in most tribal societies), but indirectly, through the division of labour. However, there is a point below which Brahmans in particular will not go in providing ritual services, an impassable barrier of pollution separating them from the Untouchables. Below this level, ritual services tend to become directly reciprocal, whether between castes or between groups of kin or affines within each caste (Das and Uberoi 1971: 38ff.). Thus 'it is not the opposition between the pure and the impure [that divides upper from lower castes] but between the principle of asymmetric exchange and the principle of reciprocal exchange' (ibid.: 41). [5]

Das and Uberoi feel that this argument detracts from Dumont's comparison between the hierarchy of India and the egalitarianism of the west: the contrast should actually be seen as one between a differential mix of these principles (ibid.: 40; in fact, Dumont had already anticipated this point; see 1966: 31 and above, Chapter 3). But are we not speaking here of ultimate values instead of 'pragmatic' conditions which, although recognized as existing, may sometimes have the status of necessary evils rather than ideals?

In this regard Berreman, writing in the same symposium (1971), unwittingly and unintentionally supports Dumont in the very act of condemning his apparent devotion to hierarchy by speaking out against the oppression he (Berreman) supposes it to entail and exalting individual freedom in its stead. For him, if hierarchy exists at all it is something to be done away with, in India as much as in the west. For Dumont, however, the relationship is as much one between individual and society as between equality and hierarchy. In each case, of course, the opposition is a hierarchical one, only the polarity is reversed. In the west, individual rights are ordinarily exalted above the social, and society is conceived merely as a collection of individuals. Nonetheless there are situations in which individualism is subordinated to the general good, as in a bureaucracy or business corporation, or in a crisis (1979: 796); we may call these subordinate levels or situations. In Hindu India, individualism is located at the encompassed pole; the only individual to be recognized is the ascetic, whose status depends on his renunciation of society, which is superordinate. Of course, another modern characteristic, the division of labour, makes the individualistic western ideal of total self-reliance impossible in practice. Moreover, individualism is itself a social fact, since it is society that values it and transmits it from generation to generation: otherwise, it would hardly be possible to characterize whole societies as individualistic. Even the values an individual adopts will almost invariably come from society too: at the most, he or she merely chooses between already established alternatives (Dumont 1982: 233 n.1; cf. Durkheim 1898: 12 n.). Even innovations must have an adequate basis in the culture as it already exists, otherwise they are hardly likely to be understood or, therefore, accepted. For the Durkheimian sociologist looking at matters etically, then, the direction of the polarity is reversed and, just as in India, society encompasses the individual.

Many have judged Dumont's association of individualism and equality and his opposing them to holism and hierarchy as presenting only half the picture even intellectually. Ingold (1986) reminds us of the conjunction of equality with holism in the concept of *communitas*. He also suggests that individualism and holism come together in the typical hunting and gathering society:

> The difference, I believe, between the individuality of Western man and that of the hunter-gatherer is that whereas the former is conceived as an autonomous agent prior to his entry into social relations, the autonomy of the latter has its foundation in his incorporation, through generalized relations of sharing, in an unbounded social collectivity. This commitment to the whole does not so much limit as underwrite the expression of individual autonomy. (1986: 130)

Howe, similarly, says that a sense of egalitarianism can be found on Bali that is not linked to anything that can be called individualism (1989: 50). Conversely, Beteille (1986: 127) has complained that Dumont 'has ignored almost completely what may be called, after Simmel, the individualism of inequality', which flourished in the 1980s in the idea of the inequalities of merit produced through the competition of individuals—essentially the economic views of Hayek and Friedman, and politically of Reagan and Thatcher.

At first sight, there seems to be a real difficulty here. In Dumont's own terms, if individualism entails distinguishing people from one another in respect of their own inner qualities and capacities—and if, on the other hand, to distinguish is to value and to hierarchize—then individualism can never be compatible with equality (cf. Beteille 1986 on the problem of the conflict between individualism and equality generally; also Dumont on German ideology, discussed below). Dumont's rebuff to Beteille consists of stressing instead the individualism of identity and of non-identity (1987: 671-2), the first perhaps being something akin to Ingold's hunter-gatherers, the second conceived as the uniqueness of each person. It is clear that, for Dumont, Beteille's tinkering represents a gross impoverishment of what is the most striking aspect of individualism, namely its association with equality, on which Dumont's whole condemnation of anthropologists who ignore hierarchy rests (and see Dumont 1980: 245 for other areas of discourse). It is interesting that Beteille himself introduces value (though he does not use the word as such here) to distinguish mere inequality from hierarchy, which, he says, 'may be described from the sociological point of view as the idealized form of inequality' (ibid.: 133). For him, therefore, the distinction is intended to take into account historical, sociological, actual factors, not merely ideological ones, as for Dumont.

One of Beteille's charges against Dumont's view of India is that it represents traditional India, in which hierarchy *was* valued, not modern India, from which hierarchy in this sense has largely disappeared, leaving only inequalities, which are inevitable but not proper. Dumont himself dismisses Beteille's argument by saying that egalitarianism can certainly be discerned in India—for example, *within* a caste, as opposed to the hierarchy which obtains between castes—but that it occupies a lower level of the ideology. In fact, hierarchy pervades Indian society even outside the caste system in the strict sense, as in kinship (through hypergamy; Parry 1979), and whatever other 'progress' has been made in getting rid of caste, intra-caste marriages persist. In any case, Beteille's objection, like Dirks's very similar one (see below), does little more than transfer Dumont's view and the validity claimed for it to an earlier period that was undoubtedly free from modern, western values.

In fact, the association of individualism and equality is not invariable for Dumont. This is more apparent in his later writings (especially 1991), in which a certain retreat from his earlier position is detectable. In particular, he goes to great pains to deny that there was any intention to privilege equality in his first major work on modern ideology (*Homo Aequalis I*, Dumont 1977), which he intended as being primarily concerned with individualism (Dumont 1991: 8). His only concession to Beteille, in fact, is to thank him for drawing his attention to Simmel's position as yet another of his own precursors (1991: 238 n.22)!

Individualism and German Ideology

One example where individualism *is* associated with inequality for Dumont—and it is an important one for the modern world—is German ideology (see Dumont 1986a: Chs. 4-6; 1986b; 1991). In contrast to French individualism, in which one is human first and French secondarily—'by accident' in Montesquieu's words—in German individualism one is human only *through* one's Germanness. In other words, French individualism has a universal, German a particular cultural basis, meaning that individualism has 'national variants' (1986a: Chs. 4 and 5; 1991: 15ff., 274). Secondly, German individualism is directly and intimately linked to the notion of *Bildung* or 'self-cultivation', itself derived from the Lutheran interiorization of sin and of one's whole relationship with God, which was driven further in Germany than almost anywhere else.

But the idea and practice of *Bildung* has a number of concomitants and consequences. First, it produces individuals who are different in themselves, in their own being and nature. In this, it is very different from French individualism, which is linked to egalitarianism through the notion of universal human rights. This means that German individuals, in that they can be distinguished from one another, cannot be equal, since we only distinguish in order to accord a difference in value: 'The individualism of difference entails inequality, while the individualism of equality implies identity' (1991: 237, also 35-6, 65, 236, 238). Secondly, and as a corollary, while the French proclaim the equality of individuals by virtue of the universal validity of basic human rights, German ideology at its best (for example, in Herder) equalizes whole nations. Thirdly, for all its importance to oneself as an individual, *Bildung* or self-cultivation by no means absolves one from one's responsibilities to society. The ideal of *Bildung* is pursued *within* society as it exists, not in opposition to it, and it subordinates itself to it (ibid.: 62, 123, 151ff.). The German individual is an 'organ' of a whole (ibid.: 238-9)—which under Hitler came to be personified as a leader (*Führer*). 'In Germany, holism is dominant over individualism' (ibid.: 244). Fourthly, the idea of the nation differs, being a collection of individuals for the French, a collective individual for the Germans. Beneath this can surely be discerned the popular if crude stereotypes of Germans as loving order and being ever obedient to authority.

Among the German thinkers whom Dumont discusses is Wilhelm von Humboldt, reformer of the Prussian education system and arch-exponent of *Bildung*, who stressed the 'originality' of each individual that resulted from it—thus immediately introducing value. Dumont continues:

> It is essential to see that this judgement of universality sanctions the intro-duction of particularity in a mode of thought which excludes it in princi-ple. In effect, in our earlier opposition of holism to individualism *strictu sensu* [i.e. the French version], the individual is directly universal and as a consequence denuded of any particularity. Here, German thought distends universalist individualism in order to place within it a measure of particu-larity, which Humboldt calls 'originality'. (Ibid.: 183)

Of course, Germany in its history has also shown the exclusivity (i.e. racism) that this particularity can lead to when transferred to the idea of a specific German culture: on this plane, there is equality for those within the group, rejection for those outside it. This can be found in Fichte, who converted Herder's principle of the equality of nations into a definite preference for the German nation over all others. The trend represented here culminated in a definite desire to dominate other nations, which characterized German policy under Bismarck and his immediate successors. The final stage was the extermination of Germany's racial enemies under Hitler (principally Jews, followed closely by Poles and other Slavs), which rapidly brought the country to disaster.

Thomas Mann traced this incremental policy to the Reformation and its interiorization of the person, which 'immunised' Germany against the universalizing pretensions of the French Revolution, but Dumont rejects this linkage (1991: 35-6, 71ff.). As the initial response to the Revolution he prefers to stress the particularism of German culture, combined with an initial recognition that all cultures were equal: 'Herder transferred equality from the plane of individuals [the French version] on to the plane of individual cultures or "peoples"' (ibid.: 24). Yet the distinction of cultures, as of anything else, implies valuing them, and it was natural to put German culture first. The difficulty was that, when Germany came to develop universalist pretensions of its own, it was one in which being German and being human came to mean one and the same thing. It was when this notion of dominance turned from being cultural into being racial that the worst excesses were committed, for this led directly to the extermination policies of the Nazis. Ultimately, therefore, there came to be a complete contrast with the French position, in which universalism was divorced from a specifically French culture.

Dumont also prefers to trace this desire to dominate not to the Reformation, but to the territorial and political coincidence of the German nation and the universal Holy Roman Empire from the Middle Ages until Napoleon put it out of its misery in 1806. Because of this lingering universalism, Germany never experienced the transition from a universal to an exclusively national sovereignty that other states, most notably France and England, underwent. Indeed, it had no national polity at all until Bismarck, and that was a Prussian imposition that Bismarck concocted to save the Junckers from class war by outbidding middle-class nationalists. This was another reason for the confusion of universalism and German national culture, which later also became entangled in regionalisms such as the Prussian and the Bavarian. And after the final collapse of the Empire in 1919, the French-style democracy of the Weimar republic, with equal rights for all, was too alien to be satisfying. Here we see the impossibility within the Germany of that time of a notion of individualism which was purely political and which was based on universal human rights, not on German culture or (by this time) race (ibid.: 293). The response was the assertion of *das Volk* against outsiders.

As Dumont acknowledges (ibid.: 39 n.11), most societies are apt to link themselves with the universe in some way to the exclusion of others, to think of themselves as 'the navel of the world'. However, they do it differently. In the French case, this is perhaps thought to apply mostly in terms of high culture. The French language, often considered the mark of Frenchness, can be learned by anyone; conversely, in terms of ethnicity if no longer citizenship, one needs to be *born* a German. In the English case, universalism is perhaps thought of more in terms of constitutional government and liberty, which again anyone may aspire to (though it does not of itself make one English). Only for the Germans, says Dumont, did universalism actually take the form of a desire to dominate other nations. Logically, if to be human was to be German, then universalism could only be achieved by dehumanizing, even exterminating, others.

This interpretation, like Dumont's account of India, has also begun to attract adverse comment. One notable critic is Llobera (1996), whose careful exegesis of Dumont's view of German identity develops into a charge that Dumont portrays Germany as unique. Agreeing with those who have pointed out that neither territorial expansion nor fascism were solely German phenomena, Llobera sees Dumont's main methodological fault as lying in an inadequate engagement with history. Not only is his treatment of German authors 'one-sided' (ibid.: 204), in stressing *Bildung* he is also focusing on 'the privilege of an educated elite' (ibid.: 199) at the expense of neglecting the popular, *völkisch* domain of ideology. The latter is where the 'religious' aspects of Nazism were located, and Llobera traces this neglect to Dumont's reluctance to associate Nazism with the Reformation.

Other criticisms quickly follow. Dumont disregards the importance of regional powers in Germany, some of which had effective autonomy and managed to free themselves from the universalist pretensions of the Holy Roman Empire, even ideologically, at an early stage. Dumont also disregards the significance of the Treaty of Westphalia of 1648, which regularized precisely this situation (and provided a precondition for the later rise of the nation state). There is therefore no discernible link between the universal pretensions of the Holy Roman Empire and German expansion in the modern period: if anything, says Llobera, the ideological bases of fascism are French (ibid.: 205-9).

Clearly, this critique raises some interesting and important questions, especially relating to the uniqueness of German aggression in the nineteenth and early twentieth centuries. Nonetheless, one still feels that, whatever the sources, or consequences, of German national ideology, it *is* distinct from the French, and from many others, more or less in the terms that Dumont sets out. What is more, this sense of distinction is clearly shared by many German commentators (see Radtke 1990: 87). It can be argued that the activities that led to Germany's downfall in 1945 need not have happened and bear no necessary relation to the continuation of what Llobera neatly calls 'the introverted individualism of the Reformation' (1996: 202), nor to the high regard for the state, nor to *Bildung*. Llobera is right to stress historical contingency; but one corollary of this is that German ideology as Dumont describes it was formed and flourishing long before it became pathological. It is in this sense too that it is relevant to examine it.

As far as *Bildung* is concerned, one could argue that if Dumont stressed it, it was in preference to the *völkisch* tendency, since it has prestige in relation to it. In fact there may be another double encompassment here, with *Bildung* being encompassed by the regard for the collective, represented by the state, but itself also encompassing *völkisch* populism in its turn. The state, of course, is transcendent here, as the nation was to become, both in Germany and right across Europe, even the world. This fits in with the frequent observation that nationalism is like a religion, despite its secular focus. This transcendence is expressed in two things above all else: externally, in the birth of the nation out of its struggle against other powers (Anderson, I would argue, effectively sees nationalism as post-colonial, and not just as imagined or an aspect of journalism; see 1991); and internally, in overcoming the division into socio-economic classes. It is also, perhaps, expressed most concretely where, as in Germany, the nation and the individual are fused into one. Thus there is encompassment by the nation of the individuals that compose it, who only emerge as distinct from it at a lower level of the ideology.

Individualism and Renunciation

A type of individualism can also be found in certain Buddhist traditions, which, with their emphasis on the interiorization of both feelings and ritual preparedness, if not on disinterested giving in place of true reciprocity, may be said to approach more nearly the western, especially German, situation. Sherry Ortner, in her study of Sherpa rituals, refers to this contrast as one between asociality and sociality (1978: 39, 53, 152, 157, 162, 180 n.11). There are arguments that this may be true of Hinduism too. Heesterman, for example (1971), queries the supremacy of the Brahman's position because of the fall in status that his gift-receiving brings about (especially if he is a priest): for him, the renouncer represents the supreme value. For Dumont, the first objection is the result of confusing 'a fall of rank within the category with a fall from the category (or of the category)' (1971a: 74). As for the renouncer, as Heesterman admits he is outside society: this leaves the Brahman supreme within it (ibid.: 74-5). Nonetheless, Heesterman clearly has a point (cf. Parry 1994: 265, 269), for despite the social obligations the Hindu is burdened with and the hierarchies they entail, individualism can actually be linked to ultimate value. The renouncer, in leaving society, is concentrating on his own salvation through liberation, and thus aiming at direct contact with the sacred, which can only be obtained through individual effort. Despite the fact that this individualism is compromised by the need to rely on the support of the general population for basic sustenance, this is surely a form of individualism that is seen as a social value.

The *trivarga*, the values of *dharma, artha* and *kama* discussed briefly in the previous chapter, shows this clearly. While each successively encompasses the next, the value of *moksha*, liberation, is the ultimate goal, one which is linked to the others partly because it is only attainable by those who have fulfilled all their earthly duties, including especially those of *dharma*. As Malamoud has pointed out (1982: 38), to take the *trivarga* in the reverse order of *kama, artha* and *dharma* 'is to go from the most subjective to the most objective, and simultaneously, from the individual to the social'. In attaining *moksha*, one again reaches the subjective and individual, thus suddenly reversing the priorities at the top of the hierarchy, but this time as a transcendent value. In this it is unlike *kama*, which can perhaps be likened to Durkheim's profane.

Although Dumont specifically recognizes the difference between the observer's and the indigenous perspectives in this very context (1972: 231), a few pages later (ibid.: 233) he shies away from a firm decision, only approaching one when he comes to conclude his discussion of Hinduism's relentless absorption of its heresies: 'If this view is correct, it teaches us something fundamental, namely that hierarchy in actual fact culminates in its contrary, renunciation!' (ibid.: 241). This equivocation has enabled Fuchs to claim (1992: 27; also Parry 1994: 265) that while Dumont finally recognized the renouncer as the ultimate value, he did not go the whole hog and treat it as the main pole of a hierarchical opposition with society.

From the indigenous point of view, the individual's renunciation is truly the renunciation of society and is opposed to society in a transcendental way. From the observer's point of view, however, this ideal, like any other, is the product of a distinctly social tradition, despite its ideological rejection of social obligations. To argue that the individual renouncer cannot be the ultimate *social* value because he has consciously left society is to confuse the two perspectives. [6] Malamoud's objection (1982: 41; also Madan 1982: 413), that different texts emphasize different values, so that each value has to be considered in turn, loses relevance if an ultimate value is recognized. For a Dumontian, each text must be seen as referring to a different level of the ideology, each being supreme in its own sphere but liable to encompassment by other, superior values in their spheres. In any case, 'the identification of paramount values is of course open to debate and is not supposed to be always easy ... it does not preclude the existence of different valuations on secondary levels, not to speak of individual opinions' (Dumont 1987a: 670). The variability of written texts in Hinduism, between both authors and schools, is well known (see especially Parry 1985).

There is another way of looking at this question. In Dumont's account the Brahmans represent the supreme value partly because they represent the greatest purity, but also because (and as a result) they are closest to the sacred. This goes along with their priestly function. But in fact, not all Brahmans are priests, nor all priests Brahmans (cf. Deliège 1992; Fuller 1988; Parry 1980: 89; Quigley 1992, 1993). This point is still apt to be neglected, perhaps because a simplistic application of Dumézil's three-function idea has routinely led to the assumption that anyone who is not either a king (in India, Kshatriya) or commoner (Vaishya, Shudra, Untouchable) must be a priest. But 'Brahman' signifies a *varna* with many castes, not a single caste. Moreover, priestly Brahmans are normally lower in status than those who are not priests. This is basically because the purity of the priestly Brahmans is compromised by their dependence on their clients' gifts, and more particularly by the transfer of the sins of the giver which accompanies acceptance of these gifts. The highest-status Brahmans are those who live off the land and devote themselves to studying the Vedas. Typically they tend to be landlords and do not farm themselves but use Untouchable labour (e.g. Chamars in the Ganges plain), thus avoiding the sin of extinguishing the life of the soil by ploughing. Although their land came to them as a gift from the king, it is exempt from that class of gifts that bear the giver's sins.

We are, of course, still in the realm of ideals here. Ideally these Brahmans are more independent than any other caste in society, and in their study and ritual observances surrounding the sacredness of the word and the text, they are most in contact with the sacred. Only renunciation can bring them closer to it, and this is indeed the normative goal of their existence, enshrined in the four stages of life: student, householder, hermit (the stage one enters after all one's social duties have been fulfilled, though maintaining contact with the community from one's forest retreat) and renouncer (see Burghart 1983). These Brahmans are thus ideologically the most superior in Indian society. [7] However, their own destinies point away from it, towards an existence in which only individual effort leads to individual liberation and salvation. It is this that brings about fusion with the sacred in India, not the function of being a priest.

Dumont does not deny the existence of either individualism or equality in India, but he places them at subordinate levels of his model. As we have seen, these levels are far too subordinate for many of his colleagues. The chief lesson to be drawn from the foregoing, however, is that if individualism is to be regarded in any sense as the transcendental value in India, Dumont's dichotomy between modern and non-modern societies on the basis of his experience of India needs qualifying. Fuchs goes so far as to suggest (1992: 37) that India is closer to the traditional west than was ancient Greece, from which so many of our values nonetheless derive. This is because while the modern individual is very much in the world, the individual of early Christianity, like the Indian renouncer, was not.

However, Dumont's later comparison focused on the *modern* west as the counterpart to India. One can hardly suggest that individualism is the same in detail in both, or that they hold the same position in their respective societies. They can only be drawn together by taking seriously Dumont's own equation of ultimate, encompassing value with that which is transcendent. For Indian society, purity may well be this value; for the Indian person, it is escape into an oblivion where purity no longer matters, vital though it may be on the road to it. In Dumontian terms, we may say that purity is encompassed by the value of liberation, though the latter requires purity for its attainment. This in turn means that, while India is brought no nearer the west, it can hardly be seen as the comparative model for non-modern societies generally, in Africa, say, or Oceania, or even other parts of Asia (excepting perhaps Buddhist societies). The Orokaiva inner person, for example, although it has a name (*jo*), is merely a residue, totally encompassed (Iteanu, in Barraud et al. 1994: 122; see also below, Chapter 7). That is not so of the person in India, any more than in the west.

Hierarchy and (In)dependence

For Fuller and Parry, the anti-transactional nature of the Brahman's existence has developed into a more general argument that the further one goes up the hierarchy, the greater the tendency to distance oneself absolutely from the castes below. The first version of this argument actually relates to the distinction Fuller makes between Sanskritic and village deities. The latter but not the former are divided further into meat-eating or, in Fuller's terms (1988), meat-accepting deities and those who are only prepared to accept vegetable offerings (cf. Dumont 1957b). This dietary distinction reflects one criterion of caste, given the low status of meat-eating in India, and Dumont treats it as a special case of the distinction between purity and impurity which he sees as the basis of the caste system. This relational aspect disappears with the Sanskritic gods (Shiva, Vishnu etc.), whose excellence is absolute and encompassing, that is, they have no low-status opposite. Again, one can initially identify a triple segmentation, into Sanskritic deities, vegetarian village deities and meat-accepting village deities, though again too, each opposition (between the latter two alone, and between Sanskritic and all village gods) has to be viewed separately. The Sanskritic gods are ultimately transcendent in nature, in accordance with that view of Brahmanism which sees it as aiming to embody the values of the ascetic, whose desire is equally transcendent, that is, to transcend social hierarchies.

According to Fuller (ibid.) this means that the dichotomy between the two sorts of village deity reflects the social order better than do the Sanskritic gods on their own, for their transcendence and Brahmanism leave absolutely no place for the lower strata of society. Thus it is the non-Brahmanical and lower-status village deities which express the very hierarchy to which they are mostly subject, a fact which leads Fuller to conclude: 'When such a model issues from the religion of inferiors, instead of superiors, the legitimation of hierarchy surely attains its apogee' (ibid.: 35).

Parry has taken up this theme more recently with respect to his own data on the holy Gangetic city of Banares (1994: 247-8, 266-9). With reference to the opposition between possession cults and their exorcism on the one hand and Sanskritic rites on the other, he suggests that while the latter have no need of the former, exorcism ultimately needs a Brahman in order to be effective. Another context relates to the actions of the two genders in mortuary rituals. Whereas women are only involved at an early stage, and as highly demonstrative mourners, men are involved mainly in the later stages, when the emphasis is on the transcendent themes of sacrifice and cosmic renewal, and there should be no expression of emotion. This, Parry argues, makes women, who are status-dependent on men at all times of their lives, closer to the social and its relations and transactions than men. Similarly, while the male householder must have a wife in order to carry out household rituals, unlike a woman he can remarry if necessary, and in Brahmanical theory can also substitute his wife with a *kusa* grass. He can therefore make himself less dependent on his wife than a woman can ever be of her husband.

For Parry, these are merely examples of a more general trend for Brahmans to reject ties with lower-status groups, an attitude which, he says, they are just as likely to express with reference to the latter's ignorance as to their impurity. But like Fuller he argues that this indicates the greater dependence of the lower castes on the higher than vice versa, and that therefore they have a greater interest in maintaining the relational caste system that writers like Berreman allege oppresses them. As Parry further remarks, this effectively counters the frequent allegation, which we shall immediately encounter again, that in adopting a relational view of the caste system Dumont has been privileging a Brahmanical view. It also affects Moffat's defence of Dumont (see below), since his Untouchables are actually replicating a view of the caste system that they only imagine is a high-status representation. For Parry's Brahman informants, complementarity with their inferiors is to be avoided; for Parry himself there simply is no interdependence or reciprocity between high and low castes. As Parry sums it up: 'the higher is more complete, and therefore less reliant on others, than the lower. Relative superiority implies relative autonomy' (ibid.: 268).

As we have seen (Chapter 3), and as Parry also argues (ibid.: 267), one consequence of this is that the Brahman as the encompasser of everything else does not represent relations, but substance. This at variance with Dumont's explicitly relational view. As an encompasser, however, the Brahman also contains everything. Does he therefore represent a single substance, as well as a single value? Or, as Parry suggests further (ibid.: 268), is it even possible to identify the latter, given the range of possibilities that have been suggested (cf. Mosko 1994a: 48; 1994b: 197, 214)? But then Dumont himself did not expect this to be easy (see 1979: 814).

Parry also points out that the denial of relations with inferiors is not without its costs for the Brahman, and that it simply adds to the 'conundrums' of Indian society that surround him (1994: 269-70). Fundamentally, Brahmans are faced with having to both affirm and deny their relations with inferiors. If they are priests, they also have to live from the gifts they manage to extort with such great difficulty from their patrons, (mis)using the transcendental ideal of sacrifice (of the patron's resources in this case) to force the latter to cough up. Finally, the ideal of death as a sacrifice renewing the cosmos is in conflict with the ideal of death as escape from such renewal (as represented by rebirth).

Parry ends his book (ibid.: 270-1) by generalizing these ambivalences to other societies, and to 'society' generally. Basically, although the sacred certainly affirms the social order, as Durkheim and, following him, Dumont aver, it also exposes its faults by setting up ideals (for example, through asceticism). So long as people are wont to regard their lives as incomplete, their societies as imperfect, the ideal will always be separated from the actual. But the ideal and the actual are also related, the former providing a model for the latter, which shows how the latter's concerns may be transcended. The form this relationship takes, of course, is that of a hierarchical opposition.

The Rituality of the King in India

Another line of attack against Dumont's theory is the argument that the king as well as the Brahman has ritual functions and is therefore not concerned solely with power (e.g. Burghart 1978; Dirks 1987; Raheja 1988a, 1988b). If religion *is* the social in India, as Dumont maintains, this would imply that the Brahman alone cannot stand for the whole. The argument that he can and does do so opposes the view that such functions were a feature of Vedic times only, since when the king has lost them to the Brahman; in other words, in post-Vedic times the Brahman has no longer had to share ritual power with the king, a situation which reinforces his hierarchical superiority. Heesterman, for example, calls this transition the 'axial breakthrough' and attributes the very genesis of the caste system to it (e.g. 1985). It solved what he calls a 'contradiction' and what Trautmann (1981: 285-8) calls 'the central conundrum of Indian social ideology', namely that the superiority of the Brahman was compromised by his physical dependence on the gifts of the king. More particularly, the king's gifts embodied the sins of the king and of his kingdom, and these were also transferred to the Brahman. For Heesterman, the axial breakthrough changed this situation by converting the gift into a mere fee for ritual services and by requiring the donor to interiorize the sin and deal with it himself by ritual action.

Raheja specifically challenges the view of such a change ever having taken place. This is partly because her own data from a village north of Meerut, Uttar Pradesh, show the local Brahmans still dealing with what she calls the inauspiciousness incurred by the Gujar, the local dominant caste. The latter are, it is generally admitted, the local representatives of the Kshatriya, not only because of their own claims to Kshatriya status, but also because of their local dominance as landowners and their 'centrality' in removing inauspiciousness from the village through their gifts of *dan*. Such gifts have clearly survived the redefinitions of what constituted a gift that Heesterman associates with the transition to the post-Vedic period. Raheja accordingly advocates a return to the Hocartian perspective of the ritual centrality of the king (Hocart 1938) that Dumont had been at such pains to deny. Hocart's view, of course, was a product of his general obsession with ritual at the expense of social structure and his insistence that kings were everywhere priests before they were kings, in accordance with his diffusionist pre-occupations.

Raheja's data show convincingly enough that the ritual prestations centred on the dominant caste cannot be reduced to a common standard. At the minimum there is a distinction between *phaslana*, payments to lower service castes out of the harvest, to which they have a right, and *dan*, which the donees have a *duty* to receive. Other payments go between affines, and the Brahman receives *dakshina* for his ritual services. Dumont and Pocock had, according to Raheja, played down the ritual aspect of these prestations in order to preserve their view of the Kshatriya's lack of ritual functions. In restoring it, she strengthens the view of the *jajamani* system as a basically ritual system overall.

Raheja's work certainly greatly increases our understanding of ritual, dominance, prestations and the interaction between them within a typical village of northwestern Uttar Pradesh. It may be doubted, however, whether it really goes far enough to overturn Dumont's thesis, at least as regards the respective positions of Brahman and Kshatriya. In the first place, the charge that Dumont and Pocock denied ritual importance to the king, and more generally to the royal function, does not stand up to a close scrutiny of their actual writings (e.g. Dumont 1962a; Pocock 1962). It can certainly be argued that they failed to appreciate the full significance of the gifts that pass from the dominant caste *jajman* to the service castes, assuming that they were all merely payments for services or retainers. Nonetheless they aver several times that *jajmani* relationships have to be seen in ritual terms and not merely as a consequence of economic or political dominance and subordination within the village (e.g. Dumont 1980: Ch. 4; Pocock 1962: 85, 89ff.). [8] Similarly, while Dumont certainly stresses power in relation to the Kshatriya, both the ritual inner qualities of the king and his concern with ritual matters as provider of the sacrifice and punisher of ritual transgressions are recognized (1962a: 58ff.). Thus it is not a matter of the ritual versus the mundane but of the respective positions of two ritual spheres: 'Whilst the king would decree a penalty, the Brahmans would prescribe—sometimes for the same action—an expiation' (1980: 168).

Secondly, even if it were correct to say that Dumont and Pocock under-emphasized the rituality of the king, to restore it would not in itself be enough to signal royal supremacy in view of the Brahman's undeniably superior ritual role ultimately, which even Raheja recognizes. There is no necessary contradiction between this superiority and the ritual centrality of the king: the king has always provided the sacrifice—the literal meaning of *jajman*—but leaves it to the Brahman or other ritual specialists to carry out. Nor does the sacredness of the king's person and the need to preserve it of itself make him the most important ritual figure. Dumont and Pocock's answer to Hocart was that the latter had tried to solve the 'conundrum' of the Brahman–Kshatriya relationship by seeing the Kshatriya as a divine king, but that there was no such easy way out: 'His [Hocart's] argument is no less "ideal" than that of the ancient texts which resolve the conflict in favour of the Brahman ... there is no question of "either-or" but of both' (1958: 58). The two ritual powers are opposed but also linked in a hierarchical opposition: those of the king are significant only on an inferior level (cf. Tcherkézoff 1994–95).

Thirdly, as we have seen, the purest and therefore most superior Brahmans are those who study and more particularly those who have the sole right to teach the Vedas, not those who work for others as ritual specialists and accept their gifts. It is noticeable that it is only the latter sort of Brahman who is involved in the exchanges recorded by Raheja for the village of Pahansu. Indeed, it can be doubted whether any largely transactional analysis such as Raheja's can take the non-priestly Brahmans into account, simply because they do not really transact anything—they do not work for others, nor do they give or receive gifts (this is discussed at some length in Fuller 1984). This fact is crucial, since it provides us with a means of reconciling Dumont's approach with the challenge of Raheja's ethnography. In effect, Dumont spoils his case by arguing as if the Brahman's basic function is as a priest, probably a reflection of the influence of Dumézil. Once this assumption is discarded in favour of the idea of the Brahman as a student and non-receiver of gifts, a non-transactor, objections that he cannot be superior because of the transactions he engages in disappear. As when discussing individualism, therefore, here too we encounter personal salvation through the rejection of society and its transactions as the highest ideal, not being a priest. And although this is open in principle to all castes, it is an ideal that the Brahman has sought to link to himself above all others.

Raheja does not by any means deny the existence of hierarchy in India, nor the relevance of relative purity and impurity in its expression. For her, however, impurity (and by implication purity) is that which *cannot* be transferred by gift-giving (1988a: 46; cf. Quigley 1992: 82). Prestations centring on the dominant caste as *jajman* concern not purity or hierarchy, but the removal of inauspiciousness—caused by sin, death, evil or misfortune—to castes at all status levels, Barbers and Sweepers as well as Brahmans. Some of the latter are certainly of low status in this village, something which may well derive from their persistent willingness to accept inauspicious gifts. The question then arises whether this low status is the product of impurity or of unworthiness. Parry (1991) and Őstőr and Fruzzetti (1991) have challenged Raheja's rather exclusive emphasis on inauspiciousness on both ethnographic and theoretical grounds, the former arguing in addition that too sharp a distinction between auspiciousness and purity produces a biased account.

At all events, it can be doubted whether the essentially non-hierarchical system of prestations that Raheja describes can tell us anything about how the hierarchical aspects of Indian society are ordered—and the Brahman–Kshatriya relationship is certainly hierarchical. As Evens points out (1993: 106 n.7), the difference in perspective between Dumont and Marriott (from whom Raheja clearly draws her basic theoretical orientation), which is essentially one between '"hierarchy" and "transaction" as organising analytical concepts', involves respectively 'a kind of structuralism' and 'a kind of systems theory'. Dumont, in incorporating the Brahman, may overstress his dominance, but at least he finds him a place, through the fact of hierarchy; Marriott, in insisting on the salience of transactions and their presumed or implicit reciprocity, has trouble properly accommodating him at all. Dumont's innovation, through the notion of hierarchical opposition, has been to accept the importance of differentiating situations while still being able to identify an ultimate value—namely purity—as articulating the whole. This obviates any talk of 'contradiction' or 'conundrum'—there are no ambiguities ultimately in Dumont's view. In that it adds to the contextualization that he too regards as vital, Raheja's data can only reinforce this aspect of his work.

Burghart also invokes contextualization in his work on Nepal (1978). He argued that there is no common version of Hinduism; instead, the Brahman, king and ascetic each have their own, which conflict with one another. This view, which has also been elaborated by Marriott (1959, 1976), amounts to a series of complementary oppositions, not a unified hierarchical sequence of them. Dumont's account has often been adjudged a very Brahmanical one (e.g. Berreman 1971: 23; Hobart 1985: 49), but on the other hand Moffat (1979) shows convincingly how, in Tamil Nadu, at least, even the Untouchables accept and act upon the prevailing status ideology of purity and impurity. If asked, many Untouchables would probably opt for being Kshatriyas rather than for overthrowing the system (see also Fuller 1988: 35). More generally, by referring to a hierarchy of ideological levels, Dumont can bring the various attitudes of king, Brahman and ascetic into a unified ideological whole.

Similar criticism of Dumont has come from historians. Dirks has suggested (1987) that Dumont's very Brahmanical view of Indian society reflects a bias in his sources that is itself a product of the changes wrought by the British. The latter removed or weakened the kings, but due to their comparative ignorance of Hinduism, they could not take over the kings' former role as arbiters of the caste system in respect of disputes about ranking, rights, etc. Accordingly the British consulted the Brahmans, who rapidly filled this function and tended to put forward their own point of view rather than a strictly royal one, a point of view which subsequently entered scholarship, where it has substantially remained. If this is so, then the Brahmanical account will be coming under challenge today not only through ideas of equality imported from the west, but also through competing accounts from within the Indian tradition itself, encouraged by the reluctance of modern Indian governments even to recognize caste, let alone arbitrate in matters concerning it.

Conversely, Fürer-Haimendorf has argued (1967: 158-9) that although traditional Hindu rulers certainly adjudicated, they were less inclined to lay down caste rules as such. Caste rules were anyway extremely variable and were primarily a matter for a caste's own assembly. Also, the 'tolerance' of traditional Hinduism (see further below, Chapter 5) would have ensured a low level of interference from outsiders, even the king. There was no neutral body of tradition to appeal to, and traditional rulers only intervened in the interests of maintaining harmony in the community. This view may simply reflect the influence of Dumont. But as Fürer-Haimendorf also points out, subsequent non-Hindu governments have on occasion been prepared to intervene in caste matters even where social harmony was not obviously threatened, in order to produce conformity with their own moral values. Thus the British put an end to *sati* (widow-burning) and tried to control child marriages, while the secular Indian government has gone further still, with laws against alcohol, dowry, polygamy and untouchability. In this view, contrary to Dirks, it is colonial and post-independence governments who have intervened the most in caste regulations. Are we then to regard these governments as ritually central to Hinduism, perhaps more so than the traditional rulers they replaced? This would obviously be absurd, but, more importantly, the interference of legislating against certain caste practices seems to be a characteristic modern phenomenon: the banning of *sati*, though humane in western terms, was also a withdrawal of tolerance. [9]

Tcherkézoff on Status and Power in India

Given that Dumont regards the ultimate values of Hinduism as those of the Brahman and that these encompass all other perspectives, his choice is at least logical. For Tcherkézoff (1994; 1994–95), the problem is more the allusiveness and hesitations of some of Dumont's writings rather than any inherent lack of substance. Many difficulties are removed once one realizes that reversing the polarity between status and power does not produce a new encompassment but simply an asymmetry. This means that the subjection of the Brahman in respect of the Kshatriya that Dirks claims is not absolute even on the second level, witness his exemption from tax and from certain punishments. This is also seen in circumstances in which the householder is assimilated to a Kshatriya and any ritual officiant to a Brahman, the former engaging the latter to perform a rite. This makes the latter an employee of the former, but only on an inferior level of the ideology, one which is associated with material reward. On the supreme level, that of ritual, he is the officiant, the householder his dependent client. A payment ideologically belonging to the secondary level is made for a ritual service associated with the primary level. To concentrate on the power factor—which is what all those writing on Indian kingdoms necessarily do—is to miss the point that caste is at once a system involving distance, through the need to shun impurity, and one involving the provision of inter-caste services. Profit and pleasure are recognized, but at an inferior level. On the primary level, the search is not for power, wealth or other worldly goods, but for purity and, through it, salvation.

One source of confusion has been the fact that Dumont opposes purity to both impurity and power (purity being the value especially of the Brahman). Tcherkézoff (1994–5) advocates the separation of the two oppositions. The dichotomy pure/impure acts in India to produce a graded hierarchy of castes and becomes operative as a hierarchical opposition at each boundary between different castes. Any particular caste is a whole for its inferiors but an opposed and encompassed part for its superiors. The idea of caste implies relation, since castes are defined with reference to rules of contact with other castes. Here a substantialist perspective would see only equality or inequality in either direction (up or down the hierarchy). In the Dumontian view, however, any two castes differ according to their relation to the whole. Further, whereas substantialist thought sees caste as a matter of absolute purity, a Dumontian structuralist sees it as a matter of a particular caste being more or less pure than others. The Brahman is not 'pure' (this would involve attributing him with a substance) but 'least impure' (this defines his supreme position in relation to other castes, i.e. to the system as a whole). In principle, no one avoids the Brahman; [10] conversely, the Untouchable has no one to avoid. Nonetheless, on the secondary level for Dumont (*pace* Parry), substance reappears: 'if purity is a relation, it constitutes its contrary as the contrary of a relation: it constitutes a substantial impurity'. Unlike purity, impurity is seen as a bodily condition or state in India, not a relation.

This, for Tcherkézoff, provides an answer to Dumont's puzzlement in *Homo Hierarchicus* (1972: 109-10) over the fact that the period of mourning was shorter for the Brahman than for the lower castes, despite the fact that one would have expected the reverse, given that the Brahman must maintain—and therefore must regain once lost—a greater degree of purity than any other caste. Where impurity is concerned, however, we are on the second level of a hierarchical opposition with purity. Here, purity as relation gives way to impurity as substance, of which one can have more or less of, in a series of inequalities. The Brahman, being the least impure to begin with, actually has an advantage when impurity increases during those life-crisis rites that give rise to it. Dumont was thinking primarily of the changes in status of the mourners. However, it is the corpse that is the source of impurity, and the corpse of a Brahman is less impure than that of an Untouchable. In cases of breaches of caste rules, on the other hand, it is the higher castes that undergo the greatest degree of pollution (cf. Parry 1991: 279). Deliberate misdoing is therefore distinguished from the consequences of inevitable life crises, just as the temporary impurity of the latter is distinguished from the permanent impurity threatened by the former.

For Parry, however (1994: 218-19, after Orenstein), the situation is more complicated, since it is partly related to the Brahman's ideal lack of dependence on inferiors discussed earlier. Certainly, 'the purer and more knowledgeable the Brahman, the less pollution he suffers.' But also, he is less affected by pollution than his inferiors to the extent that he is able to minimize contact with them. Also, when there is a status difference between those who have to observe mourning for one another, it is the inferior who is most affected, the superior less. This adds up to a situation in which periods of pollution may vary, even for the same individual, because 'bodily connectedness is not immutably given at birth, but can be diminished, enhanced or even created by one's actions...' (ibid.: 218).

Tcherkézoff also links the dichotomy between the pure and the impure with Hertz's modification (see above, Chapter 1) of that between sacred and profane. From the point of view of purity, the opposite pole is impure, antagonistic, absolute, a threat. From the point of view of impurity, there is a system of progressive distancing, expressed as rules of contact. But in respect of the enforcement of such rules, it is power and its relation to purity that come into play. This is the business of the king and, more generally, of the Kshatriya *varna*, of the locally dominant caste, not the Brahman, who is more concerned with purity. Therefore one can, says Tcherkézoff, actually see the opposition between purity and power as the key one, purity itself being divided between purity and impurity as another hierarchical opposition (thus two different relations may themselves be in a hierarchical opposition). Viewed in this light, purity sees impurity (i.e. a part of itself) as the opposite pole; from the point of view of power, one sees only purity, something different. This, of course, depends on assimilating or even reducing impurity to power, something which cannot easily accommodate the impurity arising through life-crisis rites. However, a model in contexts would have difficulty in relating purity, or status, to power at all. It would see them as in contradiction because it would place them side by side and not in a relation of encompassment, as the Indian does; for him, therefore, there is no contradiction.

The domain of power is thus located within that of status. The former is local, territorial; the latter is pan-Indian, transcendent. Thus ultimately not even Dumont views hierarchy as purely religious: it is so simply at one stage in the analysis, before power comes to be perceived as encompassed. In effect, it represents the view of the primary level alone. Even one of Dumont's longest-standing critics, Bailey, unwittingly tends to support him here, in a footnote on the symbolism of different types of leadership:

> when the secular leader folds into himself that set of activities which I have called religious, the symbols of the latter mode predominate. He can symbolize moderation and foresight and wisdom, and allow his hidden hand to busy itself with the activities of the boss and warrior. The opposite solution is not possible: if one selects the *macho* style of leadership, then someone else must be the saint. (1981: 41 n.11)

What of dual sovereignty elsewhere? In Byzantium and Tsarist Russia there was a similar situation to that in Vedic India: the Emperor or Tsar was head of the Church as well as the state (Dumont 1971a: 72 n.36). Similarly, 'comparative study of the king in Indo-European myth and epic shows him … as a transfunctional being who represents the synthesis of all three [of Dumézil's] functions' (Allen 1985: 29). Conversely, in medieval western Europe in about AD 500, Pope Gelasius put forward a formula similar to that corresponding with the post-Vedic situation in India, which later popes changed into a claim of ultimate temporal as well as spiritual authority with the help of the fictitious Donation of Constantine. This reached its height at Canossa, where in 1077 the Holy Roman Emperor Henry IV did humiliating penance in the snow to Pope Gregory VII. But as the terror of excommunication began to diminish, papal claims to secular sovereignty were increasingly resisted, and the Church succumbed to the pressures of secular politics, culminating in the disgrace of the Babylonian Captivity at Avignon in the fourteenth century. Subsequently papal claims, though never renounced, have been progressively eroded, helped by the shift towards the interiorization of religious values during the Reformation. Today the situation is entirely the reverse, and in Europe religion survives as a matter of largely private observance that has lost its former monopoly of belief and ritual (Dumont 1986a: 46ff.; 67ff.), while secular powers have given up all claim to deal with the transcendent, at least as regards traditional cosmologies (see Maybury-Lewis 1989: 14-15). Elsewhere (1962a: 54), Dumont contrasts the Hindu situation with those of China and ancient Egypt, where the king-emperor did have clear sacerdotal functions, concluding finally that the Hindu polity is truly unique.

Dumont clearly has much to say, therefore, about global trends in world history. As Kapferer points out (1988: 219 n.1), he has reversed the usual evolutionary view—of Hobbes, Rousseau, Marx etc., as well as of Morgan or Maine—that hierarchy has developed out of an original primordial equality between men. The difference is largely one between pragmatics and ideology. For these writers, hierarchy is simply social inequality through differential wealth and power. For Dumont, it is value, which is inescapable in any society; even egalitarianism is a value expressing a preference and therefore forms a hierarchy. The trend has thus been a shift in value which is only *ideologically* expressed as a shift from hierarchy to equality. In this way, Dumont manages to combine an almost exclusive focus on ideology—that is, on indigenous values—with a sociological perspective which is truly positivist. This, which has escaped so many of his colleagues, is made possible by means of a rigid model, or perhaps methodology, into which one can pour whatever values one uncovers and which can even be used in uncovering those values (see also Tcherkézoff 1994). The global variety of social life is not diminished by the constancy of hierarchical opposition.

Hierarchical Opposition and Kinship

As Dumont himself notes, in *Homo Hierarchicus* 'the notion of encompassing and encompassed ... provides a fairly general principle for ordering and understanding the data (1971a: 75)'. It also impinges on his work on kinship. One example is his treatment of the Hindi term *bhai*, 'brother'. At one level, this denotes consanguineal male relatives of ego's generation and is opposed to the male affines of that generation. At another level, it stands for all male relatives of ego's generation, whether affinal or consanguineal (1971a: 69 n.33). This particular instance has been attacked by Scheffler (1984: 562-3) as an example of the structuralist disease of preferring classes divided into sub-classes to the extensionist rectitude of seeing elements as the building blocks of every society's ideology. However, the extensionism involved is clearly metaphorical rather than literal and is therefore distinct from Scheffler's view of a kinship terminology as being made up of the semantic extensions of basic terms. [11]

In a more general sense, Dumont has regularly opposed consanguinity to affinity in order to stress affinity as a value hitherto neglected by anthropologists dealing with India (e.g. 1971b: 134). He actually calls this a 'simple, binary, or "distinctive opposition", i.e. an equistatutory opposition' (1983: 32). In south India, there is a constant to-ing and fro-ing between affinal and consanguineal statuses:

male ego's mother's brother, who is an affine to ego's father but a consanguine to ego himself, soon becomes an affine again, as ego's own
wife's father, when ego marries his daughter. The distinction in the
west, by contrast, is hierarchical (ibid.: 33): consanguinity encompasses affinity, one's wife's brother (affine) becoming the mother's
brother (consanguine) of the next generation, without ever becoming
an affine again. It is surprising that Dumont does not go the whole hog
and explicitly plump for a hierarchical opposition in respect of south
India too, one in which affinity encompasses consanguinity, since otherwise he is going against his own precept that there are no oppositions which are not unequal. This is nonetheless implied by his
frequent references to the permanence of affinity in south India.

Elsewhere in India, there are examples where affinity is not the ultimate value, for example, the Santal, a 'tribal' group of northern Orissa
and central Bihar, who ultimately recognize the whole tribe as of one
substance, regardless of lower-order affinal oppositions (Bouez 1985:
177). This is no less true of individual castes at the level of their greatest inclusiveness. Similar examples where consanguinity encompasses
affinity have also been identified relating to groups outside India, for
example, the Xingu Carib or Kalapalo of Brazil, where the kin term
ifisúandaw may refer to all kin of ego's generation; to consanguines of
ego's generation as opposed to affines; to 'real' consanguines as
opposed to classificatory ones; or to brothers as opposed to sisters
(Basso 1970: 406ff.). Other examples from Asia include the Tobelo of
Indonesia (Barraud 1984; see below, Chapter 6; also the discussion of
Toren's work on Fiji in the same chapter), and eastern Indonesian societies generally (Howell 1990b), despite the traditional anthropological
focus on asymmetric affinal alliance in the region. Indeed, Ortner
(1981) has generalized the theme to all societies with cognatic or
matrilineal descent in South and Southeast Asia. Here, she argues,
women are seen primarily as sisters rather than as wives and accordingly have a higher status than they do in the mass patrilineal societies
of India and China. The latter are dominated by dowry, and women
are first and foremost pawns in marriage alliances between groups of
men and are consequently of low status.

This claim may have to be modified in the light of Goody's more
recent work (1990) on precisely these two mass societies (and also
those of the Middle East and historical Europe). Goody argues that
brother–sister ties remain important and that not all marriage payments can actually be considered dowries, nor all inheritance as patrilineal: many examples of both are rather to be seen as long-term
transfers between generations from women to their (especially female)
children. He stresses the combination of male control of women with
dowry payments over which women have some say as a factor tending

to improve the status of women, in contrast with their African counterparts, who are often simply exchanged for cattle or other property.

Finally, hierarchical opposition can help us understand kinship from the cultural as well as structural point of view, as in Ortner's interpretation. Another example is Das's article on Punjabi kinship (1976), where she describes an acceptance of the inevitability of the sexual and procreative aspects of kinship, combined with a feeling that they are less valued than the moral ethos that surrounds wider networks of kin and affines involving exchange and other purely social strategies. In addition, there is a feeling that the former should be hidden away as far as possible, and only the latter emphasised in social arenas. Thus the level of these wider kinship networks encompasses that of procreation, and does not allow it to appear in its own domain. It only appears in domains peculiar to itself, as a matter of practical necessity rather than transcendent value, and then as part of a distinction from the superordinate level. This, although backgrounded for the time being, is still present, reminding everyone of the social ideals for which procreation is practically necessary, but to which it is ideologically subordinate.

Notes

1. According to Stanner, another precursor was Radcliffe-Brown. Stanner discusses the matter in a paper thought to have been written in the 1960s but only published posthumously some twenty years later (Stanner 1985). In Stanner's own words, 'All conceptions of "value" necessarily involve the idea of hierarchy or order' (1985: 120). He also calls value a 'first rank' concept, in contrast to structure, a 'second rank' concept (ibid.: 123). Dumont cannot have known about Stanner's paper at the time he started writing about value, and there is no evidence that Radcliffe-Brown had any influence on him in this respect. Nor does Stanner discuss Dumont.

2. Salzman's paper, entitled 'Does complementary opposition exist?' (1978), is basically about this phenomenon.

3. This version of the acknowledgement is for some reason more fulsome than that in the later collected edition of Dumont's papers on this theme (cf. 1986a: 232 n.18).

4. For Parry (1991: 281), the distinction of different sorts of impurity in Das's account, while well-founded, is too radical, and he suggests that a polythetic solution might be more appropriate.

5. There is thus a resemblance with marriage, in which the lower castes, like the tribes, are more prone to tolerate direct exchange than the upper castes, for whom the return of anything for a bride given, let alone another woman, is strongly forbidden. In both respects, the dichotomy is not between caste and tribe, but between high and low status.

6. This provides, *inter alia*, an answer to Pickering's argument (1984: 144) that because the most sacred persons are those who are outside society or are striving to leave it, Hinduism is recalcitrant to Durkheim's equation of society with the sacred. The general point is nonetheless conceded further on: 'Clearly, in terms of sociology, [the sacred] is a "social fact" and related to collective *représentations*' (ibid.: 150, reference removed). This very confusion is one of a number weakening Lynch's critique of *Homo Hierarchicus* (1977: 256).

7. Quigley's claim (1992: 87) that Brahmans who simply own land cannot represent an ideal is therefore specious. Their greater social independence relative to other castes is precisely a mark of their minimal reliance on the transactions which are so important socially but which encumber the search for salvation, which can only be individual. Quigley's more extended account (1993) of the caste system is as problematic as it is radical, but that cannot be gone into here. See Good 1993 and Parkin 1995b for critical reviews.

8. Dumont also admits (1972: 150) that he has not solved all the problems connected with the *jajmani* system so much as identified where they lie.

9. For a discussion of modern interference in traditional practices, see Dumont's discussion of the dilemma over the banning of female circumcision in North Africa (1979: 815-16, n.5).

10. This is not invariably the case, witness certain tribal groups of central India with a strongly anti-Hindu identity, such as the Santal and Munda, who may, for example, refuse to accept food from Brahmans (see Culshaw 1949: 16; Parkin 1992b: 6). In effect, they have recourse to avoidance to mark their own versions of status while inverting its application from the point of view of the dominant caste society. Is this an indication that these tribals are really outside the system, or does it indicate that they accept some of its values in the very act of trying to subvert them?

11. Jamous (1991) has recently produced a more extended account of the use of both this term and its female equivalent *bahin* among the Meo, a Muslim community south of Delhi.

Chapter 5

THE RECEPTION OF HIERARCHICAL OPPOSITION

What Hierarchical Opposition Is Not

Just how significant is Dumont's shift from the mere discrimination of contexts to the notion of a unitary ideology divided into levels? First, it should presumably be treated not as a theory but as a method, in accordance with Lévi-Strauss's view of his own work: in Daniel de Coppet's words (personal communication), a hierarchical opposition is propositional, not theoretical. According to Tcherkézoff (1985a: 61-2; 1986b: 92; 1987: 8, 125) the shift also means that reversal need no longer be seen as denoting rituals of rebellion, catharsis, the presence of 'outsiders' within the society (as Beck proposed of 'left-hand' castes in south India, 1973: 392; cf. Dumont 1979: 811), or any other form of anti-structure. It also avoids the necessity of resorting to ambiguity or ambivalence as an explanation (as in Mosko 1994b; 198-9; cf. Dumont 1959: 12, 18, on Srinivas 1952), or of postulating a substantial difference between ideology and action, ideal and real, as a way of accounting for what are really different levels of a unified but also relational ideology (Iteanu 1983b: 55). The necessity is to postulate 'inversion between ideological levels ... not between irreducible contrasts', and this represents 'the elementary relation of holistic logic' (Tcherkézoff 1985a: 61). Thus Maussian totality and coherence are exalted above Marxist or Turneresque views of social division and opposition. Gluckman's treatment of conflict is compared with hierarchy as another mode of integration (i.e. through periodic rituals stressing unity), one that is 'in keeping with the modern trend' (Dumont 1982: 239). But conflict, unlike hierarchy, is non-essential. Conflicts

---

Notes for this section begin on page 127.

certainly exist, but the parties involved in a rebellion represent not autonomous, perpetually antagonistic elements but parts of a wider whole that might be represented as society—through, for instance, the chief against whom the rebellion is for the moment taking place. Dumont's approach thus clearly recognizes conflict, but at the same time it obviates any idea of its necessity, or of treating it as a sort of game—the 'cricket syndrome', in which the parties play to certain rules in a basically friendly spirit. It is equally opposed to Bourdieu's pragmatics, in which, although there is the greatest sensitivity to context (or 'universe of practice' in Bourdieu's own phrase, 1977: 110), there is no resolution of them, nor any attempt to unite them into a unitary ideology.

Others, who have looked on from a greater distance, not without scepticism generally, have been able to hint at further advantages. One is that Dumont's idea may obviate resort to the view that aspects of culture may contradict one another but that people do not see it or do not care (Forth 1985: 109), or that informants disagree (Barnes 1985b: 11). This may sometimes mean glossing over aspects of culture that actually exist, but on the other hand it is claimed as a feature of the model (e.g. Iteanu 1985: 100-1) that the contradiction the outside observer might see is not necessarily perceived by someone within the culture. The notions of reductionism (e.g. of sociology to economics in Marxism, of descent to property in late functionalism, of affinal alliance to exchange in Lévi-Straussian structuralism) and of the epiphenomenon, of the element that is a reflection or kind of iceberg tip of something else, might also be more fruitfully explained as instances of hierarchical opposition. For instance, in the social sciences, especially anthropology, relativism is often opposed to positivism in the explanation of social forms. However, those who proclaim the uniqueness and incomparability of societies are still making statements that are intended to say something about the world as it is, and to that extent they are positivist in intention. Thus relativism can be reduced to positivism, or in Dumontian terms the opposition that is evident on one level disappears on the other, through the encompassment of the latter by the former.

The idea of a continuum, on the other hand, which blurs the distinctiveness of the poles, must be ruled out. Where Leach sees sacred and profane being related as a continuum, not a straight cut (1954: 106), Dumont and his followers see a hierarchical opposition (see previous chapter; also below, Chapter 6). One is reminded here of Dumont's early debate with Bailey over the difficulties of distinguishing tribe and caste in India (Bailey 1961; Dumont 1962b; cf. Parkin 1992b: 9). For Dumont, this was another hierarchical opposition (though he had not yet begun using such language), in that 'India is *one*. The very existence, and influence, of the traditional higher, San-skritic, civilisation demonstrates without question the unity of India. One might even think that it does not only demonstrate it, but actually constitutes it' (Dumont 1957: 9). The 'tribes' are in general no less subject to the values of caste than are the castes themselves, and even a simple dichotomy in terms of inferior and superior is difficult to establish, given that many so-called 'tribes' are considered to rank above the lowest castes in local hierarchies. In any case, a continuum does not obviate the requirement to make a definition of the two poles in which it cumulates (cf. Dumont 1962b).

It is instructive here to compare Dumont with Collingwood, whose *Essay on Philosophical Method* (1933) deals in part with what Colling-wood calls the 'scale of forms'. [1] A scale is defined as having:

> extremes, opposed to one another and representing the infinity and zero values of the variable, and intermediates, representing various degrees of their inverse combination. But if the variable is identical with the generic essence [which defines the scale], the zero end forms no part of the scale; for in it the generic essence is altogether absent. The lower end of the scale, therefore, lies not at zero, but at unity, or the minimum realization of the generic essence. (1933: 81)

Philosophically speaking, a generic essence, for example badness, still has, or contains, an opposite, in this case goodness, when at point unity on the scale; similarly, the temperature of something very cold actually consists of heat. But in the former example, 'the lowest case on the scale, when compared to the next above it, not only loses its own intrinsic goodness, but it actually becomes identical with evil in gen-eral' (ibid.: 84). This is replicated along the scale in either direction. It thus resembles the *varna* scheme and other seemingly multi-polar models involving opposition, though in fact there are only two poles and therefore a single opposition. In this repect, Dumont's distinction of purity and impurity is as good an example as Collingwood's good/evil and hot/cold.

In his treatment of opposition itself, Collingwood makes a clear dis-tinction between the scientific and philosophical meanings of the con-cept, which remind one of Dumont's modernity and non-modernity respectively. 'In its non-philosophical phase, opposition is a relation sub-sisting between a positive term and its own mere negation or absence. Cold, as understood by the physicist, is the lack of heat ...'. This is 'pure or mere opposition'. But cold can also be experienced as something dif-ferent from heat, this being 'at once opposition and distinction ... fused into a single relation' (ibid.: 75). Collingwood gives as similar examples good/bad, truth/error and beauty/ugliness. His use of terms thus differs somewhat from both Dumont and conventional discourse, since he uses 'distinction' where one would normally expect 'opposition', which for him is simply a term and its absence. Philosophically,

> a relation which subsists between terms [is] at once opposed and distinct. [...] Distinction and opposition, which in non-philosophical thought are two mutually exclusive kinds of relation, in philosophy coalesce into one, so that what at first sight seems a mere opposition—the relation, that is, between a term and its own absence—turns out to be also a distinction between two terms, and vice versa. (Ibid.: 76)

Although not speaking of anything resembling encompassment, Collingwood at least recognizes that one pole of a 'distinction' may contain something of its opposite, and that this entails a philosophical rather than a scientific view. However, he does little more than hint at differences in value and certainly does not develop this theoretically. This means that his 'false disjunction of opposition and distinction' (ibid.: 86), while privileging philosophical over scientific realities, does not really find an echo in Dumont's claim that we only distinguish in order to value. His 'distinction' is a recognition that a second term exists, but in itself this does not specifically entail a difference in value.

Originally, Dumont was also at pains to deny that his method is at all dialectical (1971a: 76-7; 1980: 242-3). As regards ritual, there are at first sight some similiarities, although the van Gennep view of ritual (1909) approaches more nearly the dialectical in that society is changed by the rite. From being perfectly ordered, society becomes disturbed by the creation or accumulation of anomalous statuses (thesis); it enters a liminal or dangerous phase (antithesis), and in coming out of it regains perfection (synthesis), but one which differs in detail (i.e. in terms of the statuses actually held by particular individuals) from the earlier order (cf. Kruyt 1973).

With Dumont, on the other hand, one starts with the whole, changes to a subordinate level through reversal or a division into levels, then returns to the original whole: there is no synthesis, in the sense of a freshly structured merger of two antagonistic poles. Nor, with dialectics, does the whole (the synthesis) pre-exist its parts, as is the case with hierarchical opposition (Tcherkézoff 1987: 142-3 n.17). Although hierarchical opposition has its own dynamics, this does not produce a new order in the same way as dialectics. 'Movement' (Tcherkézoff 1985a: 62) is provided through reversals between the whole and its parts, but there is always a return to the starting point: 'differentiation does not change the global setting' (Dumont 1980: 243). There is a combination of synchronic and diachronic factors (Dumont 1971a: 76), but in Dumont's own terms we may say that stasis encompasses dynamism. It is thus again a hierarchical view, whereas dialectics is non-hierarchical, with movement from one position through another to a third, not between two differently valued levels. In the latter case, contradiction is again resolved by agglomeration or perhaps compromise, not by restoring to the whole the part it had released through a temporary change of levels.

As far as the Nyamwezi are concerned, for instance, 'a dialectical or polythetic analogy ... would wrongly associate the white light of day ... with the whiteness of drought [and] the fearful black of night (witches) with the life-giving black rain' (Tcherkézoff 1985a: 61; see also above). This reference to polythetic classification is directed primarily against Needham (for example, 1980a: 56), who has made this idea of Wittgenstein's very much his own in anthropology: for Tcherkézoff, however, a polythetic classification can only involve context, not Dumontian levels (1994). For Dumont too ideology is monothetic, and the search for 'a cardinal value' (1982: 211), 'the fundamental idea, the mother of all others' (1979: 814), although far from easy and subject to disagreement, is explicitly approved. This value is the superordinate level or pole rather than a reduction of some oppositions to others. Anything else is simply a subordinate level, and the 'distinction of situations' that allows this to become apparent is merely a temporary phenomenon actuated by reversal or by a division of the whole.

Yet in respect of this search for ultimate but segmented values, Dumont actually has much in common with Hegel (with whom dialectic process is first and foremost associated, of course). Indeed, he has put on record his preference for Hegel over Marx as a 'precursor of sociology' (1970: 138-9), and he refers to him approvingly on occasion in *Homo Hierarchicus* (e.g. 1972: 80, 322 n.24a). In his more recent work on the nature and development of German ideology (1986b), he even seeks to interpret Hegelian thought directly as a series of encompassments. He begins by drawing attention to the conflict between an older sense of holism and the newer individualism as something arising ultimately out of the Reformation, which necessitated 'adaptation taking the form of syntheses, i.e. hybrid representations combining holistic and individualistic aspects' (ibid.: 593). In Hegel,

> the clash between the two opposed modes of valuation is avoided through the recognition of a hierarchy of levels, with reversals of primacy between levels and sub-levels. Thus, individualism reigns at the topmost level, that of absolute spirit; holism, with the state, dominates on the level of objective spirit, but encompasses in turn the individualism of civil, or bourgeois, society and abstract right. (Ibid.; also 1991: 81-2)

Thus again, there is no simple opposition, but a hierarchy involving at least three poles, though as in other apparent examples of this situation, the model must be broken down so as to be able to concentrate on each opposition in turn. Hegel's holism is, of course, no more than the holism of society as greater than the sum of the individuals that compose it, but it is similarly transcendental. More recently still, Dumont refers to the Hegelian dialectic as such as a hierarchical opposition, though leaving aside the notion of antithesis (1991: 183): the movement is 'from thesis, a simple entity, to synthesis, totality.' [2]

The Validity of Hierarchical Opposition

In pointing out what he sees as the common anthropological aversion to hierarchy, Dumont has also reminded us of the dangers of ethnocentrism (or sociocentrism, as he prefers to call it, e.g. 1982: 215; 1992: 260). At first sight, this seems to fall in line with the widespread soul-searching that characterized the anthropology of the 1980s on both sides of the Channel (not to say the Atlantic). Most of this, however, has concerned the worry that structuralism—like the functionalism it displaced, and with which Dumont is to be associated, through his concentration on relations—is merely another means of imposing our own sense of order on data about 'the Other'. Self-reflexivity, process and agency have replaced 'meaning' as watchwords. But despite his own and his followers' assertions of hierarchical opposition and its associated ideas being concrete social facts, it does not seem to have occurred to any of them that history may be repeating itself. Terence Turner, for example, while supporting Dumont generally against Needham, criticizes him for repeating the latter's failings in at least one respect, namely in his 'reduction of entire sets of symbolic polarities to a single homogeneous dimension of contrast, now conceived as that between whole and part' (1984: 369).

Such reductionism is for many precisely where structuralism as whole, as exemplified by Lévi-Strauss and his followers, has failed. This is to disregard the possibility that the notion of structuralism may take many forms and is quite capable of further development (see Chapter 1; also below, Chapter 6). Nonetheless the ultimate test of Dumont's ideas, as of all other ideas in anthropology, is their ethnographic applicability. A volume entitled *Contexts and Levels* (Barnes et al. 1985), the collection of ethnographic analyses which has already been cited often here, attempted to provide just such a test. This was the result of a joint conference of Anglo-American and French scholars (the latter being members of Dumont's *équipe*, though not he himself) held in Oxford in March 1983 (see Preface, above). Two reviewers, Good in *Man* (1987: 570) and Keeler in *American Ethnologist* (1987: 571-2), independently came to the same conclusion, namely that the contributions from the English side were much more sceptical and detached from—if not downright hostile to—these ideas than those of the French, who were, of course, defending what had virtually become their party line. This is only partly true: at the time, the clearest exemplification of what was involved was widely felt to have come from one of the English contributors (McDonaugh, on the Tharu house; see 1985). [3] Nonetheless—and despite the visitors' own determined attempts to be good guests by being rigorously empirical—the division between cerebration and empiricism that is often felt to be marked by the English Channel did not wholly disappear.

The fundamental problem was felt to be that Dumont's proposal admits of no exceptions. This was especially the case over the necessity of hierarchy. In fact, equality no less than hierarchy may itself be an abstract value distinct from social morphology, even in respect of binary oppositions in non-modern societies (e.g. Duff-Cooper 1985: 163; also his 'Manichean oppositions', ms.: 27). Of course this is implicit in Dumont's own arguments concerning western egalitarianism. But the valuing of equality is not restricted to the west. Howell (1985; also Howell and Willis 1989) could find little use for Dumont's ideas as regards the Chewong of West Malaysia, a society in which, she says, dyadic asymmetry manifests itself but rarely. In opposition to Dumont, she suggests that the recognition of difference need not entail attributing a value, in which case equality necessarily results (1985: 167, 169); indeed, such recognition *is* the dominant value here (ibid.: 169). Speaking more generally, she argues that there are nonetheless some oppositions that are inherently valued, such as good/evil and auspicious/inauspicious. Others, such as right/left, are not, and have to be valued deliberately (ibid.: 174). Of course, it is precisely this, seen as an analytical process, that Dumont criticizes, since for him value is always inherent in any distinction (1979: 810). And it is clear that hierarchy in Dumont's sense can be identified among the Chewong too (Howell 1985: 177-9). Cool is ordinarily superior to hot, though hot becomes superior at childbirth, which is followed by the common Southeast Asian practice of 'roasting the child'. The very opposition between hierarchy and equality can itself be seen as a hierarchical opposition. Although equality might be the normally superior pole, in crises, such as those caused by crossing categorical boundaries (eating two sorts of meat at the same meal, for example), some oppositions become value-laden: in other words, hierarchy is emphasized so as to return to order. [4]

This tends to confirm Dumont's association of hierarchy with value rather than just social order etc.: equality may itself be a value higher than any other, in which case it is opposed to and encompasses hierarchy, as largely in the west. Formally, in fact, one can postulate a cline from mere differentiation (equal or not unequal) through opposition (antagonism between the poles, but not necessarily hierarchy when perceived from outside) to asymmetry without hierarchical opposition, to hierarchical opposition or encompassment of the contrary (Forth 1985: 114). The first would seem to correspond with Howell's own description of the Chewong situation, and it is presented as a clear exception to the last, which is Dumont's formula for non-modern societies generally.

The second might be found in the conventional division into right and left in the politics of modern states, in which, although there is antagonism, there is no evident asymmetry, nor at first sight any obvious sense in which one party stands for the whole in most contexts. In England, for instance, we have long been used to the idea of 'Her Majesty's loyal opposition', whose leader is recognized as such by his or her special salary. Antagonism is institutionalized: the Queen stands for the whole, but she is above the parties, not also one of them. Only on specific occasions is this antagonism put aside (e.g. on Remembrance Day, or at the presentation of the Queen's Speech, though not at the subsequent debate on it), and then it appears to be by agglomeration, not by the subsuming of one pole by the other. The parties themselves oscillate between power, and neither can lay claim to permanent dominance.

However, as Dumont himself has argued (1971a: 69, after John Locke), hierarchical opposition immediately becomes evident if one focuses not on specific parties but on the idea of the majority party. The majority also stands for the whole, being the government party, as well as opposing the official opposition, regardless of which party it actually consists of at any one time. [5] This involves relation, not the substantialism of named parties, as in the conventional view. Alternatively one might choose to regard this second sort of opposition as that characteristic of modern societies, in which there is fragmentation but no hierarchical reference to the whole. In that case, one would also see it as complementary. One problem with hierarchical opposition here is the fact that the opposition is frequently split among several parties, who can hardly be said to be hierarchically organized among themselves. Conversely, Dumont is able to show, in relation to post-revolutionary France, that the values of the left have progressively become those of the nation as a whole (universal suffrage, nationalism), whereas in practical affairs the values of the right predominate (economic inequality, political power; they also accord more nearly with reality), forming another hierarchical opposition (1992).

The Distinctiveness of Hierarchical Opposition: Logic versus Ethnography

At all events, hierarchical opposition clearly exists as a separate type of opposition, characterized by the relation of ideological levels, encompassment and the latter's own polarity with distinction. One cannot therefore agree with Needham in regarding it as merely 'a peculiar form of complementarity' (1987: 102), nor with Barnes when he states even more unequivocally: 'For my part I see no reason to follow Dumont in distinguishing between complementary and hierarchical opposition, for they are one and the same' (1985b: 14; cf. Mosko 1994a: 48; 1994b: 196). It is perhaps better to regard them as alternatives that are not mutually exclusive as far as anthropological theory is concerned, though they may be so in particular ethnographic situations (Forth 1985: 112 ff.).

This is to say no more than that not all oppositions are logically of the same type (cf. Needham 1987). Barnes argues (1985b: 17) that part–whole relations that lack the dimension of hierarchy have frequently been discovered, and he relates this to Cassirer's observations on the 'confusion' of mythical thought. This is a far cry from Dumont's orderly holism, in which there is seemingly nothing out of place, and he would surely regard the idea of confusion as both ethnocentric and superficial as an explanation: as with the idea of 'ambiguity', it may actually suggest that the analyst has not managed fully to understand the situation he is examining. Tcherkézoff too, at one point (1987: 122), deliberately contrasts non-modern and modern thought as mythical versus rational, but it is clear that he is thinking in terms of contrasting 'logics' and that no conceptual disorder is involved.

Conversely, not all part–whole relationships are oppositions: they may involve the whole and one of a number of taxonomic sub-classes instead. One of Dumont's own examples of hierarchical opposition, animal/vertebrate, is an unhappy one for this reason (see 1979: 809). Here, certainly, is a part–whole relationship, with hierarchy between the poles (vertebrates are a part of the class of animals, and subordinate to it), but the poles are not in any sense opposites. Moreover, they do not exhaust this particular universe of discourse—there are also invertebrates. This in itself does not prevent the opposition from involving hierarchy: as we saw in the previous two chapters, more than two terms can be involved, even though each opposition has to be taken separately. But, unlike the *varna* example, there is no clear sense in which animal and vertebrate come together in opposition to invertebrate, despite the fact that the latter is at the inferior level.

What Dumont appears to have in mind here is the everyday association of 'animal' with vertebrates, as contrasted with its use as an equivalent to 'fauna'. Conversely, 'animal' is sometimes even more restricted in meaning in the ordinary language, being congruent with 'mammal'. Only if 'vertebrate' were to stand for 'animals', including invertebrates—which it does not—could we talk of a hierarchical opposition here. In his own terms, Dumont's error is to confuse whole (animal) and encompassing value. [6] He is also trying to see an example drawn from a scientific taxonomy as a hierarchical opposition, thus confusing the modern and non-modern perspectives. This does not work, because a scientific taxonomy, though hierarchical, separates fact and value. There is thus no 'logical scandal' of the sort that a hierarchical opposition requires (Barnes 1985b: 16; Needham 1987: 129).

Dumont's use of the Great Chain of Being of medieval Europe as an example (1982: 227-8) also presents problems. This is unitary but hierarchical, graduated, we may even say segmented, to use Dumont's own term. However, as he himself points out, there is no reversal involved. Moreover, there is no clearly identified subordinate pole. The Chain is just there, its different parts reflecting the glory of God—which gives it its unity—in different measure, according to their various abilities, and just fading into nothingness at the margins of existence. It is hard to see it as an opposition at all, though as the model of all existence it is certainly a whole.

A similar example (not mentioned by Dumont) is the linguistic equation between tree and cottonwood tree, identified by Trager (1939) as common in Indian languages of the southeastern United States. Brown (1984: 60) refers to it as an instance of polysemy, in which the same term stands for both referents. There is thus a part–whole relation, but one cannot see how the referents themselves are opposed. Although when meaning 'tree' in general the term encompasses all other types of tree, including cottonwood, its specific meaning, even if seen as appearing only at a subsidiary level, has no clear opposing term, only a series of them, which are equally specific (i.e. terms for the various other species of tree). For Brown, indeed (he does not mention Dumont), this represents a lexico-semantic innovation in the course of the development of life-form terms—an incident in linguistic evolution, therefore, not a permanent form of classification of ritual significance.

Nonetheless, the idea of encompassment is still present, even in an attenuated form, and this still allows us to speak of a non-modern ideology. Another example where there is no clearly defined opposite pole is Comte's placing of sociology at the top of the hierarchy of knowledge and his reduction of the remaining sciences to the status of social facts, which sociology can therefore study. Although the arch-exponent of nineteenth-century positivism, here Comte resorted to a non-modern model of the branches of knowledge in his attempt to establish sociology as the pre-eminent modern intellectual discipline. A comparison with Durkheim is instructive. Although influenced by Comte in the early stages of his own intellectual development, he did not follow him here but contented himself with establishing the autonomy of sociology from other subjects. In moving from Comte to Durkheim, therefore, we are finally leaving the non-modern approach to the study of man in society and entering modernity.

But are all oppositions linked in a part-whole relationship, even in non-modern societies? Apthorpe—who after all was among those who set the ball rolling—himself argues that this is not necessarily the case with reference to the frequently occurring dichotomy between joking relationships and avoidance or respect relationships (1984: 290), though one form, the avunculate, is certainly ordinarily asymmetric in allowing the 'snatching' of an uncle's property by his nephew but not vice versa. In fact, much depends on the situation. However, if ego finds him- or herself in a situation where different categories of relative are present, some of whom may be joked with and others not, a choice imposes itself. Ordinarily, it may be that respect is shown to all relatives in such situations, in which case it encompasses joking. On ritual occasions, however, joking may be prominent, despite the presence of relatives with whom one may not joke. In this case, both values may be apparent, with joking restricted to proper joking partners, but not others—a form of respect to them.

A perhaps more recalcitrant example is the animal/plant distinction, which is very generally found (Brown 1984). Man/woman may be a part-whole relationship in Genesis and the English language, but it is not in Melanesian societies, judging from Strathern's study of gender concepts there (1988), even though all persons are felt to partake of the opposite gender to some degree. She says explicitly (though without mentioning Dumont) that 'the relation [between the collective sphere of men's actions and the domestic sphere of women's actions] is one of alternation, not hierarchy' (ibid.: 319; see also Marcus 1984: 214). This might even be said of the opposition between right and left itself (see Barnes 1985b: 10; cf. Dumont 1979: 810). In the Nuer example Dumont started with, what Evans-Pritchard actually said was that the right hand 'stands for' and 'represents' the whole (1973: 94, 100); presumably, this gives it independence as a value in other contexts, and in other societies. Dumont's claim that right and left, as with other dyads, are inherently valued depends on right being *identical* with the whole, which is quite different (Barnes 1985b: 17; 1984: 240 n.8).

Gradability is another problem: as we saw in Chapter 3, it is common for anthropologists to disregard intermediate terms. This is because it may be common for ordinary folk to disregard them too (cf.

Lloyd 1966: 89-90). For example, in Kédang, right–left is a gradable opposition as regards the layout of the village (the centre is also significant) but not as regards the sexing of children in the womb (Barnes 1985b: 13; he also cites examples from North America, including the Omaha, ibid.; 1984: 63, 65). Another example is Black/White as applied to ethnic groups. This is in principle gradable because of the possibility of mixed descent. In the United States and generally in Europe it is nonetheless regarded as ungradable: people of mixed descent are defined—and normally define themselves—as Black. [7] In South Africa, on the other hand, it has frequently been regarded as gradable because of the existence of a separate Coloured community, whose identity did not simply depend on government fiat or others' prejudice but was also partly a matter of self-definition. Yet even here this mediating term has been ignored when the wider conflict between Black and White has come into focus. In the past, under apartheid, the White minority regarded Black rule as the chief threat to its own identity and interests, while the majority Black community regarded White supremacy as the chief obstacle to its own political progress. In the wider political battles between White and Black, both groups have tended to place the Coloured and Indian communities alongside the latter, where they noticed them at all. [8]

On the whole, oppositions treated as gradable are probably quite uncommon, despite logical possibilities. Lloyd points out (1966: 162ff., 434-5) that even after Aristotle's classification of oppositions—which *inter alia* distinguished contradictories from contraries—Greek rhetoric, and presumably Greek practice generally, still tended to treat all oppositions as ungradable: only contradictories, of all Aristotle's types, are truly ungradable and subject to the Law of the Excluded Middle (see ibid.: 162-3). Similarly, an opposition like light/darkness may be seen as ungradable in some cultures rather than as a positive/privative opposition as in Aristotle. [9] Presumably a hierarchical opposition would be able to incorporate any middle term as a further segment or pole, as with the *varna* example, though of course this would have to be indigenously recognized before it would be legitimate to talk about it. Otherwise, one might fall into the trap of making the opposition black/white gradable with the help of grey, which rarely seems to be conceptualized as such in most contexts (indeed, grey is very often classed with black in indigenous colour terminologies).

Other oppositions may, *pace* Dumont, divide a universe of discourse rather than be contained by it. 'For instance, the dyad white man/black man may be interpreted by the Meru not as opposite colour values attributed to members of the genus "man" but as generically contrasted subjects, of which only one has claims to true humanity' (Needham 1980a: 52). The very terms of some oppositions may change according to context: for instance, while white is most obviously opposed to black, red has no obvious counterpart, being opposed to green in traffic lights, to white in many ritual contexts (the contrast between blood and semen or milk; cf. Willis 1985: 218-20), to black in others (the contrast between blood and soil), etc.

Seen as a set of formal possibilities, however, as in Aristotle, opposition is hardly reducible to a single type. Of course, Aristotle was a logician who had to sit down and work out his types through rational thought over, one assumes, a significant period of time. This is very different from perceiving an opposition as and only as it arises in the consciousness (through the stimulus of symbolism, for example), which is about as far as most human beings ever get: and even then there are, as we have seen, many instances in which a choice is automatically made between possibilities that would be equivalent were it not for cultural interference. As Needham remarks, 'so much depends not on formal criteria but on connotations and values' (1987: 101). The power of symbolism, after all, whether it constitutes code (Lévi-Strauss), knowledge (Sperber 1975) or substitution (Lewis 1980) or is something more multivalent (Barley 1983), is its immediacy and its existence outside the realm of rational cogitation, or at any rate calculation. Yet given the considerable ethnographic variability in the nature of the relationship between the poles of different oppositions, the ways in which they are regarded, the uses to which they are put, and the forms in which they manifest themselves, it was inevitable that Dumont's claims for the unavoidability of hierarchical opposition would come under challenge.

For Needham, accordingly, the different sorts of relation that obtain between the poles of dyadic oppositions constitute yet another polythetic class (1987: 235). The faculty of opposing may itself be constant, for 'it implicates only two terms, and in this respect it can be seen as exemplifying the simplest possible form of relation' (ibid.: 3; cf. 1960b: 'the simplest form of distinction is opposition'). But 'whether the relation itself is equally simple is a separate issue' (1987: 3). A system of dual symbolic classification cannot possibly be simple, therefore, especially as it requires not just opposition, but analogy and homology too (ibid.: 221). Needham also notes that the faculty of opposition makes use of a spatial metaphor even when it is not itself spatial in content. This property is just one instance of 'a very common tendency to represent mental processes and qualities by means of images and expressions taken from mechanical operations and material objects. ... Naturally there is a spatial aspect to this tendency, for the objects referred to are three-dimensional and have locations ...' (ibid.: 232). In other words, opposition is 'a spatial relation ... that is extended metaphorically to relations between terms and between propositions' (ibid.: 58).

Thus like Dumont but in a very different way, Needham declines to see opposition as a fundamental mode of thought. Given the general and longstanding tendency in anthropology to see distinctions as primarily binary oppositions, this may seem to challenge not merely structuralism, but much of the Durkheimian, not to say Aristotelian, intellectual tradition. For Needham, though, the faculty of opposing remains important. It is just that, in the form it takes, it is ethnographically contingent: it is the resulting complexity that rules out its fundamentality. For Dumont, the limitation is that opposition is just a temporary phenomenon that manifests itself in certain temporary and subordinate situations, and even then it is only significant as a way of indicating a difference in value. Ultimately it is everywhere subsumed in a single totalizing ideology centred on its superior pole. With him, one feels that the totalizing spirit of Mauss completely pushes out the dichotomizing spirits of Hertz and Durkheim, and that Hegel triumphs over Kant. [10]

Hierarchy and Equality: How Political is Dumont?

Veena Das has neatly summed up the overall significance of Dumont's innovation: 'His main achievement must surely be judged to lie in a creative transformation of structuralist concepts and his attempt to shift the centre of gravity in structural analysis from symmetrical binary oppositions to hierarchical ones' (1982: 183; also Geirnaert 1987: 107).

Dumont himself has used this tool most fruitfully in comparing the holism and hierarchy of caste with the individualism and egalitarianism of the west. Indeed, he has taken more seriously than almost anyone else the old anthropological adage that the intensive study of other societies is the best way to learn something significant about one's own. In this respect, his career provides both parallels and contrasts with that of an earlier French sociologist who took an interest in caste, Célestin Bouglé. This early and quite independent-minded Durkheimian studied an aspect of western society first, namely the social conditions favouring the development of egalitarianism (1899), before quite deliberately going on to study caste (1908) as a test of the validity of his earlier work. Thus the trajectory of his comparison was exactly the reverse of Dumont's, who proceeded from India to the west. And although Bouglé is perhaps not as condemnatory of the caste system in his *Essais* as Vogt indicates (1983: 238ff.), he did tend to see it as the outcome of a deliberate mystification by the Brahmans, something which was directly responsible for India's supposed 'arrested development'.

Dumont has consistently refused to strike such an attitude, always placing the understanding of caste before its moral evaluation. As a result, his work on both hierarchy and individualism have attracted not merely intellectual scepticism but a degree of hostility too, often on non-academic grounds. This is perhaps not entirely surprising. *Homo Hierarchicus*, which not only seeks to understand hierarchy in its own terms but even suggests its necessity, in the sense of its unavoidability, was published in French in 1966. This was right in the middle of perhaps the most far-reaching libertarian revolution of modern times, when political radicalism in France had already become agitated by the supposed apolitical fence-sitting of leading anthropologists, including Lévi-Strauss (see Kurzweil 1980: 24-5); the first English translation was not long in coming (1972). It is surely significant at least symbolically that Berreman, whose response to Dumont is largely one of indignation at his apparent blindness to the 'oppression' of caste (Berreman 1971), was by then at Berkeley, the 'Rome' of this libertarian movement. There is also evidence that commentators have not always been able to understand Dumont even in relation to the simplest things: Lynch, for example, consistently confuses the general notion of hierarchy with its particular form in India (1977: 253, 256, 258, 260), arguing from this that Dumont regards hierarchy as a purely Indian phenomenon. Scarcely a smaller error is the assumption that Dumont's notion of hierarchy is multi-faceted (ibid.: 256). Quigley too attacks Dumont from an inadequate basis of understanding (1993; cf. Good 1993; Parkin 1995b).

The passage of time has not improved matters, as can be seen from Hart's testy exchange with Dumont (Hart 1987; Dumont 1987b) and Bailey's more recent polemic (1991). Beteille has castigated Dumont's whole method, which, he claims, 'assigns priority to contrast over comparison, to difference over similarity, and to discontinuity over continuity. [...] From the viewpoint of this method not all societies are of the same value: societies are valorized in the very acts of comparison and contrast' (1987: 675). And Needham declares flatly of Dumont:

> He is clearly against egalitarianism and individualism, as social ideals, and he is for hierarchy and totality. What kind of political system would satisfy these requirements is not our present concern, if only because the values that Dumont favors are quite likely to be of a temperamental kind that is not completely under the control of rational responsibility. (1987: 144) [11]

Such statements disregard Dumont's declaration (Dumont 1982: 241) of his own preference for the very values his critics are so keen to deny him, though the impact is reduced somewhat by Dumont himself immediately qualifying this preference as 'irenic'. But as a one-time Marxist (Daniel de Coppet, personal communication), Dumont could hardly be described as ignorant of political issues. Moreover, given his care in distinguishing 'is' and 'ought to be' in his own thought, it is hardly likely that he would confuse them when talking about aspects of the human condition in the broader sense. In the first place, he accepts more readily than most anthropologists the unavoidability of hierarchy (as he defines it), and therefore of distinctions. Modern societies are much less stable than non-modern ones in respect of the egalitarianism that mostly characterizes them, an instability that sometimes leads to the 'pathological' forms of racism and totalitarianism. As Őstőr and Fruzzetti have recognized (1991: 319), Dumont's approach allows him to say something really significant about racism and communalism (the latter being especially significant in India) in a way which is simply not open to Marriott's substantialism, for instance.

If Dumont sometimes seems to extol hierarchy above equality, it is simply because it is better able to accommodate conflict, to which it is surely preferable (see 1982: 239). Certainly caste, for instance, is not free from conflict; but disputes centre around the ranking of particular castes rather than around the existence of caste itself. Although Dumont's is hardly a 'simple consensus model' (Moffat 1979: 26), it does suggest that fundamental caste values are accepted throughout the hierarchy (Dumont 1957a: 20-1; also Fuller 1988; Moffat 1979; Mosse 1994). Indeed (and as we saw in the last chapter), Fuller and Parry would even argue that such values are adhered to most strongly by the lower castes, precisely those who are most strongly 'oppressed' by them. Apthorpe also dissociates hierarchy from conflict:

> Formally it is this asymmetry of hierarchical relationships which can be regarded as a logical resolution of the hostility that would otherwise characterize an opposition between a pair of categories which exhaust their universe of discourse [here, the complementary opposition in particular is intended, R.P.]. The sociologic of an interaction in which one party respects the other and is esteemed for this is one of hierarchy, not hostility. (1984: 290)

In other words, if it is recognized as part of the order of things, hierarchy is immune from the legitimate competition of an egalitarian society. Hostility between the poles can only take the form of rebellion, which is illegitimate, a threat to order, denying the superior (and encompassing) pole the predominance it and society need in order to survive. As we saw in the last chapter, Apthorpe had linked this earlier to the difference between ascribed and achieved statuses (1961: x), the former also being part of the order of things and therefore not subject to either the 'envy' or the competition that afflicts the latter. One might also link this to Foucault's work on the self-disciplining of those who are subject to any authority. Of course, a withdrawal of the recognition of hierarchy amounts to the legitimation of rebellion for the rebel, who will have his own ideology (in general terms). However, this simply means that he prefers this to the existing order, implicitly relating the two in the form of an inverted hierarchical opposition. Rebellion and revolution do not avoid hierarchy even when stressing equality: the most they do is raise the latter as a value over the unequal aspects of the society they are presumably opposed to.

Another characteristic of a hierarchical order for Dumont is that, unlike an egalitarian order, it is infinitely extendable. Dumont suggests (1972: 240) that non-Hindus—Christians and Moslems—have come to form a sixth category alongside, or beneath, the four *varna*s (the Untouchables being the fifth category in this argument). The caste system is thus 'a hierarchical system oriented to the needs of all' (1986a: 76). Of course this entails authority, but legitimate authority is as unavoidable as hierarchy, and certainly better than the exercise of raw power.

By being better able to accommodate difference, there is thus a sense in which caste, and indeed any hierarchy, is ultimately more tolerant than the egalitarianism of the west. Since this 'egalitarianism' has proved impossible to achieve in practice, conflict is frequently generated. This undermines another key modern ideal, namely individualism and the tolerance of others that this implies. In crude terms, the supposed 'tolerance' of Hinduism might indeed seem to be little more than a philosophy of 'a place for everyone, and everyone in their place', a matter of the recognition of different practices and observances (an 'orthopraxy' rather than an orthodoxy, says Dumont, 1972: 238) rather than the traditional liberal give and take (cf. Fürer-Haimendorf 1967: 156). This is reflected in the differences in the penances imposed, according to the status of both victim and offender (ibid.: 157). Yet despite all the prescriptions, within certain limits one can act as one pleases, at the cost, possibly, of being accorded an irremediably low status by the society as a whole:

> While the West, under the logic of contradiction, approves or excludes, traditional India under the logic of encompassing attributes a rank. (Dumont 1971a: 76)

And similarly:

> In the hierarchical scheme a group's acknowledged differentness whereby it is contrasted with other groups becomes the very principle whereby it is integrated into society. If you eat beef, you must accept being classed

among the Untouchables, and on this condition your practice will be tolerated. (Dumont 1972: 238)

Dumont attributes to western egalitarianism, on the other hand, a stress not so much on equal rights for all as on equality in those respects that form group identity—an equality of qualities rather than of rights, so to speak, though all with the first also enjoy the second. In other words, those that meet the criteria are accepted, and treated as equals through the principle of the ignoring of difference; those that do not are rejected, being defined as qualitatively different. This reflects the idea that if hierarchy is holistic and therefore relational, equality is atomistic or individualistic and therefore lacks relations, since there is no whole to relate to. Thus the individual cannot be defined relationally, through his or her place in a holistic scheme, but only substantially, in terms of his or her inherent qualities (see Tcherkézoff 1987: 11; 1993-4). In comparison with this view of egalitarianism, caste does not actually have to do very much in order to seem more tolerant. However much upper-caste oppression there might be in India, it is chiefly directed at preserving the hierarchy, not at expelling those who do not qualify for membership of the society. All groups have a place, however inferior.

This is why, however paradoxical it might seem, Dumont regards racism as the ultimate form of egalitarianism, a kind of pathological extension of it. In it, race is seen as being the qualitative difference par excellence, since it is completely irremovable. As long as this difference continues to be recognized, there is no way of accommodating it without introducing hierarchy—which in itself violates the principle of equality. Hence the 'separate but equal' slogan is modern in the sense of being post-hierarchical, but still discriminatory. Caste, precisely because it is hierarchical, can integrate as well as separate; racism can *only* separate in order to be able to discriminate and still retain egalitarianism for those left within.

Just as nationalist ideologies disregard class differences, therefore, so racist ethnic groups that discriminate against others tend to be egalitarian within. Thus although, under apartheid, Afrikanerdom contained both the super-rich of the Witwatersrand and the poor whites of the rural Transvaal, all were included within the *volk*. This, of course, excluded other population groups entirely, and the *volk* even used its control of the state to prevent 'miscegenation' in law. One result was the misrecognition, except as an oxymoron, of Afrikaner liberals (i.e. liberals in matters of race), who were treated quite specifically as traitors to the *volk*. Another was the restriction of political rights to whites, which although discriminatory, even pathological, is not inexplicable in terms of Dumont's model: the principle of democracy, practised as an ideal within (that is, given to whites only), was used as the instrument of an empirical form of power that produced exclusion without. This is reflected further in the ideology of apartheid, which, although empirically it may have increased the repression of the excluded, represented ideologically a shift from quasi-hierarchical forms of discrimination across the whole state to a principle of 'separate but equal' in its parts. However farcical, the Bantustans, formally independent states for the Black population, were the ultimate expression of this principle.

In a sense, the principle of equality was extended here in a pseudo-Herderian way to include the equality of ethnic groups taken as wholes—which may nonetheless continue to be subjected to discrimination on empirical grounds (for example, by being given micro-states with poor resources), something which is hidden away by the ideological focus on a form of pseudo-equality. Tcherkézoff discusses modern France in this context. The supreme value here is the unity and equality of mankind, the 'natural' equality, the 'rights of man' of the revolutionary period and after. This can, however, be contradicted on a secondary level, that of access to wealth and resources, where actual inequality, the result of competition, can prevail unchecked. For Tcherkézoff, this is especially striking in the case of Third-World immigrants into France and indigenous people in France's remaining colonies. Imposing disadvantage on grounds of race or ethnic origin is illegal, as it contradicts the primary level. On the secondary level, however, with competition for jobs, land and so forth, disadvantage seems less objectionable and is therefore allowed. As Tcherkézoff says, 'though strongly marked [this] does not contradict the ideology of the "left" *on the level where this is mainly situated.* One can take the natives' land, as long as one avoids racism against them, which is a statutory offence' (1994, original emphasis). Immigrants are not rejected as non-human, but incorporated at an inferior level—a characteristic of any hierarchy, which can thus be found even in supposedly egalitarian France.

There thus seems to be a departure here from Dumont's view of racism, which sees it as a pathology of egalitarianism in which those who represent substantial differences are excluded. Dumont's examples of this situation were all from societies dominated by a Protestant ethic and by definite separation on 'racial' grounds, especially the southern United States and South Africa. France's traditional claims to disregard race in favour of assimilation based on language and culture in colonial and post-colonial situations, however unreal in practice, may contribute to this difference. Fundamentally, though, the difference lies elsewhere. Clearly, both situations involve the practice of racism. However, whereas under apartheid the mystification was the ideology of 'separate but equal', in modern France it is an ideology of racial equality in a unitary state. Of course, both countries now see themselves as being in a post-racist, multicultural situation. Whereas formerly discriminating whites are still politically powerful in France, however, and are in a position to continue discriminating in other ways, in South Africa they are not, at least politically (in addition, the population imbalance is skewed in different ways in the two cases). Here, one feels, a genuine post-racist state has a better chance of evolving.

Ultimately, however, for Dumont, racism, like all forms of totalitarianism, is not an essential concomitant of egalitarianism but simply one of its possible outcomes, a pathological, not legitimate form of society. This is perhaps some indication of his own personal position. But also, we might regard this pathology as something that encourages the eventual collapse of all totalitarianisms from within, even when they remain undefeated from without. In general totalitarianism is the artificial imposition of a pseudo-holism on a social base which has already become partly individualistic, but which has not yet freed itself from holism. It is an attempt, in short, to reverse history and restore society as the supreme value by force. This does not mean that the old forms of society necessarily return, only that there may be continuities: Naziism had roots in the German Empire, Russian communism in Tsarism. Moreover, egalitarianism remains in place, obviously so under communism, but also with fascism as far as the chosen people itself is concerned (cf. the discussion of apartheid, above). The difference here might be said to lie in the fact that the internationalist claims of the former to speak for all humanity are replaced by the rigid exclusion of the rest of humanity by the latter—indeed, it might not be prepared to recognize their humanity at all.

Even at their most liberal, modern states are faced with contradictions. Partly, this is a problem of authority and legitimation:

> the moment the real being is conceived to be not the group but the individual, hierarchy disappears, and with it the immediate attribution of authority to a ruling agent. We are left with a collection of individuals, and the problem of justifying the construction of a power above them can be solved only by supposing the common consent of the members of the fellowship. (Dumont 1986a: 77-8)

This leads directly to a contradiction, given that common consent is a chimera, and consequently only a majority or sometimes 'least minority' view can be represented. This, together with the fact that elected leaders are still leaders, reintroduces hierarchy. Again here, we see that the oppositions modern/non-modern and egalitarian/hierarchical are for Dumont themselves hierarchical: 'the modern model itself becomes a particular case of the non-modern model' (1979: 795; cf. Dumont on Fichte's diagram, 1986a: 123-4).

Similarly, says Dumont, individualism is not fully able to replace holism even in modern society. He gives as an instance the transition from Hoover's laissez-faire economic policy in the United States to Roosevelt's New Deal policy when business confidence collapsed (1991: 21-2). Here holism had to be brought back to make up for the deficiencies of naked individualism. The phenomenon receives a more permanent form of expression in socialism, which Dumont regards as a 'hybrid form', one which combines the individualism of universal rights with the holism of the planned economy. Equality survives, though it is 'no longer an attribute of the individual but ... of social justice' (1986a: 76-7): a strenuous attempt is made to turn the ideal into fact. Yet such hybridizations of individualism and holism are 'as dangerous as they are intense' (Dumont 1991: 30). The 'only way they can come together without danger' is for them to enter into a hierarchy with one another (ibid.: 31). Thus in socialism, the individual becomes subordinate to the whole and equality comes to encompass liberty—otherwise the state can scarcely survive.

The attempt by all parties to combine socialism with liberty in Britain between 1945 and 1979 may stand as one example of the 'danger' Dumont is referring to, though he does not actually discuss it. If the state claims to be able to provide everything under such circumstances, it will become the target of every grievance and its stability may be threatened. In Britain this attempt culminated in nation-wide strikes of workers in the nationalized industries during the 1970s. The decline of union power under Thatcherism was of a piece with privatization, which amongst other things can be seen empirically as a policy of 'getting the people off the state's back' (as much as vice versa—the actual Thatcherite slogan ideologically speaking). The socialist states of eastern Europe avoided this problem only by suppressing any overt manifestation of liberty, especially by trade unions, which were mostly arms of the state and almost invariably closely controlled (cf. Solidarity's shadowy legal existence in Poland). One result here, however, was the extreme atomization, or rather individualism (since the former term is really an exaggerated self-stereotype), which formed one popular response to an ideology which took only slender root at a popular level. In the one case, therefore, liberty undermined a polity that sought to be liberal and egalitarian at once, to which the state eventually reacted by preferring the former to the latter and scrapping nationalization altogether. In the other case, popular individualism conspired against an official egalitarianism which also eventually imploded, with the same outcome. In both cases, conflict arose out of attempts to do away with hierarchy. [12]

We might conclude, then, by arguing that hierarchy is better able to realize its ideals than equality, and even that it is ultimately more tolerant. This is not an argument in favour of one or other, merely a recognition of the fact that hierarchy is, of necessity, simultaneously a fact and an ideal, while equality seems destined to remain only the latter. In particular, the tolerance of equality, though equally an ideal, is always liable to be compromised when it is asked to accommodate what it does not want to accommodate. But also, it is ultimately no objection to Dumont's argument to insist that egalitarianism predominates in this or that society. For the Dumontian, it is not enough to say that people *believe* in equality or *are* egalitarian. They do more, they tacitly *prefer* equality to something else—to hierarchy or inequality, say—which they try to ignore but are nonetheless forced to recognize on occasion. Accordingly, the objection disappears as soon as one sees the matter as another hierarchical opposition.

Tolerance was also what Hertz displayed towards the end of his article on right and left (1909) in approving the modern trend against subordinating the left hand to the right. Again, however, this was the modern tolerance of widening the criteria of equality by choosing to disregard the difference between the two hands. Hertz was a true modern, in the sense that he believed in the scientific socialism and the science of sociology that was being developed by French intellectualism. This was maintaining French culture as the highest on earth, and Hertz, in his pamphlet on depopulation of 1910, condemned the idea of foreign immigration into France as a cure for the country's depopulation because it would threaten this culture. Today we would call this chauvinist, even racist, though it was not uncommon at the time, even among anthropologists (who frequently talked of the 'inferior' societies and the like). Behind it in overall terms is a greater concern for equality at home than for conditions in overseas spheres of influence—a posture typical of democracies expanding abroad, from ancient Athens to the post-war history of the United States. In that these spheres of influence are not part of the home country, democracy in them is unnecessary.

There are various manifestations of the world's more recent attempts to overcome this and other colonial legacies. One is the direct claims to the equality of all ethnicities for equal access to political and economic power, claims which increasingly threaten the nation state's very existence in some cases and are rapidly replacing merit or democracy as their basis (Tambiah 1989). A similar aspect, especially in Africa, has been the attempt to suppress tribalism in favour of identity with the post-imperial but multi-ethnic state. A third example, identified by de Coppet (1990: 143-4), is the modern stress on equal human rights, which refers the individual directly to the generality of mankind without the society to which he or she belongs and which lies in between being involved. Indeed, the notion of human rights explicitly blinds itself to all social, cultural or racial particularities as criteria for awarding them.

Dumont himself traces this development to the Declaration of the Rights of Man in the French Revolution (1986a: 92ff.), which, in eliding subject and sovereign, deprived the state of its 'ontological reality' (ibid.: 145). Indeed, he sees it as a peculiarly French (as opposed to British or German) phenomenon, the undoubted recognition of other states by the French existing at a secondary ideological level (1992: 260-1, 267). The contemporary trend has been to remove the notion of human rights from this uniquely French historical and cultural environment and to apply it to all humanity, in accordance with its universalist pretensions. This procedure is often resisted not only by certain recalcitrant governments (for example, China, certain Islamic countries) but often by whole peoples. This is at least partly because it is apt to be seen as being a new form of western domination in disguise. As de Coppet points out (1992b: 62), the concentration on 'universal' human rights, which are in reality based on European individualism, disregards the right of societies to be different: in particular, not all societies place the individual on the supreme level.

But in parallel to this, more tolerant trends can be discerned. To some extent, this is the result of the arrival of postmodernism, itself a consequence of the freeing of the world, both western and non-western, from the problem of direct political control of the latter by the former. Dumont himself defines this as the reintroduction of non-modern characteristics into modern thought (1986a: 18-19). But there is another way of looking at it, one which, moreover, does not directly involve the supposed relativism of the current age. Generally, we may say that the world is moving not backwards towards hierarchy but forwards towards widening still further the criteria of equality by eliminating any remaining recognition of difference.

Thus the discourse of the international bureaucracy, in its relentless search for common ground, glosses over cultural differences as much as possible, recognizing their existence as something which sometimes demands attention for practical reasons, but not invoking them in decision-making as a matter of principle. This contrast in itself is another hierarchical opposition. Similarly, as far as race is concerned, it is rapidly becoming *de rigeur* not to allude to it at all. As we have seen, Dumont has argued that racism is an outcome of egalitarian ideologies which ground equality in substantive terms rather than the relational terms of a hierarchy. The problem is that, despite being egalitarian, they are not freed from the compulsion to discriminate. Ethnic others may be defined in racial, that is, in somatic or physical terms, or in Dumont's terms, substantially. This is the basic reason why Dumont declines to see racist societies, such as, formerly, the southern United States or South Africa under apartheid, as caste systems. Any integration was economic only. Politically, ideologically and ritually, there was complete separation in what were really variants of the notion of the late-colonial 'plural society' discussed by Furnivall (see Eriksen 1993: 48-50). This is another key difference from the caste system.

The contemporary response to racism from the point of view of 'progress' or 'political correctness' has therefore been to drop unnecessary references to race altogether. If Dumont is correct in saying that we only distinguish in order to accord a difference in value to what are being distinguished, then it is logical to attempt to remove discrimination by declining to recognize difference at all. This is only partly possible so long as any discrimination continues to exist, since the issue still then has to be discussed for practical reasons. Immediate relevance, therefore—which may include identification in urgent cases—is just about allowable. In probably most multiculural societies that are also 'non-modern' in Dumont's terms, it is not unusual to include some ethnic label when referring casually to individuals. In the west this usage has become increasingly unusual in 'politically correct' circles, at least in the direct hearing of those it refers to. It has also come to be associated with at least covert racism, of seeking to make a point about race, of the 'I'm not a racist but...' type of racism. A refusal to make casual use of ethnic labels, on the other hand, goes along with a willingness or desire to include all people within the community of equality, regardless of ethnic difference, that is, to widen the criteria of differentiation by ignoring difference.

In the present politically correct climate, other discourses are going the same way. One is gender. One aspect to the removal of discrimination in this sphere is linguistic, expressed in the tendency to dismantle the hierarchical opposition between 'man' and 'woman' in, especially, the English language (cf. above, Chapter 3). Where earlier male pronouns also stood for females if both genders were involved, now both forms are required in the interests of abolishing discrimination: thus 'he' has become 'he or she' or 's/he'. Another alternative is the substitution of 'she' for 'he' as the pronoun covering both genders, though in fact this merely represents an inversion of the earlier discriminatory situation. In the first alternative, by contrast, the shift is not from one form of hierarchical opposition to its reverse but from hierarchy to equality.

Nonetheless, with gender it is more usual, and even considered desirable up to a point, to retain a sense of difference, because, quite simply, the most basic aspects of gender relations are still those that are felt to make the world go round. But in other areas, such as employment and access to resources of all kinds, discrimination is now thought to be wrong, and overt expressions of it problematic. Drawing attention to gender differences in such contexts again implies making a discriminatory point, though here too reference to them is allowable where corrective action to remove them is being discussed (employment policy, for example).

Other areas in which the expression of gender difference has been reduced are in dress, at least casually, with jeans, T-shirts and trainers near-universal wear for young people, but also at work ('power dressing' etc.). There are also certain cross-gender linguistic usages, such as the extension of the American colloquial term 'guy' to women. Actually there is still a certain bias in these changes: women have adopted trousers, not men dresses, while the standardization on 'guy' has meant universalizing the male, not the female term (the former equivalent to 'guy', namely 'gal', sc. 'girl', is anyway problematic when used for women, since it juniorises them).

Another exception is gay discourses, where 'gay' often refers to both genders, while 'lesbian' refers to just one and is often contrasted to 'gay' as male. This shows how pervasive hierarchical oppositions are even in these supposedly liberating situations. Sexual orientation per se, however, is another case where there has been a reduction in the number of situations in which difference may be expressed, including a certain tendency to avoid the familiar jokes and innuendoes. This is not to say that there is no more homophobia, but from once being routine it has become marginalized, or at least politically incorrect. There has been a similar shift in attitude in relation to the distinction between health and disability. In all these cases, the only permissible discourse of difference is that directed at overcoming the discrimination that the difference gives rise to. [13]

Notes

1. I am grateful to Wendy James for drawing my attention to this text. As far as I have been able to determine, Dumont himself does not mention it anywhere.

2. Only one author to my knowledge has opposed a Hegelian approach to a Dumontian one in interpreting ethnography, namely Toren, on Fiji. This is basically because, in her later work at least, she sees the values of Fijian society as being antithetical to one another rather than hierarchically related in the Dumontian sense. Her work is discussed in more detail in Chapter 7.

3. The French were among those most impressed, so much so that they soon invited him to Paris to spend six months with their *équipe*. A later article on the same theme is McDonaugh (1987). As noted in the Preface, I am writing here partly as an eyewitness.

4. There is also some implicit criticism in Howell's paper of the tabular representations of data of her former supervisor Needham. Since the distinctions the Chewong make 'are not vehicles for meaning beyond themselves', save to denote equality, 'to link them all into a long table of pairs would be at best uninformative, at worst misleading' (1985: 175). On the other hand, if the dyads are mostly symmetrical, as is said to be the case, there could hardly be much contradiction of the sort that plagued Tcherkézoff, since all the usual dynamic value of such oppositions in analysis would be lost.

5. Cf. Jennings (1959: 390): 'the Government for the time being, though supported by a section of the people only, is the instrument of the whole.'

6. Cf. the Nuer example, where right and left are linked in a hierarchical opposition, and the body is the whole to which right refers, not itself one of the poles or values. The present case is like constructing an opposition between body and the right hand and seeing that as hierarchical, which would be a false representation of what a hierarchical opposition would involve.

7. Parsons remarks (1975: 75-6) that this amounts not only to emphasizing the Black elements in one's descent but also to forgetting the supposedly White ones. For the Dumontian, there is yet another hierarchical opposition here, one in which Black encompasses White except on occasions when the fact of mixed descent is being stressed specifically. The American politician Jesse Jackson suggested that 'Black' was a discriminatory term and proposed replacing it with 'Afro-American', a modern formulation defining the person more definitely in substantialist terms, in which nothing is 'forgotten' (and therefore nothing encompassed).

8. The situation is actually more complicated, especially following recent political changes in the country, and as just described was essentially a product of apartheid. Coloured self-definition is reduced to some extent by the desire of many members of the group to assimilate to Afrikaners, especially if they speak Afrikaans as their mother tongue. Jamaica and many other Caribbean islands make a similar distinction between supposedly pure Blacks and those who are obviously the product of mixed descent, the latter often being elites in effect too. This is verbalized by using the terms 'Black' and 'Brown' as well as 'White' (Eriksen 1993: 83).

9. See Needham (1980a: 52). Needham is saying here that day/night may be treated as a contrary by the Meru, but as Barnes points out (1984: 240 n. 7; 1985b: 13), in Aristotelian terms he has defined contrary on the previous page (Needham 1980a: 51) as ungradable rather than as gradable—its normal meaning in this sort of discourse.

10. Cf. Bataille (1988 [1938]: 117): 'Hegelian phenomenology represents the mind as essentially homogeneous. [...] It seems to me that the marked heterogeneity estab-

lished between the sacred and the profane by French sociology, or between the unconscious and the conscious by psychoanalysis, is a notion that is entirely foreign to Hegel.'

11. There then follows a reference to some earlier remarks of Needham's deploring the influence of temperament on academic argument.

12. The actual situation in the UK was, of course, more complicated. Generally the private sector was quieter in the 1970s, since the survival of some market competition ultimately gave employers and workers little choice but to reach settlements over pay and conditions. In the nationalized industries, on the other hand, the largely nationalized labour force that came with them tended to take the view that wage demands could be made up out of general taxation. Since this increased government borrowing, inflation resulted. It also meant that every trade dispute in the public sector tended to develop into a political fight with the government (whether Labour or Conservative), in which the formal employers, the various public corporations, were ignored by both sides. The actions of the unions, who became overmighty subjects in the eyes of many, but whose own members were being affected by this same inflation, were therefore actually conditioned to a large extent by the structure of the situation. By 1979, however, the perception was widespread that a weak Labour government was becoming overwhelmed by such issues, and it was the trade unions that took most of the blame. This brought Thatcher to power to end the post-war left-of-centre consensus over public ownership of most of the means of production, which in practice had been maintained by mainly right-wing governments since the war. It is noticeable that, since 1997, the Blairite Labour government has shunned re-nationalization and, indeed, seems intent on pushing forward remaining privatization wherever it can. In effect a new consensus emerged in 1997 (apparently confirmed in 2001) that now favoured privatization, though taking the form of a right-of-centre consensus being maintained by a left-wing government that had successfully stolen Thatcher's clothes from her successors. As for the taming of the unions under Thatcher, privatization was probably ultimately more permanently effective than the unemployment it created or the piling up of restrictive legislation. Of course, one should also not discount such factors as the impact of adverse public opinion on the unions—who quickly decided to discipline themselves—an improvement in methods of collective bargaining (though coupled with a trend towards casualization and part-time working), and the re-establishment of a less inflationary form of prosperity. The essential change, though, was that privatization took the pressure off the government by removing it from trade disputes in these industries. However monopolistic the latter, their labour forces can now do little to harm the government by striking, and have become almost as toothless as the unemployed (which the new consensus has effectively disenfranchised).

13. The world of entertainment represents certain exceptions in this regard. Although liberating in many ways through their ability to manipulate images and give them fuzzy boundaries, such media are also highly conservative in other ways. Many of the symbolic devices used in media and film clearly represent or refer to male models, not to say male fantasies. Representations of gayness are also discriminatory. There has been a long tradition in theatre and more modern forms of entertainment of male performers camping it up, with decreasing subtlety, perhaps, though a sense of ambiguity concerning sexual orientation is still valuable in enhancing this imagery. Male gay performers also consciously exploit this angle for their own purposes (though there have also been straight imitations). Lesbian equivalents are much more unusual in the media, and rarely last even when they do manage to gain a brief acceptance: somehow, they have not managed to establish a distinctive tradition of humour like male campness. (However, lesbian audiences may

themselves react to this by appropriating media images such as Xena the Princess as lesbian icons.) As for race, in Britain the Black and White Minstrel Show of an earlier period has given way to Ali G, whose imitation of Black people is based on dialect, accent and stereotypical mannerisms, not on blacking up. Thus stereotyping is still present, but although it has been sanitized as cultural, not racial, it has still generated controversy (cf. Watson 2000: 67). In addition, Black musicians still find it difficult to obtain the same exposure in the mainstream media as the White musicians who, for decades, have been stylistically dependent on them, while Black actors still all too frequently play characters that are not just Black, but poor, criminal or cussed as well.

Chapter 6

THE SCHOOL OF DUMONT
FROM CLASSIFICATION TO RITUAL ANALYSIS

ERASME

In the 1980s, a group of Dumont's supporters became involved in the CNRS-funded Equipe de Recherche en Anthropologie Sociale—Morphologie, Echanges (ERASME), formed in 1981 (though now much changed). Its members have included, at times or more or less permanently, Cécile Barraud, Dominique Casajus, Daniel de Coppet, André Iteanu, Raymond Jamous, Denis Monnerie, Simonne Pauwels and Serge Tcherkézoff. Over the years the *équipe* has attracted a number of more temporary visitors from outside France, including Signe Howell, Christian McDonaugh, Jos Platenkamp and Masao Yamaguchi. In addition to numerous articles, there have appeared five major monographs utilizing these ideas in a fairly extensive and systematic manner (Barraud 1981; Jamous 1981, 1991; Iteanu 1983a; Tcherkézoff 1987 [1983]), as well as joint and edited volumes (Barraud et al. 1994 [1984]; de Coppet and Iteanu 1995). Howell and Platenkamp have subsequently introduced the key ideas in Oslo and Leiden respectively, and they were also given an airing at the first conference of the European Association of Social Anthropologists held at Coimbra in 1990. More recently, in May 2000, they became the subject of a conference convened by Roy Dilley at the University of St Andrews, Scotland.

This publicity may compensate to some extent for the fragmentation of the original circle. In June 1992, Casajus, Jamous and Pauwels left with the intention of running a seminar of their own together with Tcherkézoff, who had already gone his own way in 1984. This split reflected a certain parting of the ways theoretically. Those who have left ERASME, although remaining sympathetic to Dumont's ideas generally, tend to see them as being capable of further refinement (especially Tcherkézoff) and/or as not excluding other approaches. Those who remained within ERASME (i.e. Barraud, de Coppet and Iteanu) have tended, on the whole, to follow its original programme more closely, the main concern being the analysis of ritual and the applicability of Dumont's ideas to it. This has been an interest of Tcherkézoff's too, though it was one Dumont himself worked on far less. However, for the rump of ERASME the approach has now become focused more on cosmology, and on what they call holistic, sociomorphic or cosmomorphic societies, whereas for Tcherkézoff the level of comparison is a more universal one.

In addition, differences have arisen between Tcherkézoff on the one hand and de Coppet and Barraud on the other concerning basic issues of comparative method, culminating in a debate as to which interpretation is the more objective, the most truly structuralist (in the general sense of that word; see above, Preface; below, Chapter 7). Tcherkézoff stands out from the group as one deserving, on Dumont's own admission (1979: 817 n.22), the status of fellow traveller rather than follower, given his simultaneous but quite independent working out of the same fundamental ideas from the mid-1970s on (see above, Chapter 4). The cross-fertilization this evidently led to has already been mentioned, as have certain later clarifications of Dumont's thought made by Tcherkézoff himself (see above, Chapters 3, 4). But the latter has not been alone in developing these ideas further: in particular, he himself credits de Coppet with the initiative in their application to ritual analysis (personal communication).

It is clear that Dumont himself was always more interested in developing the notion of hierarchical opposition in relation to classification (of the *varna* scheme, the *trivarga* etc.) and in his global historical writings on the genesis of individualism than in, for example, ritual analysis. He quite explicitly left further developments to others (see 1979: 806; 1980: 239), though sometimes returning to deal with particular issues once it became clear that this had not happened and the matter had become pressing. Dumont was thus, perhaps, an inspiration more than a leader in the narrow sense, unlike Durkheim, for example. Many of those who continued his approach were not originally his students and only discovered these innovations at a comparatively late stage in their own intellectual development. In their earliest articles, for example, Barraud and de Coppet make no use of Dumont's special notions of value and hierarchy and talk of the latter only in the usual sense of social stratification: one might call their analyses conventionally structuralist without being slavishly Lévi-Straussian (see, for example, Barraud 1972; de Coppet 1968, 1970a, 1970b, 1976,

1977; de Coppet and Zemp 1978). It was not until the late 1970s and early 1980s that they and others began to draw on Dumont's lessons in print.

An early example is Iteanu's article on feuding among the Ossetians of the Caucasus (published in 1980, though written in 1977 from published sources). Here, the father/son relationship is a metaphor for the relationship between legitimate and illegitimate violence, the first encompassing the second. Women, on the other hand, stand for peace and the equality of groups. Feuds may be ended by one party entering the village of the other and suckling a woman of the latter, thus becoming her 'son'. This is, of course, also an act of submission to the other party to the feud, now the 'father'. Women also mediate through marriage, which is isogamous and may end a feud. However, since it is men, typically fathers, who control the disposal of women in marriage, the egalitarian ethos of the feud is ultimately encompassed by the hierarchical ethos of relations between generations. 'These two types of relation structure Ossetian society and form the basis of the circulation of beings and things' (Iteanu 1980: 80). This statement represents an early version of what was to become a key element of the approach in the analysis of both ritual and of whole societies.

Another example is de Coppet's article 'The Life-giving Death' (1981; also de Coppet in Barraud et al. 1994: 40-65). Here, the starting point is Hertz's article on death of 1907, which de Coppet approves of in general, although arguing that its main lesson is that premature comparisons must necessary entail ethnocentric assumptions. The first step should be to determine 'the interrelations between ... rituals in the overall framework of the main values of a society' (de Coppet 1981: 176). More specifically here, his ethnography of the 'Are'are of the Solomon Islands shows that inauspicious deaths should not be regarded as being completely outside the ritual process: indeed, in the present case they form a full part of the exchanges and transformations that transitions between life and death involve. There are no natural deaths in 'Are'are thought: instead a dichotomy is recognized between those caused by the ancestors or by foreign spirits (through illness, accident etc.) and those caused by men (murders, to which suicides, infant deaths and the deaths of women in childbirth are assimilated). In the second case, the 'murders' interfere in the sociocosmic order by pre-empting the ancestors' right to take lives—hence the need for ritual. The ritual responses to the two basic types of death certainly differ, but they always concern the problem of dealing with the consequences of death. Oddly enough, however, it is not the dichotomy between types of death but that between 'killing one's own people and eating or leaving to rot' (ibid.: 186, emphases removed), that is, between the act and the ritual responses to it, that de Coppet introduces as hierarchical, the former encompassing the latter. Phrased in this way, the example would seem to have no real resolution, since it leaves out of account murders committed against 'other people' and dichotomizes phases in a ritual sequence, not symbolic values applicable differentially to the whole sequence.

Clearer is the encompassment of breath and body by a person's 'image', which is linked to the ancestors. Similarly, the peacemaster encompasses the murderer, the two being related as life to untimely death, as the social to the individual. The ancestors, however, are the supreme value. De Coppet also makes the more general point (following Annette Weiner and others) that the view of exchange as something involving reciprocity between individuals is ethnocentric when applied to Melanesian societies. In the first place, as Mauss and Malinowski both stressed, exchange is clearly a social task with social ends and is not shaped by individual goals. In the second place, those ends may have more to do with transformation than with reciprocity, whereas exchange, or rather the transfer of values through what we would regard as symbolic interchanges, is merely the mechanism leading towards that goal. Ultimately it is the necessity of turning the decay of death into the fertility of regenerated life that shapes these ritual sequences, here and elsewhere in the region, not to mention further afield.

De Coppet thus also offers some considerations on the use of ritual to create society rather than simply to reflect it, as in Durkheimian (and Hertzian) orthodoxy:

> ... I should like to dispute the statement of Hertz that 'society imparts its own character of permanence to the individuals who compose it' [reference omitted]. We could say, regarding the 'Are'are, that the society builds up its own character of permanence through the repeated dissolution *into* the ritual and exchange process of the main elements composing each individual. (1981: 176, original emphasis; cf. Bloch and Parry 1982: 6)

However, Hertz was speaking generally; what the 'Are'are think they themselves are doing need not contradict it, being on a different level of discourse. De Coppet also challenges (1981: 198) the idea of 'representations', since it suggests a distinction between real and unreal that may not be indigenously recognized (an objection which has often been raised as regards symbolism itself). What is retained of the *Année sociologique* tradition here seems to be little more than the holist perspective of Mauss and the general doctrine of the social determination of human action.

A similar general message, of the importance of ritual as the means of a society's survival, can also be drawn from Iteanu's ethnography on the Orokaiva of Papua New Guinea (1983a, 1983b). The argument here opposes the traditional anthropological attitude that the facts of kinship provide social continuity almost automatically. For the Orokaiva, kinship is labile. There is no rule of recruitment through unifiliation; genealogical knowledge is purely a matter of which names are currently remembered; and even what the anthropologist might identify as the inheritance of land is less a matter of transferring the land itself than of transmitting knowledge about it (knowledge of boundaries, names of places and plants, ritual knowledge etc.). The transmission of one's name is particularly important as the only means of avoiding social oblivion after death: 'its genealogical value depends on its ritual value' (1983b: 55). Here, it is initiation, at which the spirits are present, that effects the continuity and is thus the ultimate value, encompassing kinship.

> Among the Orokaiva, to honour the spirits is to carry out the initiation ritual while conforming to a complex and hierarchized logic of levels, and not by privileging descent, which is only one element among others. In other words, it is the repetition of the ritual cycle, not descent, which assures permanent contact between men and spirits, which the society needs to survive. (Ibid.: 55)

And further:

> Initiation, as a manifestation of the spirits, subordinates and encompasses the domains of kinship and locality. It is therefore not for nothing that the spirits are neither in a relation of kinship nor localized. (Ibid.: 54)

As with de Coppet's objection to Hertz, here too one might identify a difference between a particular indigenous perspective and a more general view drawn out of the accumulation of comparative work. For Iteanu, however, the reasons for this situation not having previously been realized for what it is lie in the anthropologist's neglect of hierarchy and in his or her preference for a model that is sociological, not indigenous. It is only by resorting to a false distinction between ideology and action, in which the former stands for informant's statements and the latter for the supposed sociological reality that goes under the name of kinship, that traditional anthropology can overcome the conflicts involved. In the Orokaiva case, the solution lies implicitly in incorporating both in a total ideological scheme that manifests itself at different levels of that scheme and in which the values represented by initiation and names encompass those represented by genealogy at the ultimate or superordinate level. In this way, a contradiction in perspectives yields to the segmentation of a unified ideology.

Tcherkézoff also stresses ritual over social structure in the indigenous thought of many societies. An example is his paper on the treatment of twins among the Nyamwezi of Tanzania (1986b). The Nyamwezi ritually expose twins in the bush and then bring about their rebirth in the royal court (royalty, like twins, is associated with the number two, 1987: 49, 50). Their initial inauspiciousness is thus transformed into the supreme auspiciousness of being royal children. After they have been taken into the court and the gate has been closed behind them, the key event of the ritual process takes place: their parents charge the gate and break it down, whereupon the king, waiting inside, informs them that all has turned out as expected and that they (the parents) may return home. This event amounts to a change of level in the ritual sequence, which Tcherkézoff refers to as a 'hierarchical threshold' (1986b: 92, 104-5). Before it, the twins are charged with a negative value, afterwards with a positive and ultimately encompassing one. The threshold that is crossed in breaching the sanctity of the royal court may be crossed not only by those who have brought twins into the world, but also by the killer of a lion or by a murderer seeking refuge from his victim's kin. In forcibly entering the court, they are committing a second delict, one which is akin to the murder of the king himself; but in doing so they also achieve access to and union with the sacred. The price is the loss of personal liberty for the killer or the twins, plus the gifts that must be offered—money, the skin of the lion, the twins' placenta—to restore the cosmic order. 'If the initial gesture reveals the interdict, the transgression that follows animates the hierarchy through its vertical orientation. A change of level takes place' (1980: 56; also ibid.: 53ff.).

Another example of a ritual threshold is the patient's bed in healing ritual: he or she lies on it, and in spitting into a vessel beneath removes the evil that has been causing the trouble (1985b: 69). The evil must be reintegrated; it is not expelled, as in the traditional structuralist view based on binarism. Ritual is thus an operator of transformations, not of compensation; the cutting in two of a sacrificial animal, with each side in a dispute holding one end, is another instance of effecting a change of level, another hierarchical threshold (1980: 50-1), the parts themselves, of course, being conceptually unequal (1991a: 200). Violence and vengeance are thus both encompassed by ritual, the latter being 'a system of transformations guaranteed by the king' (1986a: 107). This is the only way in which the king can control violence in his kingdom, that is, with values, not with a police force or army imposing direct control (1991b: 181-2). Indeed, that royal power is itself encompassed by ritual is shown by the fact that the king is killed (sacrificed) when his powers fail. Tcherkézoff regards this as a rite of renewal, one which does not close a reign so much as inaugurate one (ibid.).

A still more graphic demonstration of the notion of a threshold, and its connection with encompassment, arises from a consideration of kingship in medieval and early modern Europe, including Tudor England. Tudor political theory regarded the king as having two bodies, an earthly, mortal body natural, and an eternal, evanescent body politic (or in some formulations, body spiritual), which is never infantile and never ages, but represents permanent royal authority, which the present physical king only temporarily inhabits (Kantorowicz 1957: 7). In normal times, the two bodies form an indivisible whole (ibid.: 9, 11): the former is encompassed by the latter, possession of which makes the king what he is, different from other men and women. It is only at the death of the body natural that the fact of encompassment is revealed, thus effecting a change of level. With this change, the encompassment becomes mere asymmetry, and the existence of two royal bodies is made evident. But also, this asymmetry temporarily makes the body natural, which alone is the subject of the royal funeral, the superior or dominant pole of the opposition. In this sense, the dissolution of encompassment is coordinate with the liminality that the death of the king's body natural has occasioned. That part of the royal funeral which separates the king's two bodies, in giving expression to this, can be seen as one hierarchical threshold, that is, the point where the encompassment dissolves into an asymmetry. This step is necessary in order that the body politic may be reunited with a new body natural. Only with the new monarch's (i.e. the new body natural's) consecration is another threshold crossed and this encompassment restored, so that the new body natural comes to be re-encompassed by the body politic (ibid.: 49).

Although Tcherkézoff appears to view only ritual transitions that restore unity as thresholds, this example indicates that there is no obvious reason why transitions that remove this unity and change an encompassment into an asymmetric opposition should not also qualify for the term. At one point, indeed, Tcherkézoff himself calls these thresholds 'operators', or generators of changes in level, which themselves effect 'transformations' (1986a: 92, 107). Reversal is also involved in producing changes of level; elsewhere (1987: 117, 124) he calls reversal an 'operation', not a 'contradiction', as in the substantialist view. For Tcherkézoff, indeed (e.g. 1995), ritual and the reversal it entails supply the necessary dynamic to the holistic scheme of hierarchical opposition, controlling and removing impurity before restoring the 'non-antagonistic superiority' of the encompassing value.

Thresholds thus not only effect a transformation or a change of levels, they also bring about transcendence in the sense of access to the sacred (see above, Chapter 3; Casajus 1985: 76). The sacred here, of course, is 'the whole of society' (that is to say, not just what is left over after the profane has been abstracted) and, moreover, it is the ultimate value in the society: it can, in a broad sense, be termed 'religious', in tune with Durkheimian orthodoxy (cf. de Coppet 1990: 147: 'ultimate value and society are one'). For the Nyamwezi the ultimate value, the expression of the social, the religious, is what Tcherkézoff calls 'ancestrality' (*l'ancestralité*, 1986b: 94). The ancestors—above all, of course, those of the king—influence everything and are the source of everything: they represent much more than the 'ancestral cult' of the traditional anthropological view, in which they are seen as being merely one aspect of the society's activities among many.

This contact with the sacred is also found with others' candidates for the ultimate values of the particular societies they have studied, such as ancestors among the 'Are'are (de Coppet) and the spirits among the Orokaiva (Iteanu; the spirits are especially active during initiation; see above). This is conceptually distinct from the question of authority. Nyamwezi kings are not the ultimate value or the sacred, but they are nearest to it, and it can only be approached through them (hence the importance of breaching the royal court and being accepted in key ritual processes). Dumont denies holism to the Hobbist state precisely because, despite appearances, it lacks this quality of transcendence: 'the hierarchical ordering of the social body is absent because the State is not oriented toward any end which would transcend it, but is subject only to itself' (1986a: 84).

Whether it is actually legitimate to talk of *access* to the sacred has been questioned by Houseman, who defines transcendence as 'a relation with the *inaccessible*—ancestors, spirits, divinities, God etc.' (1984: 308, my emphasis). But the aim at contact, even oneness, with the sacred surely forms a large part of human ritual activity. In Durkheim's words (1915: 340): 'Sacrifice was not founded to create a bond of artificial kinship between a man and his gods, but to maintain and renew the natural kinship which primitively united them.' One is reminded here of Eliade's *Myth of the Eternal Return* (1949), with its suggestion of the constant renewal of an original past time. In the Durkheimian view too, sacrifice precisely brings about not only access to, but union with, the sacred (see Hubert and Mauss 1899).

But more generally, thresholds can be inserted into the Durkheimian insight that social rules only become apparent when they are broken by individuals. Through such violations, not only do we move from social harmony and conformity to social division and contestation, but also from society encompassing the individual to the individual becoming distinguished from society through his or her disobedience. This is just one threshold that is crossed. Another is encountered in remaking the society after this breach, possibly through ritual action (the meal the offender gives his caste council in

India in order to be admitted into the caste, for example), which restores encompassment. Indeed, given that rituals generally are about handling the transitions made necessary by events that threaten or rend the social fabric, not just offences but social crises generally (cf. Hertz on death, 1907), thresholds separating encompassment from distinction are always being crossed in one direction or the other.

Tcherkézoff's analysis shows clearly why a simple binary opposition is not enough and why the usual list of such oppositions tends falsely to elide contexts in suggesting the attribution of a fixed value to each pole: 'the logic of the ritual is not that of a binary (that is, distinctive or substantialist) opposition: there is not death *or* life, the twins are not good or bad, accepted as a benefit or rejected as monstrosities. They are both; it is necessary to impose an order' (1986b: 104, original emphasis). A substantialist analysis would describe them as being destroyed, then reborn; a structuralist analysis describes them as being transformed, together with the values they bear. It is this embeddedness of value that ensures that the transformation is not simply dialectical in the manner of Lévi-Strauss. What appear elsewhere as different phases in the rite emerge here as different relational orderings within a unified whole. The dynamics of the different phases of transformation relate to this whole as much as to each other.

Sacred/Profane as a Hierarchical Opposition

These observations bear on the sacred itself, which is explicitly seen as a holistic value. The earlier dichotomy between sacred and profane was certainly asymmetric, with the sacred pole superordinate, but the Durkheimians did not use the language of encompassment. For the Dumontian, however, sacred/profane is precisely a hierarchical opposition, one in which the sacred or religious or social may be taken as the analytical, cross-cultural or comparative category, values such as ancestrality or initiation being their local or culturally specific reflexes. This identification of the sacred with the ultimate value is also found in the priority Dumont gives to the Brahman in the caste system, despite the mistaken assumption that he is necessarily a priest.

A similar line is followed by Iteanu, who criticizes interpretations of sacred and profane that are a 'transposition of our western separations between conceived and perceived or between ideology and reality' as inapplicable to 'the reality of the societies studied by anthropologists' (1990b: 169, 170). This is again a proposal for a view of holism focused on the sacred:

> ... paramount values must simultaneously be immanent in the social organization as a whole and transcendent with regard to this whole ... This

double dimension may justify our calling them sacred. But our attempt to generalize must stop here since, wherever the subordinated domain is to be found, it can never be considered as purely profane. In fact, it is always encompassed by the sacred, and thus partially partakes of sacredness although, on a subordinated level, it escapes to a certain extent. (Ibid.: 182)

This coming together of sacred and profane is necessary for the distinction to be seen as hierarchical, for otherwise the profane cannot affect the sacred or 'contradict' it in its own domain; indeed, says Iteanu, it is the profane that approaches the sacred rather than the other way round. Unfortunately he does not define what counts as profane for him, but one infers from an example he gives, drawn from Hubert and Mauss's work on Hindu sacrifice (1899), that it is again the individual subject—here, the provider of the sacrifice—who nonetheless stands furthest from the sacred centre, further than the officiating priest. For Tcherkézoff (1994; cf. previous chapter), a place must be found for this individual, 'under pain of confining anthropology in the idealism of a Durkheimian society reduced to the sacred'. For the latter, the opposition between sacred and profane does not represent a clean cut 'but an asymmetry in relation to a whole'. It is rather a question of 'more sacred' and 'less sacred'. That which is most sacred is superior because it defines the whole and is also the most separated and protected (Tcherkézoff 1989: 275). The Durkheimian sense of separation is thus retained, but relativized (or made relational). The sacred is compromised by profane contact, and the less sacred it becomes the less separate it is. As for Iteanu, he feels (1990b: 173) that his account may distort Durkheim's views but hopes nonetheless to be able 'to give new life to this distinction'. Tcherkézoff, more positively, not only has no doubt of the status of this famous dichotomy as a hierarchical opposition, he also believes that the Durkheimians themselves came very close to seeing this, without ever quite getting there. [1]

Although sacred/profane is conventionally seen as a simple dichotomy, this neglects the idea of totality that is also present in Durkheim (e.g. 1915: 442) as 'the abstract form of the concept of society', but also as something 'including' everything else. As distinct from culture, which is reducible to specific aspects of the social (the linguistic, the economic etc.), society is a system, and *ipso facto* hierarchical. On the other hand, society resembles, indeed, is co-ordinate with, the sacred, since both are wholes: they include everything and are included by nothing. However, for Durkheim hierarchy is taxonomic, not encompassing: with kinship, for example, one has a series of graded categories: clans, lineages, families, generations and individuals. In addition, there is the circularity of argument one encounters in

Durkheim with respect to the relation between the sacred and society. While the sacred represents and even reproduces society, it is society that makes things sacred. Similarly, with respect to the relation between society and the individual, while society shapes the individual consciousness with an awareness of its totality, individuals come together to form a society in the first place because of this very awareness. This qualifies Durkheim's usual insistence on the priority of the society over the individual. Given a taxonomic view of hierarchy, moreover, it actually makes this relation symmetric, that is, it is a distinctive opposition, whereas what Durkheim apparently intended would actually suggest a hierarchical opposition.

A similar remark applies to sacred/profane. In his revision of this opposition Hertz, although retaining the taxonomic view, made it more thoroughly relational (see Chapter 1). From the profane point of view the sacred (pure + impure) is the opposite pole. From the sacred point of view the impure + profane is the opposite pole, meaning—given that the sacred can be impure as well as pure—that it is a part of itself too. The transfer between perspectives indicates a change of level. Moreover, the primary level is relational, the secondary substantial: there is contamination (by the impure) from the sacred point of view, but separation (from the sacred) from the profane point of view.

Something very similar has been argued with respect to Dumont's interpretation of India (Tcherkézoff 1994-5; see above, Chapter 4). What links Durkheim and Mauss with Dumont is therefore not the idea of totality or the dissolution of the individual, as is so often thought, but the observation that 'integration … is always inclusion plus contradiction' (Tcherkézoff 1995: 63 n.3). Hertz's modification also allows us to see, says Tcherkézoff, that the inclusiveness of the sacred encompasses the separation of the profane. The sacred tends to extend itself, through the operation of *mana*, into the profane. The profane, on the other hand, only endangers itself by approaching the sacred, risking either destruction or its own sacralization without being able to alter the sacred itself. [2]

Similarly, the dichotomy between soul and body in Durkheim is best seen as a hierarchical opposition, because this restores the individual to Durkheimian sociology, contrary to the usual assumption that he fits into it only with difficulty, if at all. Durkheim himself called the soul '*mana* individualized' (1915: 264), and he appears to have conceived it as that part of the individual that is equivalent to the whole. Certainly it is sacred, in opposition to the body, which is profane. The soul exists together with the body in life and therefore encompasses it, while often being treated as the essence of the person (certainly in the Christian tradition); but at death the two separate, and the body is never a part of the soul. More importantly, perhaps, it is the soul that survives, whereas the body decays into nothing. What is more, the soul, or an aspect of it, frequently returns to the transcendent collectivity seen as the undifferentiated mass of ancestors, and may return from it again to enter a new body, through reincarnation. One might object that bone too, a part of the body, often represents permanency. One might also question to what extent the soul needs the body, especially since dependency would logically diminish its status as the supreme value. Souls may search for bodies to inhabit on their return to earth, but society as such is concerned with life—and it is this that the soul gives to the body.

A final example here concerns the individual in Polynesia, who is *noa* by virtue of the fact that he is not dangerous and can be touched. He also stands in a hierarchical opposition to the chief. However, while he must avoid contact with both the chief (who is pure) and the corpse (which is impure), the chief need only avoid the corpse. Viewed from the outside, this yields a taxonomic hierarchy of three terms: corpse > chief > individual. Hertz, however, in giving us the interior perspective of such oppositions, allows us to perceive another hierarchical opposition, despite his own silence on this point. The chief, who encompasses everything else, sees only the impurity of the corpse—that is, the negative aspect of the purity that is his own nature—as a danger. The individual sees the threat of something qualitatively different to himself in whichever direction he looks, the purity of the chief as well as the impurity of the corpse. On the first level, the chief is everything, the individual nothing. On the second level, the individual recognizes himself as different in substance from both chief and corpse. In such examples the bidimensionality of Dumont's model is preserved: we still have sacred and profane, but the profane now only manifests itself on a subordinate level.

Mosko also discusses sacred/profane as a hierarchical opposition in some of his work on Polynesia (especially 1994a), but with much more scepticism than the authors we have just been discussing. His reasons are not entirely clear, but he appears to see pure/impure as being the only form of hierarchy that appears in Dumont's thought, and certainly he seeks to reduce it to sacred/profane even in India. In Polynesia, at any rate, this is said to rule out hierarchy, on the basis that in Dumont's interpretation of the *tabu/noa* opposition, pure and impure are both included in the former (1994a: 40). He also suggests that pure/impure are actually equivalent to the profane in India itself, on the basis of a single passage in Dumont (1971a: 75; cf. Mosko 1994a: 43), in which the latter places sacred, pure and impure in a hierarchical series (see also above, Chapter 4). In fact, what Dumont appears to mean is that in one situation the whole opposition pure/impure is encompassed by the sacred, since they are only 'modes under which men come in relation to it [sc. the sacred]' (Dumont 1971a: 75 n. 41), but also that in other situations 'the first two terms can be seen as encompassing the impure (*as ... for the varnas*)' (ibid.: 75, my emphasis).

Valeri dismisses Dumont's account of Polynesia for a similar reason—in his case, because Dumont, following Steiner, assumes that pure and impure are not distinguished there. However, he is more accurate than Mosko concerning Dumont's account of India, citing a passage in a different article (Dumont 1959: 31) that identifies purity as the state a human must be in to approach the gods rather than an attribute of the sacred that the gods represent. For Dumont as for Fuller, therefore (see above, Chapter 4), in India humans are more dependent on gods than vice versa. In Valeri's terms, the relationship between gods and humans is non-reciprocal in India, where purity and power are disjunctive, but reciprocal in Hawaii, where greater purity denotes greater power (including the power to pollute inferiors, unlike in India) and vice versa (Valeri 1985: 89-92, 361 n.11).

Primordial Unities and Unilateral Figures

Elsewhere, Tcherkézoff refers the notion of the sacred to the explanation given by many peoples as to why there should be dichotomies at all. He points out (1986b: 93) how many origin myths portray primordial time as the time of the unity of heaven and earth, and how they frequently relate how historical or social time began with an event that pushed them apart, creating the present social order. The latter is likely to be seen as imperfect, since there is now also disequilibrium and asymmetry. Contact with the sacred through ritual transformations and reversals which cross hierarchical thresholds thus provides more than just an assurance of the continuity of normal life here on earth: it is an attempt to recover something of the excellence of that primordial, but also ideal and transcendent order.

This can be recognized at the height of many rituals, for example, Orokaiva initiation: after the spirits have destroyed the village, that is, the social, there is, temporarily, no social differentiation in this world (only between men and ancestors; Iteanu 1990b: 177). Similarly, on the walls of the Nyamwezi initiation hut the primordial ancestors are depicted as unilateral figures, that is, as undifferentiated, and the stars are also shown as a uniform and undifferentiated mass (Tcherkézoff 1987: 63). In some West African societies, such as the Dogon, a one-legged figure represents the ancestors and the universe, whom Manding ritual officiants symbolize by tying their legs together (Dieterlin 1968).

Examples of reference to a past and better age characterized by unity can also be found in European ethnography. One example were Polish peasant farmers and their supporters under socialism, who remembered the pre-war period as one of rural harmony between all classes, before the socialist state came along and caused divisions among them (Nagengast 1991: 199, 201, 202). Given the fractiousness of an increasingly racist and fascist state in Poland in the late 1930s, this is clearly an imagined view. Another example are Cretans who compare their island's original autonomy and internal harmony, embodied in its links with Venizelos, the inter-war Greek nationalist politician who was born there, with Crete under Greek rule, an experience which has coincided with the fragmentation of the Venizelist tradition (Herzfeld 1992: 65).

Here is one possible answer to Needham's earlier puzzle over unilateral figures (1980a: Ch. 1), which he finally decided could only be treated as another polythetic class. For him, such figures represent simply an asymmetry which has been generated out of an original symmetry (cf. Tcherkézoff 1994). This has been followed by Schoffeleers (1991), who associates symmetry with 'lawlessness or anomie', asymmetry with 'social order' (ibid.: 346, 350). For Tcherkézoff, on the other hand, what is at issue is the generation of a hierarchical opposition out of an original unity, whose attainment as something sacred remains the goal of ritual action and is expressed as a value in that very form of opposition. Unilateral figures thus represent unity, not asymmetry. They are made asymmetric in becoming bilateral, since this introduces differentiation (e.g. of the right and left hands), which for the Dumontian is necessarily asymmetric (we differentiate only to accord a value).

Schoffeleers comes close to recognizing hierarchical oppositions in discussing other transcendent figures, namely the images of those who have returned from the dead and who are therefore both dead and alive, or of those who can be asleep and awake at the same time (1991: 360). Another example is the myth of the Kumbi of Rwanda, which features a unilateral figure in the form of a cripple: 'the missing side of the cripple was not missing in the sense of being non-existent. It did exist and it was part of him, but it was kept in a superior sphere where, one imagines, it had access to experiences that no symmetrically shaped individual ever has' (ibid.: 351-2).

However, in contrast to Tcherkézoff, Schoffeleers reverses both the order of events in mythical time and their nature. In his account, the unilateral figure was created by the gods in order to replace a previous period when humanity consisted of twins, who brought about an access of disorder through their unrelenting competition and hostility. But unilateral figures were rapidly found to be sterile. Thus a compromise was sought in creating humanity as it is today, one of bilateral but non-twinned individuals (ibid.: 353).

In a common Kumbi variant, man proves to be sterile until woman is invented out of his body (cf. the Adam and Eve story). Man still had a tendency to be aggressive, however, making unilateral figures useful as a way of symbolizing a return to order. Twins, on the other hand, are regarded as negatively anomalous because their appearance threatens disorder. Across cultures, solutions to the problem they pose range from their murder or expulsion to their recategorization as non-twins, which in its turn may mean stressing the unity they can also be made to represent, or separating them, so that they are no longer regarded as twins but as different individuals. Schoffeleers refers to all these possibilities, but for him unity is never more than positively anomolous, and sometimes (following Girard) the lack of differentiation represented by twins signals disorder. For Tcherkézoff, on the other hand, unity represents rather the sacredness of primordial time. From the latter's point of view, one problem with Schoffeleers's interpretation is its apparent confusion of unity and symmetry in passages dealing with twins, and of unity and asymmetry in passages dealing with unilateral figures. In fact, unity and asymmetry are opposites, in the sense that they are the respective properties of the two levels of the model of hierarchical opposition. Symmetry exists only as a cultural value which may feature in a hierarchical opposition and is not an intrinsic part in the model itself.

The notion of primordial unity also offers an answer to Müller (1986), who produces the now familiar complaint, in opposition to Tcherkézoff, that among the Rukuba of Nigeria one can find both equality and hierarchy, it being neither possible nor necessary to decide which predominates. The Rukuba are divided into two exogamous moieties, neither being superior in respect of affinal alliance, although in particular villages there is a hierarchical opposition between first comers and later settlers. Similarly, the account of two particular villages alternating in the holding of rites appears to rule out hierarchy until one is told, first, that whenever the rite is held it is the host village that is superior, and secondly, that in the dim and distant past only one village possessed the rite. Despite the lack of detail, we thus get a glimpse of a mythical process of division following an initial period of unity, which one pole continues to represent. Müller thus appears to be weighed down by a substantialist view in his focusing on specific groups and villages rather than on the relation between them. The pairs may alternate in being superior in such a way as to suggest that neither is ultimately dominant, but in each village a hierarchical opposition clearly obtains between the two moieties, and at each rite also between the two villages, one of which appears to have a mythical priority. Müller's claim that his account is based on informants' statements is no encumbrance to a Dumontian view and simply shows how insufficient, if necessary, such statements are on their own.

We have already linked the encompassing pole of a hierarchical opposition and transcendent value on more than one occasion, and there are many other examples of this in the ethnographic corpus. One such example is the Rifian notion of *baraka*, which encompasses honour (Jamous 1981). Stewart (1994: 205-6) associates the values of honour and sanctity on the Greek island of Naxos with distinct ideological levels, referring explicitly not only to Dumont, but also to a passage in Hertz's essay on sin (1994: 104), where the latter links honour to the world of individual pride and worth, and sanctity to the transcendence represented by a divine being. A related series of examples come from Dumont's late work on German ideology (1991), which all concern forms of art. Dumont imputes to Goethe's hero Wilhelm Meister the idea of the stage as a whole on which the player can fully be himself, like a noble or monarch; this is contrasted with the specialization, that is, fragmentation, of bourgeois life (ibid.: 221, nobles and monarchs being assimilated to the whole). And similarly, in discussing the writings on aesthetics of Karl Philipp Moritz, he refers to the latter's definition of a work of art as something complete, as 'constituting a whole in itself' (Dumont citing Moritz, ibid.: 94) and as subordinating the individual to it, whether as artist or observer (ibid.:104 ff.); in this sense, it is transcendent. One can say the same of a piece of music: Mahler used to call the symphony a world.

According to Tcherkézoff (1994), this equation between the sacred and the transcendence of dichotomies is yet another reason for the inadequacy of the Needhamite approach, since the latter places sacred beings at one pole of a dichotomy with secular ones and associates them with the feminine because of their supposed sexual modesty. One possible objection to this is that women are just as often represented as sexually loose—what might be called the 'two Marys syndrome' (Magdelene as well as the Virgin). But even were this not the case, for Tcherkézoff it is the substantialist complex that Needham frequently suggests between the feminine, the mystical, the hidden and the passive (e.g. 1980a: Ch. 3) that leads him to associate the Mugwe with the feminine. Given the presence of the last three attributes and the absence of any obvious sexuality, this attribution almost imposes itself. However, says Tcherkézoff, this is to ignore the phenomenon of the third sex, androgynous figures whose ritual efficacy is connected with their ability to transcend distinctions. Sexual abstinence denotes not femininity, but the absence of any distinct sexual role, male or female. A complementary opposition sees the whole as the mere addition of sacred and secular. A hierarchical opposition sees it as the sacred encompassing the secular.

Hierarchical Opposition and the
Comparability of Societies

Another paper, on Nyamwezi alliance (Tcherkézoff 1993b), also brings out clearly the difference between the two perspectives, distinctive and hierarchical opposition, substance and relation. Radcliffe-Brown's distinction between the payment of brideprice signalling patrilateral rights and its non-payment signalling matrilateral rights (1950) is rejected as being a substantialist view, precisely because of its emphasis on rights over something or someone (wife, children etc.). Among the Nyamwezi, these payments (*kukwa*) in fact unite the two sides in relation to the ancestors. One side, the wife-givers, in being associated with the gift of life, are closer or assimilated to the ancestors and thus represent the whole, the sacred, primal unity. There is thus no element of devious strategy involved in avoiding payments in order to secure a different allegiance for the children, as a traditional interpretation might imply. In fact, marriage without payment is universally disliked, and marriage without any at all is practically impossible. The husband in such a case would be assimilated to a murderer, and indeed marriage payments and sacrifices are assimilated to payments for delicts such as murder or bringing twins into the world; all such payments restore social peace and cosmological harmony.

Marriage payments in the form of circulating livestock are therefore ultimately not concerned to establish rights but rather constitute 'the metaphor of the social, its permanence and its reproduction. As such, the beast-money is not at the service of the lineage as essence or as any other value. It is "the" value' (Tcherkézoff 1993b: 58). In other words, 'the relation to a value is repetition, not acquisition' (ibid.; cf. Iteanu in Barraud et al. 1994: 38, discussed below). This repetition, signalling as it does social continuity, is the point of such payments and of the ritual that accompanies them, and not, for example, to ensure grandchildren to honour one as an ancestor. Although the latter is important, the 'grandchildren' need not be lineal descendants: they can be collateral ones, and the relation therefore links generations rather than individuals.

Opposed to the above are the further payments that have to be made in the case of divorce or the remarriage of a widow in other than her original affinal group, payments which breach the (initial) affinal relationship. Naturally, the relation is hierarchical as to value, not least, one supposes, because divorce and widowhood are not as auspicious as marriage. There is thus a hierarchical opposition between 'the ritual act that creates the relation of affinity' and 'the substantialist procedures (the accounts) which preside over the cancellation of the relation of affinity … or which concern the space not yet *kukwa'* (i.e. marriages without full brideprice; Tcherkézoff 1993b: 75). The encompassed level is, for Tcherkézoff, one of simple asymmetry between the parties, one on which neither represents the whole—hence the appearance, temporarily, of these 'substantialist procedures'. The transcendence, which is equivalent to encompassment, here takes the form of 'monetary circulation' (ibid.) between affines and payments, in the form of sacrifice, to the ancestors who, embodied in sacred kingship, represent the whole. Thus the ritual 'is not the "whole" (the encompassing level), but it is the (re)creator of the [social and cosmological] configuration' (ibid.: 52 n.4).

Thus hierarchical opposition has provided a new way of examining rituals. Another advantage claimed by Dumont and his followers is the usefulness of the notion in comparing societies with one another. For Dumont himself (1986a: 7), it is no less essential in this task than in ethnographic analyses directed at single societies. Among his followers, however, a division has developed as to how this comparison should be carried out, a division which in broad terms matches the institutional separation outlined earlier. We shall come to these differences in the next chapter, after reviewing the statements of the various participants separately, as they arise out of their work.

First, however, Krauskopff (1987: 163), an outsider to this group, has identified some more general difficulties. In making such comparisons, does one choose types of opposition or of hierarchy, or pick societies having or lacking a dominant value, a hierarchical opposition? For the adherents of the method, however, this misses the point, since all oppositions are hierarchical and all societies have a dominant value. Krauskopff nonetheless approves of the approach in Barraud et al. (1994 [1984]), a long article comparing four different societies with emphasis on 'the notion of circulation between the levels of the ideology' (Krauskopff 1987).

De Coppet, naturally, defends the comparative potential of this 'universal tool', the concept of hierarchical opposition, more vigorously. Using it, 'societies can be considered as different wholes, precisely through their different hierarchical values'. As a result, they can be directly compared, thus obviating relativism, which proclaims the essential incomparability of societies (1990: 142-3). The genesis of sociology in the modern world, which itself puts the stress on individualism, tends to obscure this. Indeed, de Coppet sees sociology, though the science of society, as an outcome of that individualism, in that the latter had reached such a pitch by the end of the nineteenth century that it provided an exterior vantage point from which society itself could be studied (1992b: 60). [3]

In essence, therefore, comparative sociology arose as 'an effort to marry the individualist ideal with the existence of the communal social dimension ...' (1992b: 62). At the same time, individualism was but one manifestation of the modern world's tendency to separate fact and value. For the sociologist, this meant that the ideal of individualism was distinguished from the fact that man lived in society. For de Coppet, this also has a bearing on the notion of representation, originally meaning renewal (of the supreme value, of the totality etc.), but later coming to mean substitution or symbolization, in which the symbol as idea was separated from its referent as fact. Thus the empty coffin or empty litter at French royal funerals, which came to stand for the dead king during the ensuing interregnum, was originally linked with the notion of the renewal of the kingdom and, more generally, 'the universe in its totality and mystery' (ibid.: 67ff.).

A return to the creative version of 'representation', says de Coppet, is one answer to the problem of comparing the modern world with other societies and cultures. This problem of comparison has been tackled so far either by ethnocentrically reducing all societies to the sum of individual acts and actors, or by relativizing the truth: 'In either event, the universalist assumptions of science appear bankrupt' (1992b: 70-1). Resorting to the original definition of 'representation' would restore the unity of fact and value, allowing a shift in focus to the hierarchy of values in each society. Comparison between societies on a 'feature by feature' basis inevitably produces contradictions since it is carried out on a single level. If societies are seen as wholes, however, that is to say, as 'hierarchies of value', they become comparable. 'The result is the active comparison of two "hierarchies of value", the only "facts" (or value-facts) which are commensurable in social anthropology.' This phenomenon is a 'relational universal' (ibid.: 71-3).

It is through ritual that these values may most readily be approached: in that they express a society's values, they provide a means of comparing the latter cross-culturally (ibid.: 9). For de Coppet, the distinction between the ritual and the non-ritual—which can be seen as or related to other distinctions, such as symbolic/real, religious/secular or ceremonial/everyday—'constitutes the social dimension par excellence' and as such forms 'the necessary and sufficient condition for the comparison of societies' (1992a: 2). He links this simultaneously to Durkheim's situating of the ideal within society (1915: 422-3) and to Dumont's view of hierarchy and of the unity of fact and value as being non-western. 'The distinction between ritual and non-ritual is a constituent of the hierarchy of values which shapes our western society's social relations' (de Coppet 1992a: 3).

De Coppet also makes the important point that what counts as non-ritual varies from society to society as much as what counts as ritual. For him, this is important as a means of avoiding Eurocentrism. How far are we really justified, however, in thinking that all societies neces-sarily have a clear sense of the ritual as something opposed to the non-ritual? For any society where that were not the case, one would necessarily be thrown back on an essentially Eurocentric judgement as to how to define ritual before one could set about establishing the val-ues of the society and developing any comparison involving them.

De Coppet's line of thought is also pursued by Barraud and Platen-kamp (1990) in their joint article concluding two special numbers of the Dutch journal *Bijdragen tot de Taal-, Land- en Volkenkunde* on ritual in Indonesia (145–4, 1989, and 146–1, 1990; by no means all the arti-cles involved treat ritual in a Dumontian fashion). They start by stress-ing the importance of ritual in expressing a people's own identity, a throwback to the *Année sociologique* school. But ritual is not something to be studied in isolation from other aspects of the society, since 'ritual activities seem to have a bearing on its basic structure' (1990: 103):

> Societies should be studied as wholes, and a comparative analysis of several societies requires that their elements be understood in terms of the partic-ular place they occupy in each of them. Each society is ordered by the val-ues it assigns to all social facts (its social morphology, its representations and actions); this order constitutes its system of ideas and values. This places the given social facts in a specific hierarchical order, an order which Dumont calls 'ideology'. Because societies differ from one another in their systems of ideas and values, the comparison of societies requires a com-parison of ideologies and not of elements a priori selected. (Ibid.: 104, ref-erences and footnotes omitted)

In Indonesia, the closest previous model was that developed by van Wouden (1968, originally 1935), in which Maussian holism was linked to the integration of social morphology and cosmology in a wide-ranging comparison of eastern Indonesian societies. Unfortu-nately—perhaps following Durkheim and Mauss (1903) in the prior-ity they gave to social structure over symbolic classification—van Wouden prioritized matrilateral cross-cousin marriage as the funda-mental feature of these societies and therefore chose it as the axis of his comparison. For Barraud and Platenkamp (1990: 105; also Bar-raud et al. 1994: 2), this is methodologically faulty:

> This would imply the primacy of socio-morphological phenomena, select-ing a priori from among all other phenomena, over the given society's cos-mology, and consequently a selection of societies for comparison on the basis of the occurrence of the same cultural element in what may be dif-ferent social systems.

The same can be said of other phenomena that have been suggested more recently as definitive of certain Indonesian societies, such as 'the flow of life' (e.g. Fox 1980) or the house as descent group (Lévi-Strauss 1987: 151-9): however common they might be, their exploitation and therefore their place within the whole ideology differ considerably from society to society.

It is this relative difference of position in an all-pervasive ideology which makes concentration on isolated elements inadequate and necessitates the comparison of societies as wholes (Barraud and Platenkamp 1990: 106). In one sense this is a continuation of the Maussian insistence on holism rather than cut-and-paste description in the manner of Frazer. But it also reflects Dumont's complaint about 'classification by independent features' as a basis for inter-societal comparison (1982: 215), the complaint being against the independent features, not the classification: 'If classification is to be introduced later on, it will have to start from wholes and not from internal features' (ibid.). This in its turn ensures that 'holism is a method, not a type of society' (Tcherkézoff 1994). [4]

This is logically distinct from the search for 'ultimate values' in single societies. As we have seen, as 'ultimate value' Tcherkézoff selects ancestrality for the Nyamwezi (1986a: 94), de Coppet the ancestors for the 'Are'are (1981: 176) and Iteanu initiation for the Orokaiva (1983b: 54-5). Such values are, of course, encompassing ones, and thus they represent a unity which is expressed as both primordial and axiomatic. One possible focus for comparison is to see these values as the ultimate authority in each society, through which whatever is sacred in the society must be approached (Barraud et al. 1994: 102-3). Another is through an assimilation of society to the universe which is effected through value: 'Each society ... seems to bear a particular way of being the entire universe. It is precisely in this regard that societies may be compared: in their efforts to administer a universal which is theirs alone' (ibid.: 101). This leads to a focus on cosmos plus society as a seamless whole (Barraud et al. 1994; de Coppet and Iteanu 1995, both discussed in the next chapter). Tcherkézoff also shows a determination to follow a positivist path without neglecting informants' statements (1994). For him, even concepts like religion and power are at root cultural, inviting talk of contexts rather than of levels. A true structuralist approach would concentrate on 'the order of relations and not the order of ideas', in other words, on the encompassments and (in)equalities that these ideas entail.

Ritual and the Circulation of Values

Thus for its supporters, hierarchical opposition certainly has the potential to combine a comparative model with a heightened degree of sensitivity to the real nature of indigenous values. In true holistic and structuralist fashion, too, society is seen as composed of relationships rather than of discrete groups. This affects these authors' view of ritual, which is no longer seen as (or purely as) a means of effecting changes in status (the 'rite of passage' tradition) or of separating or keeping apart categories that should not be mixed, as in conventional structuralism. Instead, rituals are seen as effecting both relationships and the circulation of ideological values through the society. Indeed, these two concepts are directly linked: among the Tobelo, Platenkamp found that 'the system of relationships constituting village society as a whole was itself conceptualized as a system of circulation' (1992: 86). Here, two levels of circulation are distinguished, one concerned with the reproduction of crops and people, the other with the management of death and the need to convert its products back into life. These can readily be seen as two levels of an ideology linked by encompassment. Another instance is the distinction, also ritually expressed, between the emnity of 'houses' to one another and the affinal relationships they nonetheless create in order to link them.

The values being circulated mostly take a tangible form, such as foodstuffs, ornaments, human heads or women: in other words, tangible goods are endowed with values, which they carry with them through the society. Thus the idea of value is wedded to Mauss's theory of exchange, in that it incorporates his view of the gift as carrying something of its giver with it. 'In these circulations, which take place time and again, and at different levels, the permanence of society is articulated' (Barraud and Platenkamp 1990: 117). And since the society has external relationships as well as internal ones, the whole bundle of its relationships 'constitutes the socio-cosmic universe, hence "society" as a socio-cosmic whole'. Further, 'through this circulation, and in reference to the whole, the relationships are specified and hierarchically ordered among themselves ...' (ibid.). 'The rituals, therefore, show how a hierarchical order of relationships is established, and it is in this respect that societies can be compared' (ibid.: 118).

This view of exchange, a development of Mauss, also depends on a partial merging of subject and object through their relation, in place of their neat separation as in the west (Iteanu 1990a; Strathern 1988). This can be seen as a development of another Maussian theme, the person (Mauss 1938). 'How can we understand their exchanges [i.e. those of non-modern societies] when the substantialist approach most commonly adopted, attentive only to the passage of objects between subjects, turns its back on the very relational logic which we seek to lay bare?' (Barraud et al. 1994: 3). It is freeing the subject from the object that encourages a view of society as a simple collection of individuals both in modern societies and by anthropologists born into them. Fredrik Barth is particularly singled out here, but also Rivers, Gluckman and Fortes, the latter for the arch-substantialism of making the descent group a moral person (ibid.: 106). Lévi-Strauss is also criticized for turning affinal alliance into a system in which women as objects are transferred between men as subjects (ibid.: 104-5). Naturally this rejection of classic structuralism does not involve a break with relation. Indeed, the criticism does not apply to all earlier academic traditions: Casajus has argued (1984:73 ff.) that Mauss himself implicitly recognized the blurring of subject and object in these societies in his own work on exchange.

But as we have seen (Chapter 3), one still needs to establish what counts as an encompassment and how the various levels of the ideology and the shifts between them are to be identified. 'This encompassment is expressed by a shift from one level of relationships to another in the rituals. This shift is signalled by a change in the way the circulating elements are designated', for example, pigs now as the dead, now as food. Thus:

> a conversion of elements takes place, which results from their transposition from one relationship level on to another level. This conversion can be described in terms of exchanges as well. An element is withdrawn from one type of relationship, and made to circulate along another, in return for elements which are both identical and non-identical. Heads are made to circulate as game, in return for an abundance both of game and of progeny [etc.]. (Barraud and Platenkamp 1990: 118)

There is thus a tendency ultimately to convert the Maussian theory of exchange into an aspect of the transformation and circulation of values. Contrary to the substantialist view, reciprocity is not to be expected, since this stifles the momentum of exchange, in that it sees each exchange as self-contained and limited (de Coppet 1981: 199-200, after Annette Weiner). Instead, a perpetual transfer of values through the ideology takes place simultaneously with the transfer of goods through the social system (Tcherkézoff 1987: 130). This is of course not the familiar question of whether a truly disinterested gift can ever exist. Among the Orokaiva, for instance, the return of equivalent items in equivalent quantities signals not reciprocity in exchange but the repetition of rituals, that is, the continuance of ritual activity (Iteanu in Barraud et al. 1994: 38). Similarly, it is exchange that creates houses on Tanebar-Evav, not vice versa (ibid.: 71-2).

Two points arising out of all this need to be expanded immediately. First, not only are subject and object blurred, so too are the person and other entities in the universe, at least in Melanesian and Indonesian societies. For de Coppet, all such activities represent different combinations of the same sorts of elements and relationships (1990: 148).

In some of his work, the person is represented as constituted of different elements, which separate, temporarily, at death (e.g. 1981; also Geirnaert-Martin 1992: xxx, 401ff.). In the Kei Islands, on the other hand, the 'elements which make up a person are not substances, they are elements of relationships constitutive of the socio-cosmic universe' (Barraud 1990c: 214, abstract). The Durkheimian distinction between the soul and the body as revealing the social aspect of the person par excellence, that which makes the person human, is thus ethnocentric (cf. Tcherkézoff 's comments, above). In that it gives a distinct criterion for identifying the person, it promotes oppositions between individual and society, man and nature, that are not necessarily appropriate elsewhere.

In the Kei Islands, this construction would certainly be misleading. Here, 'the distinction between the two principles [i.e. body and soul] lies in the differentiation of the relationships, that is of the levels of value, in which the principles are involved' (Barraud 1990c: 217). Similarly, 'the passage from life to death is marked not only by a physical transformation of the person [but] by a change in a person's relationships, and by a change of level in the ideology expressed by the separation from the house taken as a set of relationships' (ibid.: 225); 'the death of a person may be interpreted as the progressive extinction of all its [*sic*] former relations' (ibid.: 216).

Secondly, society as a cosmomorphic whole is more than simply the sum of its relationships: it itself engages in them, something which hierarchical opposition, as a part–whole relationship, makes possible. This is exemplified in Tanebar-Evav, where, although different houses have different functions in ritual, 'what is relevant is not their interrelationships but their relation to the society as a whole' (Barraud 1990c: 226). In short, 'the whole, *to which all social actions are geared*, is society and universe combined' (de Coppet 1990: 148, my emphasis).

The relations to the dead, to ancestry, to the society's founders, assume a special importance for the authors, at least in respect of these Indonesian and Melanesian societies. Although Mauss's theory of exchange is incorporated into the model and is made to include relations with the dead as well as between affines, there is an explicit challenge to the notion of affinity as exchange, since relations with ancestry, in stressing the society's oneness, encompass relations between spouse-exchange groups, which highlight its internal divisions (this oneness may also signify some approximation to primordial time, before man needed affines: cf. Tcherkézoff, above).

A good example of this approach is another paper of Barraud's (1990b; not in the collection) on affinal alliance—broadly asymmetric prescriptive—on Tanebar-Evav in the Kei Islands. Here, one honours the ancestry not of one's own line but of one's wife-giving line (thus one's wife-takers will honour one's own line). One's mother's brother is one's intermediary with the dead, and indeed the relationship between wife-takers and wife-givers is 'primarily' (ibid.: 209) one between the living and the dead:

> in the framework of the relationship to the mother's brother, the god, the dead and the mother's brother together form a whole, while in all other circumstances the god and the dead are distinguished into two different classes of supernatural beings. (Ibid.: 204)

And further:

> More than ensuring an arrangement of groups in the society, the marriage rules organize the relations of the living with the dead. The relationship to the dead thus encompasses intermarriage proper in extending it beyond the matter of marriage. Indeed, 'wife-givers' are more than wife-givers, they are ancestors, and marriage may be seen as an aspect of the relationship between the living and the dead'. (Ibid.: 223)

In yet another paper (1990c: 218), Barraud remarks: 'The superiority of wife-givers over wife-takers is not due to the fact that a woman is given away, but to the fact that they represent fearful ancestors, associated to the god and responsible for the life of their descendants, children of married-out women.'

Although ancestry is valued, however, it is ancestry through a group of affines, one's wife-givers: this is no descent-oriented view being reintroduced from a previous period of anthropology. Affines thus are important, but the categorical division of society which their existence makes possible—and which the anthropologist's notion of exchange artificially perpetuates—is ultimately transcended in favour of an original unity, recreated through ritual action.

A paper by Geirnaert (1987) is also relevant here. The two rituals she discusses can be distinguished through such oppositions as male/female, dry/wet, reputation/fertility and rice/meat. One ritual is concerned with fertility and therefore with female values, though ultimately reputation is the encompassing value, acquired through hunting, especially (traditionally) the taking of heads—a purely male activity. This is evident from the usual eastern Indonesian distinction between wife-givers and wife-takers at rituals: rice (a product of female agriculture), associated with fertility, can only go to wife-takers, while meat (a product of male hunting) can go in both directions. This, of course, identifies the wife-givers as the origin of life: they give their wife-takers life through the fertility-associated foods they transfer to them, while they in their turn receive from their wife-takers foods associated with decay, the latter transfer representing not an exchange but a recirculation for purposes of regeneration. There is also the usual seniority/juniority divide: wife-takers are pre-eminently daughters' husbands, wife-givers mothers' brothers.

However, there seems to be a conflict between reputation as encompassing value on the one hand, and wife-givers as the source of life and therefore presumably closer to the sacred on the other. This is not found in Barraud's work on this theme, where unifying relations with ancestors through wife-givers encompass affinal relations that depend on a distinction (we shall meet with some further diffidence in Geirnaert's work, discussed below). Elsewhere, in her comments on a paper of Platenkamp's (1984) on the Tobelo of Halmahera—the latter itself makes no reference to hierarchical opposition—Barraud shows that here too, marriage, being 'the transformation of non-kin into kin' (1984: 194), is encompassed by a unifying value. But that value itself, cognatic kinship, is subject to dichotomization, in that it involves both descent (parent–child links) and collaterality (sibling links), that is, respectively the transmission and the sharing of flesh and blood. Normally the former encompasses the latter, but at the level where co-residence is emphasised sharing is more marked.

In that these papers stress the life-giving significance of one's wife-givers in eastern Indonesian societies, they also emphasize access to the sacred. In this same commentary (1984), Barraud remarks of a paper by Traube (1980) that the Mambai also see affinal alliance as less important than relations with ancestors (here, wife-takers have a key ritual role in ensuring the transformation of their deceased wife-givers into ancestors). However, this devaluation of affinity can at best be only relative, if one's sole access to the life-giving past runs through one's wife-givers. Of course, the society's internal relations are not necessarily the predominant value at all levels of the ideology. But whatever the level, rituals are seen as providing a mode of communication between categories running through objects circulated in exchange, not as maintaining categorical boundaries through ritual separations, as in the traditional structuralist view.

In fact, there is no reason why they should not be both, since categories are partly identifiable through their boundaries, and ritual certainly emphasizes distinctions too. Nonetheless this model, like all theories of ritual, seeks to establish the common pattern underlying all ritual action, regardless of the cultural specificities of surface expression or immediate purpose. This aspect of the cross-cultural comparison thus seeks similarities rather than differences between societies. This reflects the uniformity claimed for hierarchical opposition itself, something which has already come under frequent critical scrutiny (see above, Chapter 5).

Nonetheless, Tcherkézoff (1987: 131) claims that using hierarchical opposition as a tool for comparison enables one to avoid the ethnocentrism of invoking such western values as equality and symmetry or the reciprocity of exchange, as well as 'psychological' explanations involving ritual substitutions, such as money for a murdered man, an animal for a man in sacrifice, etc. Sacrifice, for example, can no longer be seen, following Hubert and Mauss (1899), as mere '"communication' between profane and sacred or a "communion" between the various participants in the ritual' (Tcherkézoff 1987: 130): 'its efficacy, its operative character, derives from the fact that it manipulates a class of particular objects, which participate in *both of the two levels* on which sacrifice is situated' (ibid.: 129, original emphasis; also 1986b, 1989).

In general, therefore, the supporters of hierarchical opposition claim that not only does it provide us with a new comparative tool, it also gives us new perspectives on exchange and ritual (cf. Tcherkézoff 1987: 127-31). These perspectives can be summed up in one word: transformation. Sacrifice and expulsion are not ritual ends in themselves; but attaining the sacred is, and they are therefore modes of transformation directed towards it. Exchange is another transformation, and as such it is non-reciprocal, a continuous flow: the process does not end when reciprocity is attained, as in more conventional perspectives (ibid.: 130).

Notes

1. But cf. Durkheim (1915: 229): 'when a sacred being subdivides itself, it remains whole and equal to itself in each of its parts. In other words, as far as religion is concerned, the part is equal to the whole; it has the same powers, it is equally effective.' Elsewhere (1995) Tcherkézoff examines the question more closely in relation to both sacred/profane and other classic Durkheimian dichotomies, such as society/individual and soul/body.
2. Contrast this perspective with another recent commentary (Pickering 1984: 148-9), where the sacred is again seen as predominant, but only because of the supposedly 'residual' nature of the profane: the author regards sacred and profane as an exception to the 'equal status and power' of the poles of most dichotomies. Jones, on the other hand, calls the relation 'reciprocal' because of the relative weakness of the sacred in some circumstances and its dependence on the existence of believers (1986: 123 n.13).

3. Cf. Hertz, in an unpublished lecture (1911): `The social and intellectual evolution of the nineteenth century has had the effect of restoring the idea of society considered as an organic entity distinct from individuals....'
4. This represents a shift from an earlier position (Tcherkzoff 1987: 73), where it is said that 'the Nyamwezi represent a society of the holistic type'. It nonetheless reminds one of Lévi-Strauss's claim that structuralism is a method, not a theory.

Chapter 7

RESIDUE, COSMOS AND ECONOMICS

The Individual: Residue or Agent?

The differences between Tcherkézoff and the one hand and de Coppet and Barraud on the other regarding some aspects of the Dumontian innovation have already been alluded to in the previous chapter. We shall take the discussion further here, principally with reference to a joint text already referred to (Barraud et al. 1994) and Tcherkézoff's reactions to it. Afterwards, slightly later work promoted (though not wholly written) by this group, which focuses on cosmologies, will be discussed.

A basic difference between the two camps concerns the notion of 'residue' as used particularly by Barraud et al. This term was used by Dumont in *Homo Hierarchicus* to describe those aspects of Indian society that a western sociologist might identify but that an Indian, according to Dumont, would not (1980 [1966]: 37-8, 353-4 n.22c). In his text, the residue is whatever part of the phenomenon being observed by the analyst which does not enter the ideology. In India, this means power and territory as against considerations of purity and impurity, that is, religion. In the accompanying footnote, it is presented as the contrast between the conscious and the unconscious or, one might say, between the explicit and what is taken for granted. This is elaborated in another text published the same year (Dumont 1966: 30-1), in which the metaphor of a 'threshold' between residue and ultimate value is introduced (cf. Tcherkézoff 's 'hierarchical threshold', above, Chapter 6). In Indian society this residue can also be seen to include the individual; in western societies it is society itself. This leads to a comparative point:

We had better speak of a residue of the kind *x* every time we encounter below the threshold something which reminds us of an *X* above the threshold. At the same time ... I simply transcribe the idea of the unity of mankind if I say that, if *X* has been identified in one society, all societies that do not have it must have something of the kind of *x*. In other terms, I shall hold at the same time that all 'features' or 'elements' are deeply altered by their position, and that the sum total of all 'features' or 'elements' is constant in all societies. They may be conscious and differentiated, or non-conscious and undifferentiated, but they are there. (Ibid.: 31)

In this formulation, therefore, while absolute, transcendent values are the most conscious ones, others that are opposed to them but which they encompass form the 'residue' beneath the 'threshold' and only manifest themselves in subordinate circumstances. Moreover, societies can be compared because they have a differential mix of values, which are always present but in different relations. The threshold may shift its position from society to society, but it is always there.

This allows Dumont to reincorporate *artha*, the Indian value which deals among other things with the creation of wealth, back into the ideology in certain situations. It is also why, sociologically speaking, modern societies are but special cases of non-modern ones and not absolutely different in type. They, like India, exploit a hierarchical opposition, one in which the individual encompasses society as far as indigenous values are concerned; but because individualism is itself a socially determined value, here as elsewhere it is society that encompasses (a more traditional Durkheimian might have chosen a phrase like 'determines the actions of') the individual (see above, Chapter 4). In this way, Dumont distances himself from the traditional Anglo-Saxon empiricist approach, which tends to see ideology as an epiphenomenon of the level of facts.

The notion is not without its problems, most of which have come to revolve around the question as to whether the encompassed level is to be seen as within the ideology, outside it, or either, according to circumstance. Tcherkézoff (1994) identifies the residue explicitly as both the empirical and, in more formal language, the encompassed level. This tends to disqualify this level as any sort of value, especially since Tcherkézoff also says that there is no hierarchy of values, only one fundamental one, that which encompasses its contrary—and the contrary itself is not a value, since it cannot stand alone. He also calls the residue 'simply what remains when all our observation has been referred to the ideology we have encountered: not everything is directly explicable by the "system"' (1994; cf. Dumont 1972: 75, where this is treated as a process of 'subtraction').

We can therefore see the residue as the scarcely considered manifestations of the actual that the ideal, encompassing value is seeking to transcend. Although modern western societies have equality as a transcending ideal, there is still inequality: for example, the world of work is one where employees are subject to their employers' instructions and vulnerable to their dismissal of them. This is often represented as a necessary but undesirable, thankfully temporary situation that does not intrude into one's private life and/or leisure time. It nonetheless creates a sense of tension, which business corporations may try to mystify through consultation procedures, having just the one rest area for all staff, etc.

On the other hand, while one might accept that the Kshatriya is the encompassed level in relation to the Brahman, is one justified in reducing him to the merely empirical, in depriving him of ideological value, in seeing him as 'not ... directly explicable by the "system"'? This devaluation of the Kshatriya's alloted place in Hindu thought has caused Dumont more problems than probably anything else. As Tcherkézoff himself points out, Dumont's hierarchical opposition between priest and king in India does not square with his placing power outside the Hindu ideology (see above, Chapter 4). Tcherkézoff's own work has plenty of examples of hierarchical opposition in which the two poles are within the ideology, such as black/white among the Nyamwezi and sister/brother in Samoa. Such examples are enough to account for the occasional use by Dumont, and by Tcherkézoff himself (e.g. 1986b: 113 n.11), of 'values' in the plural, despite the principle that there should be only one real value. But if there are two, is there any residue?

As Tcherkézoff himself realizes (1994), the lack of clarity here goes back right to *Homo Hierarchicus*, something which he regards as having contributed to Needham's difficulties, in *Counterpoints*, in understanding Dumont's writings as well as Tcherkézoff's own (Needham 1987, e.g. 141-2). The problem centres around Dumont's distinction, rather vaguely worded, between 'articulate hierarchy' and 'hierarchy in the strict sense', which is also defined as one between hierarchies involving a set and those involving a whole respectively (see 1979: 809). For Dumont, the difference is that, in the former, both levels have a place in the ideology, whereas in the latter the secondary level does not. Thus the dichotomies between priest and king, in India or elsewhere, or between *baraka* and honour in the Rif, are of the articulate type (1982: 225), while that between status and power in general is an example of hierarchy in the strict sense. Similarly, the opposition between individual and society is of the strict type in both India (but see above, Chapter 4) and the west, regardless of the fact that the supreme value differs in the two cases. Here, one leaves the ideology upon reversal, but this is therefore a movement that the ideology does not recognize. Tcherkézoff associates this 'strict' hierarchy with the model in which the superior pole of the opposition is coterminous with the whole, which brings it line with his own 'unity' variant (see below).

For Tcherkézoff it is in relation to India that this confusion especially arises. Seeing the opposition between priest and king here as a 'hierarchy of the articulate type' as defined above contradicts Dumont's desire to see power in India as non-ideological. The opposition between status and power, on the other hand, would fit the model perfectly. Yet it is not possible to push all lesser values in India into the non-ideological. *Artha* is recognized by the ideology, though it is inferior, as are royal rights and powers (cf. Dumont 1972: 321 n.22c). Similarly with regard to the association of the residue with what is unconscious, this is contradicted by Dumont's own admission (1962a: 66) that Brahmans have always been conscious of their dependence on the king in his domain. Tcherkézoff realizes that such contradictions, if left unresolved, would weaken the rigour of hierarchical opposition as a tool of comparison.

The different definition of residue given in Barraud et al. (1994: 121-2) is no less problematic. The authors say that the encompassed 'is never simple to define, since, albeit encompassed, it is never totally integrated. A part always remains which the dominant values do not succeed in assimilating fully, what we call a residue.' The plurality of 'values' in this passage, when taken together with the distinction between encompassment and integration, suggests that the encompassed pole can never stand for the whole in practice. This would appear to contradict Dumont's use of the term 'residue', which varies according to whether the encompassed pole is within or outside the ideology, but not according to the degree of encompassment that is possible. The one unequivocal statement to be drawn from this part of this joint text is that the residue is that 'which can encompass nothing' (ibid.: 122), though as we shall see immediately, this is apparently contradicted elsewhere in the same text. The most difficult thing to decide here is whether the residue is or is not subject to being encompassed, which is also a question of whether or not it has a place in the ideology.

Further examination of the text clarifies some points at the price of raising others. The authors retain the view that in a modern society the residue is seen as society itself, while in non-modern ones it is some aspect of the individual. The latter situation is typical of what they call 'cosmomorphic' societies, that is, societies that regard themselves as 'co-extensive with the universe' (ibid.: 118). One indication of this is that they lack any words for their values: 'a society which "speaks" its values implicitly accepts a universe wider than itself' (ibid.). However, this is evidently not thought of as a determinant: of the four societies dealt with in this text, only the Orokaiva and the 'Are'are are said to be cosmomorphic on both criteria, while Tanebar-Evav are cosmomorphic on the first but not the second, and the Iqar'iyen of the Rif are not cosmomorphic on either (ibid.: 122).

There would seem to be a further difference, in that the first two societies allow the individual a genuine but subordinate place in the ideology, whereas on Tanebar-Evav he or she is all 'residue'. It is true that in one place (ibid.) the authors describe the Orokaiva *jo* or individual subject as 'residual'. However, given that this has a name (not to mention a recognized location, the liver), it is clearly recognized by the ideology. Indeed, this is explicitly confirmed a few pages earlier, where it is referred to as 'an integral part of the encompassing social order' (ibid.: 119). It is difficult to square this with the later description (ibid.: 122) of the residue as that 'which can encompass nothing'. At all events, there does not seem to be anything comparable on Tanebar-Evav, where 'the residual element is constituted by the individual subject' (ibid.). This 'individual subject' is clearly the analogue of the Orokaiva *jo*, which itself is contrasted with the 'fully social subject' (ibid.). In the former case, however, it would appear to be outside the ideology, in the latter within it. This difference resembles that between Dumont's 'strict' and 'articulate' forms of hierarchy respectively (see above).

As for the Iqar'iyen of the Rif, they are not cosmomorphic at all, partly because they name their values, but also because the key hierarchical opposition involves two archetypal individuals, not straightforwardly a relation between society and individual (ibid.: 118-22). There is also a reference to the outside in the form of the Moroccan Sultan, which—unlike the case of the Tanebar-Evav opposition between *lor* and *haratut*—is not easily incorporated into the society's own values. Yet here too there is a transcendental value, that of *baraka*, represented by the mystic, mediating *cherif*, which encompasses the value of honour. *Baraka* encompasses honour at the primary level, on which feud gives way to mediation, but honour becomes distinguished from it on the secondary level, on which feuding takes place. Honour reaches its highest pitch in the *amghar* or 'great man', the 'man of honour *par excellence*' (ibid.: 91), whose pursuit of honour necessarily involves them in the pursuit of power too. What is again not clear is the exact relationship between residue, encompassed pole and ideology. Although both honour and *baraka* are a part of the ideology, the 'residue' is defined here as that 'which escapes from this encompassing order', and it is referred to '"great men's" pursuit of power' in Rifian society (ibid.: 122). However, since the pursuit of power arises directly out of the pursuit of honour, it must be within the ideology.

Thus the residue is variously seen as being within the ideology, but at a subordinate level, encompassed; or else as lying outside the ideology altogether, eluding ideological (i.e. subjective) encompassment, but still subject to structural (i.e. analytical, objective) encompassment. Both versions can be read into Dumont's work, as well as into the joint text of Barraud et al. (1994), even though this seems to be partly at variance with what they actually think. This itself is at points anything but certain, partly because of direct contradictions between consecutive statements and partly because the conclusions to be drawn from particular bits of data are not always made explicit to the reader.

Tcherkézoff, on the other hand, is quite explicit in seeing the second case as the only fruitful one. One might say that in this case, encompassment is envisaged as taking place between the ideology itself and what is left outside it. Despite the uncertainty as to exactly how it should be interpreted, the notion is useful in showing why Dumont's idea of hierarchy is not reducible to simple social stratification. Tcherkézoff defines the latter as 'unequal access to things [e.g. property, wealth] external to the whole constituted by differentiated terms' (1993b: 62, brackets removed; also 1994). As well as being matter of fact rather than ideological, such 'things' can clearly be regarded as the residue as defined by Dumont originally.

Tcherkézoff sees the tendency of Barraud and de Coppet to construe hierarchy as residing totally within the ideology as blurring the distinction between the ideological and the empirical. Hierarchy of the 'strict' type places the residue outside the ideology and entails an encompassment that is purely structural, a reversal that distinguishes not two levels of the ideology but the ideological from the empirical, the mother idea from the residue. This is the model that is truly comparative for Tcherkézoff, truly structural, truly objective. The sociocosmic or cosmomorphic idea, conversely, in that it attributes to any particular ideology the view that its society is coextensive with the universe, ignores the individual unless he or she receives explicit recognition in that ideology. Tcherkézoff 's double perspective allows him to give place to the individual at all times and in all societies, in contrast to the opposing view, which entails that human society was and remained holistic until the appearance of individualism as a value in modern Europe (see Tcherkézoff 1993–94). This view tends to reduce the basis of individualism to its supposed origin in a historical and therefore contingent event, making it untypical of human society generally, even, perhaps, pathological. For Tcherkézoff, however, individualism is and always has been present, though often ideologically subordinated. The revolution wrought by European society at the Reformation took the form not of an innovation but of a shifting of values between the two levels. The individual is always objectively recognizable, whether supreme value (i.e. ideological) or residue (here, empirical, non-ideological). For de Coppet, Barraud and Iteanu, he or she is either ideologically recognized (this includes the Orokaiva *jo* and Rifian great man as well as the western *ego*, though the latter is given the supreme value in western society) or ideologically non-existent (Tanebar-Evav): the empirical dimension does not count.

In eliding the empirical individual, the alternative approach of Barraud and de Coppet is closer to what is often taken to be Durkheimian orthodoxy. It also pluralizes value, since the two levels are both located within the ideology: the single key value, the mother idea, no longer has the ideological field to itself. 'For those who use this vocabulary, the levels observable in the society can be of different types of ceremonial exchange etc., and one does not then see how only certain of them would be in the ideology ...' (Tcherkézoff 1994). In turn, charges Tcherkézoff, this encourages the pre-selection of those values that are to be placed in the encompassing relation, whereas what one should be doing is to use encompassment and the reversal associated with it as the tool by means of which the supreme value is to be identified. This also entails comparing ideologies rather than structures.

It is also possible to object to de Coppet's claim that individualism is essentially the value of the modern west and that conversely the idea of society always obtains in non-modern, non-western societies. Strathern (1988; also 1992, addressing de Coppet's arguments more specifically) shows Melanesia to be a graveyard of such assumptions. This does not involve her in a denial of individualism to the west. Here, birth creates a unique individual, one whose individuality survives death, as a memory, as the bundle of his or her achievements. But there is also a consciousness of society as something into which that individual first has to be incorporated, or in the words of mid-twentieth-century anthropology, 'socialized', a consciousness which also corresponds to a western folk model.

In Melanesia, this may not always be the case. Every life-stage, initiation, marriage or death, is liable to take the form of the deconstruction and reconstruction of relationships, but there is not necessarily any sense of an individual joining society at birth or initiation, or of leaving it at death. At death, for example, relationships are newly formed and therefore have to involve different individuals. What this leads to, *inter alia*, is a situation in which different things or persons may be seen as simultaneously similar and dissimilar, for example, male and female members of a matrilineage, initiates and the newly born, the men who are handling initiates and a woman giving birth (the examples are all in Strathern 1992: 85). A Dumontian would presumably be able to make yet more hierarchical oppositions out of these examples. The point Strathern is making, however, is that there need not be a notion of society at all. Society, therefore, like individualism, begins to be seen as an essentially western notion. Moreover, it is essentially a modern one, the late twentieth-century problem being no longer individualism but the deconstruction of the notion of society (see her contribution in GDAT 1990; also de Coppet, previous chapter).

Tcherkézoff too, therefore, clearly sees hierarchical opposition as an important tool of comparison, a truly structural model in the sense that it is applicable to any society, modern as well as traditional, yet is also objective, that is, independent of the particular tradition of any one of them (1994). This objectivity depends crucially on the phenomenon of reversal, which indicates the change and therefore the difference in level. Remove it, and 'we lose the advantage of formal proof in order to fall back on culturalist interpretations'. In other words, we are presented with 'a clear choice between an anthropology of interpreted ideas and an anthropology of structures'. Encompassment is thus a formal device to locate the mother idea, which should not be pre-selected, lest one fall into ethnocentrism and end up with 'relativism rather than a tool of comparison'. Encompassment as a 'properly anthropological concept' is contrasted with culture-centric, one might say Eurocentric notions such as inequality and power.

Anthropologists themselves contribute, if unwittingly, to the development of such ethnocentric ideas. Religion is another example. The primary level is by definition identified with the ideology. Dumont does not define ideology as such, but for him it clearly approximates to religion, at least as regards India. Given especially the difficulties in defining religion at all neatly, there is the danger of imposing our view of religion on the indigenous situation, perhaps including, for example, the notion that religion is absolutely distinct from politics. In any case, this is pre-selection again, the model directing rather than reflecting the evidence. The order of the ideology may then be missed: and what is significant is 'the order of relations, not the order of ideas' (Tcherkézoff 1994).

Dumont's particular development of the Maussian sacred has not, therefore, been uniformly appropriate. Of course, says Tcherkézoff, sacred/profane is certainly a hierarchical opposition, as even Durkheim and Mauss came close to realizing. What they did not realize was that the encompassed profane—represented, for example, by the individual and his interests—is allowed an existence, if a subordinate one, with hierarchical opposition. This does not contradict the doctrine that society is more than just a collection of individuals, nor that the individual must be deduced from the group and not vice versa. But the individual need not be engulfed by society, as the strictest Durkheimian orthodoxy has always tended to assume, nor does the individual appear solely as a transgressor of social norms, as for Durkheim. The sociality of the sacred encompasses the individualism of the profane, but this also means that the latter has a level of distinction of its own: 'The system of inclusions encompasses the system of distinction, adherence encompasses the empirical difference between individuals' (Tcherkézoff 1994).

It all comes down to the difference between contexts and levels once again. The first is the view from within the culture, indigenous, emic, seeing the encompassed level as something outside the ideology, as the 'residue' (at least with hierarchy 'in the strict sense'; see above). The second is the structural, objective view, the view of the observer, the etic view, seeing the encompassed level as a logical contradiction, but one with dynamic analytical value. Although the observer also places that level outside the ideology, it is because he too is outside it that he notices the contradiction, which the view from inside the culture obscures. This in its turn renders objections to the applicability of hierarchical opposition on grounds of informants' statements ultimately futile. Being emic and 'cultural' in character, they relate to a different area of discourse than the analytical area in which hierarchical opposition resides. Indeed, as we saw with the example of France, such statements do not provide an objection to anything, but only new material from which fresh analyses using hierarchical opposition can be generated. Egalitarianism contradicts hierarchy culturally, ideologically and subjectively; but where it is the dominant social value, it actually constitutes a hierarchy structurally, analytically and objectively.

Cosmos and Society

The shift from ritual to cosmology as the focus of discourse on hierarchical opposition is continued in another recent work generated by this group, the last we shall notice here. This is a volume edited by de Coppet and Iteanu (1995) entitled *Cosmos and Society in Oceania*, the outcome of a 1990 conference. In many respects it is a fascinating volume, since, in relation to the relevance of hierarchical opposition, it brings together aficionados and refusniks, sceptics and fence-sitters, plus some who might be described as the innocently neutral. Its main aim is to challenge, using data from Oceania, the frequent tendency in anthropological theory to separate cosmos from society, the argument being that this frequently does not correspond to ethnographic realities. Of course, being among the aficionados, in their introduction the editors are also keen to identify hierarchical oppositions wherever possible, even in the work of the remaining categories of author.

Apart from the editors, who themselves contribute papers, most of the authors are well-known anthropologists in this ethnographic area who have led careers separate from ERASME. Many of them make reference to hierarchy, encompassment and hierarchical opposition, often without explicit reference to Dumont. This is perhaps further evidence that, in some circles, Dumont's ideas have begun to take root independently of his own scholarly personality.

The first chapter in this collection is a partly comparative work by Alfred Gell on Polynesia, which mainly refers to Samoa and the Marquesan Islands (Gell 1995; he does not make any reference to Dumont and his ideas). The sort of origin myth found very widely, whereby the world emerged from an original unity, which thus gave way to division, is represented in Central Polynesian myths by the story of Ta'aroa, the creator god, who divided the world in order to increase his own scope for action. [1] The first and most fundamental division he made was into *ao* and *po*, respectively earth and sky, day and night, light and darkness, life and death, etc. Successive divisions are marked by *'apu* or shells, which Gell describes as being 'nested' within one another (cf. the *varna* scheme as described by Dumont), and the various divisions are linked by 'pathways or ladders'.

One key difference from many mythico-ritual situations of this sort is that ritual action is not directed towards restoring or returning to this situation of primordial unity, but towards preventing the re-merger of the cosmos into one. Tattooing is significant here. Although its exact meaning varies in different parts of Polynesia, its main function for Gell is that it preserves men (women are not affected) from this merger. On Samoa, it does this by sealing or closing (Gell uses the image of 'wrapping') the body, thus ensuring its integrity. In the Marquesans, tattoos are linked not just with the closure of the body but also with its fragmentation, which the very patterns of the tattoo indicate. Tattoos are also a means of avoiding the sacred and thus the cosmic merger associated with it (gods are anyway viewed as over-sanctified and therefore dangerous in Polynesia).

As just noted, tattooing is a male activity and only protects males. Why are women not affected by the concern for integrity with which tattooing is associated? Unlike the Christian account of the emergence of the separate genders, which Dumont uses as a simple example of hierarchical opposition, in Polynesia men were created by an originally unitary woman. This is expressed in the idea that, since women give birth to both men and women, they encompass men. Women pose a greater danger to men than vice versa; they are also closer to the sacred. They therefore need protection from merger less than men— indeed, they are more closely associated with it to begin with. More precisely, women mediate between the worlds of *ao* and *po* in a way that would threaten the integrity of men. In fact, women at the moment of parturition are likened to the cosmos at the moment that Ta'aroa separated it into *ao* and *po*.

Another type of representation that Gell talks about at length are the 'Siamese twin' images that are very common in Polynesian art. These Siamese twins are usually portrayed as being joined at the back. This makes them quasi-unitary figures, not dissimilar to Needham's unilateral figures, in that they are actually portrayed as lacking backs and can therefore also be said to lack one horizontal distinction, that between the back and front of their bodies. But in addition one's back is vulnerable, since one cannot see it (Gell also mentions strong prohibitions against walking behind chiefs during ceremonies). Since gods are shown as being joined at the back and thus as having no backs, they are presumably invulnerable (over-sanctification again?), but also unitary, representing the encompassing nature of the original cosmic order. However, these figures can also be seen as the god at the moment of the primordial division of this order into *ao* and *po*, like women giving birth.

Women have another role in relation to men, namely to transform their husbands' corpses after death. One missionary account of Polynesia from the nineteenth century that Gell cites (1995: 51-3) reports the widow of a Marquesan chief picking the tattooed skin from his body piece by piece. It is tempting to see this as the unwrapping of the body, making it vulnerable to the re-merger that was fought against so vigorously in life. In fact, Gell sees the practice as one of a number, including exposure of the corpse, human sacrifice, various forms of cannibalism and offerings to the gods of the *po*, that are designed to ensure that the deceased reaches his proper destination, and avoids improper alternative destinations, as quickly as possible. These aims and practices are unexceptional in terms of worldwide ethnography. However, what is involved ultimately is avoiding the 'immanence' that the deceased would suffer if the gods themselves were to consume and therefore re-absorb him. The offerings are thus made to induce the gods to desist from this practice; similarly, human sacrifice and being cannibalized are preferable to consumption by the gods (exposure is presumably linked to consumption by wild animals). Even in death, therefore, we meet the Polynesian's 'refusal of transcendence' (ibid.: 50).

In this same volume, a younger writer, Denis Monnerie, focuses on the Mono-Alu society on Alu, one of the Solomon Islands, a traditionally stratified society, with nobles, commoners and, in the past, slaves. It is also a society with matrilineal descent, in which men are said to produce nothing, unlike women, who are the bearers of both male and female children (cf. Gell above). There is a division into *latu*, roughly but not consistently matrilineal, exogamous, descent groups, though with a tendency to endogamy among the nobles. The *latu* are connected with food taboos relating to different animal species, though they are not consistent. Monnerie deliberately avoids the term 'totemism' for this reason, though the species are also partly ancestral. There are more fundamental divisions for present purposes. One is that between two different sorts of *nitu* or ancestors: orginal *nitu*, who have never been human, and recent *nitu*, the souls of the recently dead. Before discussing them further, we must bring in another opposition, that between *tua* and *tete*. These terms also denote ancestors, and Monnerie glosses them respectively as 'grandfather' and 'grandmother' (obviously in a general, non-genealogical sense). They are also associated with the animal world, *tua* with creatures of the air or of trees, *tete* with creatures of water or beneath the earth (the earth's surface that lies between these two is the domain of humans). Both *tua* and *tete* are of consequence at mortuary rituals, at which both are made offerings, *tua* by hanging an offering in a tree, *tete* by feeding the remains of the dead after cremation to fish in the sea. So far, all we have is a series of complementary oppositions. But the dead also become recent *nitu*, who, despite the above distinction, quickly turn into original *nitu*, who are themselves associated with *tete*, the original grandmothers. This suggests a double encompassment, of recent *nitu* by original *nitu*, and of *tua* by *tete*, the latter encompassment also according with the descent mode. However, since the recent *nitu* are distinguished by gender, it would appear that the division between *tua* and *tete* relates to them. This in its turn means that the level of the recent *nitu* is one of complementary opposition between *tua* and *tete*, the level of the original *nitu* one of both encompassment and the absence of opposition, with *tete* encompassing *tua*.

Monnerie himself is quite explicit about these encompassments, and refers to Dumont as an inspiration. At one point, he calls the original *nitu* the 'most encompassing level' (1995: 123), and he also says that they encompass the recent *nitu*, who are at a 'lower level [of the ideology]' (ibid.: 125, also 126). The original *nitu* are also associated with *darami*, meat and vegetables used in rituals, recent *nitu* only with *sanaka*, meat used in rituals. In addition, while the two sorts of *nitu* are similar in that they 'have no spatial limits', 'they have different temporal extensions' (ibid.: 124). While Monnerie only refers this to work elsewhere on 'ways of expressing the "past"' among the Mono-Alu (ibid.: 130 n.20), it is clear that the original *nitu* are eternal, whereas the recent *nitu* have a temporary existence on their way to becoming original *nitu*. He also realizes (ibid.: 127) that the recent *nitu*, being distinguished by gender, are connected with an internal relationship that is 'complementary and asymmetrical rather than hierarchical', that *between* the two sorts of *nitu* being hierarchical.

Daniel de Coppet's contribution in this volume continues his long-term examination of the values of 'Are'are society, also in the

Solomons, which he claims have sustained the society for the past four hundred years, despite colonialism (1995: 235). The basic opposition here is identified as that between peace-masters and killers, this evidently being a society governed in part by feud. Parallel to this is an opposition between those who died 'normally', of illness sent by the ancestors, and those who suffered violent or premature deaths. This includes not only victims of murder, but also suicides and women who died in childbirth, as well as dead foetuses and stillborn children— that is, two categories of the immature. This can be associated with the parallel circumstance that rituals held to deal with the former entail the use of areca nuts and coconuts that are riper, more 'mature', than those used in rituals dealing with murder victims. Another contrast is that the peace-masters act for the dead of the whole community—indeed, one becomes a peace-master by signalling a readiness so to act, and not just for the dead of one's own kin group. By contrast, in expiating their killing, killers direct their rituals to their own agnatic ancestors alone. Finally, there is a difference in bodily ornamentation: whereas ornaments worn by peace-masters are open in shape, signifying their openness to all the social relations of the community, those worn by killers are closed, signifying the more particular aspect of their agnatic relations, as well as the ultimate sterility of their activities.

The main difference, however, between the peace-master and the killer is their involvement in a hierarchical opposition whose encompassing level is that of sociocosmic renewal. The rituals in which the killer is engaged are designed primarily for his own expiation (de Coppet uses the term 'ablution'). Those of the peace-master, by contrast, are linked to prosperity (which de Coppet explicitly contrasts with 'ablution'), and more particularly are intended to ensure that all the dead, including the murdered, are successfully reincorporated into the sociocosmic order. This is the main sense in which the former ultimately encompasses the latter.

The importance of funerals is that they resolve distinctions set up by earlier rituals in the life-cycle, especially marriage. These distinctions are symbolized by different exchange goods, namely taros, pigs and shell money. Mortuary rituals remove these distinctions through the conversion of the first two into shell money, which therefore stands alone as a unitary value. But the distinction between pigs and taro is also important, the former being associated with the 'normal' dead, the latter with murder victims. This is also a distinction that is resolved in favour of the encompassing value of the 'normal' dead: murder victims, whose bodies are not given funerals but left to rot in the forest, also come to be associated with pigs, who eat them. These pigs will later be offered at the peace-master's ceremony that is held for all the dead. Here shell money will also be offered for this same purpose of reincorporating all the dead into the sociocosmic order. This particular shell money also originates in the forest, where it is given to bachelors by unmarried women in so-called 'flirtation campaigns' organized by the peace-master. Finally, most peace-masters themselves have made a transition from earlier existences as killers. It is therefore they and the symbolic values they are associated with that represent encompass-ment, the killers and their values being on a subordinate level.

Hirsch's chapter, on the Fuyuge of Papua New Guinea, engages with others' use of hierarchical opposition without, in the end, entirely accepting it. The main opposition he concentrates on relates to notions of ancestrality and achievement in ritual. Ritual is designed to bring about 'increasing collective unification' and the 'coalescence of ancestrality and achievement' (1995: 220). There is a further dichotomy between forest and gardens, in which the latter, at least, is associated with an ancestral life-force and being called *tidibe*. Theoret-ically, Hirsch links ancestrality with the sociocosmic idea of de Coppet etc. (cf. Barraud et al. 1994), and therefore with an 'emphasis on an encompassing image of the social whole as derived from ancestral ori-gins and as realized through the performance of ritual' (Hirsch 1995: 214; also 229). Achievement, conversely, is linked to Marilyn Strath-ern's 'emphasis on the revelatory nature of social practices' (ibid.: 215; also 229), that is, encompassment as 'the encapsulation of another's viewpoint, a containment of an anticipated outcome' (Strathern 1988: 259, cited in Hirsch 1995: 230 n.2). This refers to encompassment not as an aspect of hierarchical opposition, as for Dumont, but rather as the interpenetration of persons and the actions that can be predicted and expected, even compelled, in others. It is also, therefore, a matter of agency rather than ideology alone.

Hirsch himself ultimately declines to see this distinction between ancestrality and achievement as a hierarchical opposition, apparently preferring to regard the two as complementary. However, he does sug-gest that images of achievement are always uncertain and contingent, whereas ancestrality is 'certain and unproblematic'; in addition, he talks about 'an imagery of achievement that [is] predicated on notions of ancestrality' (ibid.: 229). It is perhaps this that leads the editors of the book to suggest more confidently the existence of 'a form of hier-archical relation between two domains: the subordinate achievement and the encompassing ancestrality' (de Coppet and Iteanu 1995: 15).

This is not the only attempt to contrast the perspectives of Strath-ern and Dumont. Mosko has been a persistent critic, not so much of Dumont's model per se, but of its wider ethnographic applicability, especially in the western Pacific (1992a, 1992b, 1994a, 1994b). Indeed, at one point (1992a: 110 n.8) he suggests that 'Dumontian formulations of hierarchy are very likely poorly adaptable to Austronesian societies generally and both Melanesian and Polynesian societies specifically'. Although he has tackled Dumont directly (1994a; cf. above, Chapter 6), he has also channelled his criticisms through some of those who have adopted Dumont's ideas, especially Valeri (see Mosko 1994b) and Sahlins (see Mosko 1992a, 1992b). Mosko's criticisms of both writers seem to be chiefly ethnographic. As I discuss Valeri's work at some length in the next chapter, here I shall concentrate on Sahlins.

One aspect of Sahlins's account of Polynesian kingship (1985) is his suggestion that kings and chiefs embodied the peoples they ruled in a relationship of transcendental encompassment corresponding theoretically to Dumont's model of hierarchical opposition. He has been followed in this by Lutkehaus's account (1990) of chiefship among the Manam of the Sepik in Papua New Guinea, an area normally associated with big men and great men, not hierarchies of chiefs, let alone kings. Here we find ourselves in the midst of a classic distinction in anthropology between political formations in Polynesia and Melanesia, to which Sahlins contributed in an early paper (1963), but which has often been challenged since as too rigid. Lutkehaus reflects this later perspective in claiming to have found an embryonic 'Polynesian' situation among the Manam, because of the authority they invest in their hereditary village chiefs. Mosko, conversely, appears to see both 'Polynesian' and 'Melanesian' features among the Mekeo of the Central Province of Papua New Guinea, who, in speaking an Austronesian language, seem to be associated at first sight more with Indonesia and Malaysia to their west than to either of the other ethnographic areas. While they have a more elaborate, 'Polynesian' system of chiefs than the Manam, their concept of the person, Mosko claims, is more typically Melanesian in being partible, in the manner described by Strathern for big men and great men societies (1988).

So far, this is simply another case of ethnographic variation undermining previous theoretical models. However, for Mosko the very partibility of chiefly persons among the Mekeo rules out their encompassment of either one another or of the people they rule: the argument seems to be that, since they are not wholes, they cannot represent a whole in the way Sahlins describes for eastern Polynesia. This does not mean, however, that there are no hierarchical oppositions here. I have already discussed this briefly as regards the relationships between the chiefs themselves, where war and peace, and chiefly rule and sorcery, are opposed, with Mosko's own description indicating that one pole of each pair is quite likely to be transcendent in practice (above, Chapter 3).

A clearer example is provided by the Mekeo origin myth, which Mosko discusses at some length as evidence for the partibility of the chiefs (1992b: 706ff.). This represents the Mekeo as having originally been entirely male, and as lacking women, birth and death. These three aspects came into their lives once they met Akaisa, the god or culture hero, who gave the men his own daughters (so that they inter-bred, whereupon both birth and death entered the world), along with other cultural artefacts like fire, and apparently also installed chiefs among them (ibid.: 706). A page later, we are told that 'the four types of hereditary clan official initially appointed by Akaisa, in their per-sons or in their ritual actions, effectively return or decompose Mekeo society to its autochthonous, strictly masculine origins'. Thus there appears to be something transcendent about the exclusive maleness of the primordial time, to which Mekeo society periodically returns sym-bolically, though needing women to reproduce in ordinary time. What is more, it is precisely the partibility of the chiefs that is the instrument whereby this happens, since it enables them to rid themselves of one gender so as to emphasize the other temporarily. Despite Mosko's reluctance to think in these terms, we are actually confronted with a perfectly good example of hierarchical opposition in this myth.

For an even more trenchant rejection of the value of Dumont's ideas, we must return to the volume being discussed earlier (de Coppet and Iteanu 1995), before this interpolation of Mosko's material. This is found in Josephides' chapter on gender relations among the Kewa of Papua New Guinea. For Josephides, the approach cultivated by Dumont's followers involves privileging the ritual and the social over what she calls 'positional viewpoints' (1995: 190-1)—in other words, it offers a single view of 'the true account' of society as superordinate over the plurality of perspectives that ethnographers have come to expect in the field. This can be seen in gender relations, where hierar-chical opposition reproduces the predominant male model, neglecting the political reality that women's models are also autonomous and self-generated, although they are masked by the male ones. Joseph-ides's criticism is thus partly directed against earlier work on the Kewa that neglects the reality reflected in the myths on gender relations that she examined. Josephides therefore focuses on empowerment, agency and politics more than on ideology and ritual, though songs sung in ritual contexts are also important.

Another basic opposition dealt with here is between present and past with respect to forms of empowerment, which is itself gendered. Specifically, men need the past to validate their activities, while women do not. Land is agnatic and therefore links men to the ancestors. Men are also involved in exchange relations with affines, mediated by their married sisters, who live elsewhere. A favourite male saying is: 'All wealth comes from sisters'. For Josephides, accepting this at face value neglects the use men make of this saying to mask the reality of their wives' physical production of wealth through work in their husbands' gardens. This is further mystified by another common male attitude, devaluing such work because it takes place on the husband's land, and therefore prioritizing male exchange relations over it. One practical consequence is conflict between husband and wife over the disposal of the pigs she raises on his land, the husband seeing pigs as a means of raising his prestige by increasing the possibilities for exchange with important affines, the wife wishing to include other important relatives in the gifting. Josephides makes the strong point that this conflict is not merely symbolic but actually felt as conflictual by husbands and wives, to the extent of weakening marriages in some cases.

Another consequence of these different attitudes to wealth, however, is that women's production can be claimed to be inherent in them: they do not need ancestrality to empower them as men do. This contrast is also seen in the ritual songs. Female songs are basically songs of courting, which, being connected with love and marriage, are timeless and involve both genders. Male pig-killing songs, by contrast, are strongly linked with agnatic values and therefore with specific ancestral histories. However, men also have their own courting songs. But whereas women's songs again inhere in them, men have to purchase the magic associated with them from women to begin with. Again, therefore, men's agency depends on something external to themselves, while women's agency is intrinsic to them.

Josephides concludes by decisively rejecting hierarchical opposition as an approach to understanding this material. In reality, there are two models: a male model, privileging pig-killing to marriage; and a female model, regarding both as equal but separate domains. In fact, despite Josephides's reluctance to have anything to do with it, it seems possible to argue that there *is* encompassment here, but that it is female values that encompass male ones, not vice versa. This is partly because men are shown as being dependent in respect of their agency in many situations in a way that women are not. But there is also the question of the differential relation to the transcendent values of the whole sociocosmos. The pig-killing ceremonies, which are basically male, give way to night-time exchanges of courting songs that not only involve both genders, but are premised on the female-connected values of love and marriage. Women may regard this as a separate but equal domain of activity and discourse; but their songs also deal with the continuation of society as a whole, as opposed to the (purely male) celebration of specific pasts in the pig-killing songs.

In part, Josephides is also arguing against André Iteanu's chapter in this same volume, which continues his own long-term interest in the Orokaiva of Papua New Guinea from a consistently orthodox Dumontian perspective. Again rituals feature strongly, initiations being associated with encompassing values, mortuary rituals with subordinate ones. Initiations are associated with *jape* figures, who represent ancestry but are also 'thought up' by the elders (or more strictly, people with the most extensive experience of initiations). Mortuary rituals are associated with ancestors, either *ahihi* or *onderi*. A fourth term, *hamo*, refers to the living.

More precisely, *ahihi* are children at birth, until they become *hamo* or full persons through ritual action; and they are also what the dead turn into initially when mortuary ritual has stripped them of the relations they have built up in life, so that they cease to become *hamo*. In course of time, *ahihi* join the undifferentiated body of ancestors as *onderi*. *Ahihi* are thus transitional. They are also personal, like *jape* but unlike *onderi*. Unlike *jape*, however, they are somewhat despised because the mortuary ritual also leads to their over-identification with the material objects that are exchanged rather than with immaterial persons—who themselves are treated roughly in these rituals. *Onderi* are seen as 'a subordinated representation, at a lower level, of the otherwise valued *jape* characters'. Reversal occurs in that, 'while *jape* is dominant at the ritual level, at the lower level, under the diminished guise of *onderi*, it is subordinated to the living' (Iteanu 1995: 159). As for the relation between *ahihi* and *onderi*, presumably the latter, being a manifestation of *jape*, have a higher value than the despised former. *Jape* figures thus encompass both *ahihi* and *onderi*. In fact Iteanu sees the three sorts of supernatural taken together as forming a nested hierarchy of successively encompassing relations like the *varna* scheme in India.

Another distinction between initiation and mortuary rituals is the collective nature of the former (the focus being on the whole community), while the latter focus on deceased individuals. Within initiation itself, there is a gender contrast, since men represent individual *jape* figures who are associated with particular families, while women collectively represent just one such figure, called Sivoropoka. There is also a distinction between this ritual, at least, and the circumstances of everyday life: the elders are respected for their knowledge of initiation, whose performance depends greatly on it and on their authority; but in day-to-day life they are, if not despised, then at least exposed to the gibes of the younger generation.

Toren's chapter in this same collection focuses on relations between hierarchy and equality as values in Fiji. She makes explicit reference to Dumont's ideas in one place (1995: 78 n.2), though also using terms like 'hierarchy' and 'encompassment' in an apparently normative fashion. In fact, though, here and elsewhere (e.g. 1990, 1994a, 1994b), she has repeatedly declined to see the relationship between hierarchy and equality on Fiji as an encompassing one, and even denies any usefulness to Dumont's model (e.g. 1994a: 212). In fact, she prefers the Hegelian dialectic, since she sees the relationship between hierarchy and equality on Fiji as antithetical rather than one of encompassment, on the basis that each depends similarly on the other (ibid.: 197-8). This presumably produces synthesis in the manner of Hegel rather than a Dumontian encompassment. For Toren, who makes extensive reference to the changes introduced by colonialism and Christianization, Hegel is also more sensitive to history than Dumont.

Right at the start of her chapter in the volume edited by de Coppet and Iteanu (1995), Toren points out that, while in Christianity 'hierarchy is an encompassing value' (ibid.: 57), in Fiji it is challenged by the value of equality. Another fundamental division for Toren is that between compassion and desire. Initially, these are linked respectively to the distinction between relationships within the household, which are hierarchical but involve compassion; and relationships between cross cousins, which link households through marriage—itself a manifestation of desire—but which also involve a competitive expression of equality that is explicitly considered inappropriate within the household. This desire is presumably expressed also in the snatching relationship between cross cousins. Marriage, which takes place axiomatically between cross cousins, produces a reversal in that it creates a formal, public hierarchy between husband and wife, which may be marked by the violence of the former's jealousy and therefore by desire. Informally, however, there may be equality in the relationship, governed by compassion.

Not only does this level of marriage therefore reverse the connection of compassion with hierarchy and of desire with equality with which we started, it also appears at first sight to be one of complementary opposition. However, the informal level of compassionate equality appears to be much more contingent than that of the formal level of male authority, which is also presumably a matter of the ideal being opposed to the actual. An essential part of Toren's argument is that cross-cousin marriage also creates a new household—in other words, desire creates the locus in which compassion is appropriate. This means that the exercise of compassion depends ultimately on the operation of desire, with its associated notions of equality. Conversely, in its turn that household will create cross cousins for the wife's kin group, thus allowing a fresh marriage and reversing the dependency.

This is why Toren sees the relationship as antithetical, not hierarchical. A Dumontian might say that, while marriage entails this distinction between informal equality and formal hierarchy, the household does not, being solely associated with formal hierarchy. In Toren's favour is the assumption we can surely make that a married couple also forms a household, in which case the compassion and equality actually *both* become associated with it too. In reading this particular article, therefore, a Dumontian is left with the informal nature of equality in this context to support a claim that this is actually a hierarchical opposition in which the formal value of hierarchy is encompassing.

In fact, an examination of one of Toren's earlier articles, on gifting and commodification (1989), reveals much clearer evidence of encompassment and hierarchical oppositions in Fiji. This is despite the fact that she does not mention Dumont here, is apparently not influenced by him, and does not use the language of encompassment. Indeed, it would seem that Toren has only discovered Dumont and his failings relatively recently, and that she has not much liked what she has seen. This is a pity, since ironically it seems to have had the effect of producing a much muddier picture of what really goes on in Fiji than her earlier work.

For a start, the earlier article on gifting is less ambiguous with regard to kinship. Discussing the distinctions revolving around the household and cross cousins, for example, Toren's position here is that 'The term for kin, *veiwekani*, *subsumes* affines and friends as well as consanguines; ideally all Fijians are kin to one another' (ibid.: 144, my emphasis). Here too, the equality between cross cousins is opposed to the hierarchy of all other kinship relations, but Toren goes on to say that the threat this presents to the hierarchical order is

> de-fused by the fact that, when two cross-cousins marry ... the equality between them *gives way* to the axiomatic hierarchy of husband over wife. In effect this means that kinship hierarchy is able to '*contain*' the equality of cross-cousins by *subordinating* it to the hierarchy of the domestic group. Thus hierarchy is *dominant* in 'the way according to kinship' which is itself synonymous with 'the Fijian way'. (Ibid., my emphases)

In other words, hierarchy is the supreme value of Fijian society.

For the editors of this volume (de Coppet and Iteanu 1995: 5-7), however, it is the myth Toren discusses that is most significant here. In it, men are transformed into gods by being cooked like food in an earth oven. Since they willingly submit (and perhaps too because the gods restore them as beings of their own kind), de Coppet and Iteanu argue that compassion is involved. But since eating is linked to sex, desire is also present. 'This intimate intermingling of two otherwise distinguished forms of relation seems to be the exclusive attribute of *mana* holders (the God and chiefs) ...' (ibid.: 6). Moreover, just as the myth started with the men's wives defying their authority, so it ends with the restoration of proper gender relations and the formation of proper households (which are linked with hierarchy).

Toren also discusses the changing role of the chiefs in Fiji (1995). Traditionally, the hierarchy of chiefs was not fixed but rotated among them, and was subject to the claims of the same challenging equality as is represented by cross cousins and their relationship. In the modern period the pervasive influence of Christianity, to which so many chiefs and their followers have converted, has introduced the idea of permanent hierarchy, with the Christian God at the pinnacle. Christianity is thus encompassing tradition, hierarchy equality.

Elsewhere in her work (1994a), Toren discusses the opposition between sea chiefs and land chiefs, who are superior in rank to, and must install, the former. Their relationship is therefore evidently hierarchical, though it is actually the former who are the paramount chiefs. However, the sea chiefs are also related as commoners to the land chiefs, who are chiefs unambiguously (ibid.: 209). It is not clear if, or how, this opposition may be related to that between *sau* or war chiefs and *tui* or ritual chiefs. For Toren, any superiority that the *tui* might claim is neutralized by the naked force the *sau* frequently used to displace *tui* in pre-colonial times, which represents the value of equality between contestants for power (ibid.: 199, 211). In that case, one must ask why the war chiefs wanted to become ritual chiefs in the first place—presumably because the values of war, though admirable in their way (or on their ideological level), did not compare with the transcendent values represented by the *tui*. As we saw in Chapter 4 in discussing a remark of Bailey's, ritual leaders can act politically in a surreptitious manner while actually claiming ritual excellence; secular or war leaders can only do the former, and usually do it more openly.

Economics as Cosmology

For yet another theme that illustrates the presence of encompassment in Fiji, we must return to Toren's earlier paper on gifting, and the opposition between gifts and commodities (1989). For example, *yaqona* or kava is given as tribute to chiefs on ritual occasions, called *guna yaqona*. Indeed traditionally, if not today, *yaqona* was the prerogative of chiefs: while junior males could prepare it on such occasions, neither they nor women could drink it. Its consumption is therefore linked to hierarchy as represented by the chiefs, who are seated in accordance with their respective statuses. Commodities, on the other hand, are associated with money, which is remote, to say the least, from the transcendantal values associated with gifting to chiefs, or with *yaqona*. Normally, only Indians in Suva or elsewhere on the two main islands sell *yaqona* for cash.

Nonetheless, there is one occasion on which *yaqona* appears to be treated like a commodity by Fijians themselves, in that it is bought and sold for cash. This is a relatively modern form of drinking ceremony designed to raise money for sports teams and the like—thus it has a clear community focus. This ceremony is called 'drinking cash' or *gunu sede* (cf. *gunu yaqona*). Those present buy drinks for one another, but never include themselves in their own purchases. The occasion is one of much hilarity and good humour, in which sociality is more evident that the economic selfishness that is usually associated with buying and selling commodities. In addition, the values of equality are represented by the fact that most of the *yaqona* purchased is given to one's affines, who are of course also cross cousins. We are therefore confronted with a set of ritual reversals, in which the gift par excellence is treated as a commodity, commodification is applied to a community activity, and *yaqona* is associated with equality rather than hierarchy. However, the chiefs are also present at these events, and are supplied with *yaqona* outside the process of buying and selling: that is—and as with the 'drinking *yaqona*' ceremonies—because they *are* chiefs. Toren concludes: 'In *gunu sede* money and monetary transactions with their potential for disruption are explicitly *subordinated* to kinship relations, which *subsume* the relation between cross-cousins ... within an existing status quo' (1989: 159, my emphases).

Many of the other contributions to the volume from which this particular article comes (*Money and the Morality of Exchange*, Parry and Bloch 1989) is about this same relationship between two commonly occurring spheres of exchange, concerning respectively notionally disinterested gifts which have a selfless community reference, and explicit commodity exchange, often against money, conducted by self-seeking individuals. In their introduction (Parry and Bloch 1989), the editors go to some lengths to question the received wisdom that changes in indigenous economic systems are solely the result of modern conditions, in which they include especially colonialism, but to which we might now add economic globalization.

More particularly for our present purposes, they challenge the neat distinction commonly made between these two spheres, describing, with reference to the articles in the collection, the respective values attached to them and the intimacy with which they are in fact related. Typically the sphere of the gift is associated with the transcendental values represented by the social good, ritual and cosmic well-being, while the sphere of commodity exchange is connected with the acquisitive economic activities of individuals. In fact, of course, the former depends on the latter: although non-capitalist discourses may prioritize community goals in economic activity, they must leave space for individual acquisition, while ultimately finding ways of subsuming it.

In addition, there must be both separation, in order to preserve the integrity of the ritual sphere, but also contact, so that the ritual sphere can draw on the acquisitive sphere.

The perpetual risk is that the acquisitive sphere fails to support the ritual one, or even that it exploits it instead, like those Brahmans whose avarice prevents them from passing on the gifts of their inferiors to their own superiors with increment, so that their bodies rot from within. Often, wealth acquired acquisitively in the form of money or European or other outside goods is felt to be unsuitable for ritual purposes and first must be converted (cf. the practice of the wealthy in the Middle Ages building or decorating a church in preference to simply handing over money to it). One is also reminded here of Foster's work on peasants, and particularly the 'image of limited good' that he associates with them (1965). This relates to the widespread belief in peasant societies that there is only so much wealth in the world, and that if one individual succeeds in obtaining more, others must go without. As a consequence peasants hide what they have, lest they be criticized for their cupidity. Of course, some peasants succeed in becoming wealthy nonetheless. One way they can maintain or restore their reputation among their fellows is to donate some of their wealth to community projects, such as temples and festivals. The despising of, for example, the Jews by peasant societies in Europe, or of Chinese minorities in Southeast Asia, must have been partly due to their failure (in reality, impossibility, because of religious exclusion and difference) to act in this transcendent manner (cf. Llobera 1996: 202, on the Nazi distinction between German wholeness and polluting Jewish individualism, the latter being grounded in the occupation of the more self-centred economic niches of the merchant and shopkeeper).

It is clear that the relation between the two spheres of exchange as Parry and Bloch describe it is fundamentally hierarchical and encompassing. The sphere of disinterested giving is linked to the transcendent ideals of the society, while the acquisitive sphere, though necessary to the maintenance of the former and legitimate on its own level, is subordinate in value. The latter also represents the world of actual economic relations, whereas the ideal nature of the ritual sphere is compromised, and therefore emphasized, by the oft-repeated question as to whether there can ever be truly disinterested giving. At this level, no reference is made to the sphere of acquisition that actually supports ritual activity, whereas the distinction between the two spheres is apparent at the lower level, precisely because the devaluation of acquisition is usually explicit in non-capitalist discourses about economic activity.

Ideologically, however, a superior level is not undermined in its superiority merely because of its practical dependence on the subordinate level which it encompasses as the transcendent value. Parry's view that the Brahman in India bases his superiority, at least in part, on his relative lack of dependence on his inferiors (cf. Chapter 4) can be seen in this context. Parry's Brahmans are making an ideological statement in rejecting their dependence on inferiors, though they are dependent on them physically either as clients (if the Brahman is a priest), or as kings to donate the land and as possibly Untouchable labour to work it (if he is a landowner).

The superiority of the ritual level is also affirmed by its conversion of the acquisitive goods of the subordinate level into ritual and spiritual wealth that is transcendent. We have already seen this with reference to Toren's work on Fiji. Another example is Langkawi, Malaysia, where men are involved in fishing and other commercial transactions. However, they hand over the money they earn in these activities to women, who 'cook' it by using it to provide for the household and through it, at least symbolically, the wider community; thus it is converted into a morally acceptable medium. The analogy with food is highly symbolic, because commensality is strongly linked to household unity and to sociality generally here (Carsten 1989). On Sri Lanka, by contrast, money earned in an acquisitive way is the preserve of women, and is linked with disorder (Stirrat 1989). Another example is the Brahman 'digesting' the gifts he obtains from patrons, which also contain the latters' sins (Parry 1989). Yet another is White's work in a suburb of Istanbul, Turkey, where the value of women's piecework in small sweatshops is masked as social obligation by being restricted to clients within their kinship networks, in contrast to men's, which is explicitly for profit. 'The money and labour involved in the short-term cycle of economic activity (which involves a desire for individual profit) is thus, through the alchemy of kinship, converted to serve the reproduction of the long-term cycle of social solidarity (where money and labour become morally positive)' (White 2000: 126).

Before leaving the wider theme of economics, let us turn to a factory in Hungary, which Czeglédy calls Krebb Smith Co. (1999). This is a joint venture set up in 1989 involving 'a western European group of companies and a Hungarian heavy engineering enterprise [called Krebb National] (which itself possessed a complex corporate history incorporating two "parent" companies)' (ibid.: 144). Employees formerly involved in the latter tend to continue to identify with Krebb National rather than the new company, which is associated with foreigners, while Krebb National retains direct links, through memory, with the socialist past. However, Krebb Smith also embraced all employees, of both origins. There was thus a subordinate level of distinction encompassed by a superior level of transcendence. But what exactly is being transcended here? Basically it is the socialist past, this conjunction of ideas being opposed to the presentism of capitalism. The superior level, by contrast, represents a future dominated by privatized, capitalist companies, in which the inadequacies of both socialism and the past have been overcome. [2]

Notes

1. Gell makes the point that, unlike in Christianity, the myth does not describe the origin of the cosmos as such, but assumes its existence already as a unity.
2. Czeglédy found that the much older distinction between Krebb and National, the former being a private firm dating from before socialism, the latter being a socialist creation, was still retained too—an even more graphic demonstration of the power of memory. Employees who associated with Krebb were more likely to favour reprivatization than those who linked themselves with the National company.

Chapter 8

INNOCENCE AND POSSIBILITY

Ambivalence

So far, the adoption of Dumont's model in analysis outside France has been piecemeal and often partial, many writers being reluctant to adopt it in its entirety. I started to document this in the previous chapter. In the present one, I shall chart a few more of these developments before going on to suggest one other possible but so far largely unexploited application, in the field of ethnicity. The focus in this and the next section is more on the influence of Dumont's ideas on those outside, or on the edge of, the core group.

As we saw (Chapter 6), Platenkamp introduced the Dumontian perspective on hierarchy and value at Leiden in the mid 1980s, apparently inspired by Cécile Barraud, whose comments on an early paper of his (1984; cf. Barraud 1984: 193ff.) pointed out the potential of Dumontian ideas of hierarchy and of levels for analysing his data. Since then, a number of Dutch anthropologists have sought to incorporate them too, while others have been more diffident in doing so.

For example, Visser (1988) has used them to study the interplay between the distinctions elder/younger and land/people on Sahu (Indonesia), Zanen and van den Hoek (1987) to study the relation between the distinctions village/cattle camp and expiatory sacrifice/confirmatory sacrifice among the Bor Dinka (Sudan). The latter paper is of interest in the greater transcendental value it attributes to confirmatory sacrifices, whose aims are to achieve union with God and to return to an undifferentiated primordial world in which 'the sacrificer ... attains a more sacred state of being' (Zanen and van der Hoek 1987: 190). Such sacrifices take place in the cattle camp, where God is always closer than in the village, and therefore they also transcend

---

Notes for this section begin on page 212.

this distinction. Perhaps in this encompassing of the village by the cattle camp, human society is itself encompassed by the sacred, so that the return to primordial time is also a return to pre-social time (cf. Tcherkézoff, above, Chapter 6). The association of the cattle camp with origins is confirmed by its association with youth and by the concern to keep death away from it. The cattle camp is also associated with the unmarried state and with the absence of sexual relations. This would also suggest the primordial status of the camps, although the authors are not very explicit on this point.

We have already discussed an article by Geirnaert briefly in the previous chapter. Her more recent book on the Laboya of Sumba (Geirnaert-Martin 1992) introduces the concept of ideological levels further but defers a decisive account until more field data can be collected. The main focus of her work is weaving, which she examines 'in relation to systems of classification in cosmology and social organization through the study of rituals' (ibid.: xxi), especially the distinction between Padu and Nyale, which 'relate to the foundation of Laboya society as a socio-cosmic totality' (ibid.: xxxii). Weaving is carried out primarily by women, but men are also associated with it, through their greater responsibility for 'religious matters' (ibid.: xxiv), which impinge both on weaving and on women's role as procreators. The author examines technique as well as pattern, but what is significant in the present context is the association of weaving with ritual, the constitution of the person and the maintenance of the sociocosmic order. 'The participants' models relate to the circulation of *mawo* and *dewa*, which are the components of a person and, more generally speaking, "principles of life"' (ibid.: 401). *Mawo* circulates through humanity and through the cosmos, its incorporation into the body at birth and release from it at death being primarily the responsibility of women. *Dewa* is connected with one's relations with one's house's ancestors, with whose own *dewa* it is merged after death. The contrast would therefore seem to be one between the general and the specific too, giving grounds for believing that their opposition is a hierarchical one.

Thus *mawo* and *dewa* come together in the living person and separate from that person and from each other at death. But they should not be separated permanently, it being women's task too to reunite them, through weaving and through procreation, for the maintenance of the cosmic order. There is a related dichotomy between the pig, connected with the wild but also with women and their fertility and therefore implicitly with *mawo*, and the buffalo, connected with society but also (and more explicitly) with *dewa*. The pig and the buffalo belong respectively to the classes of female and male goods exchanged in affinal alliance, though they are sometimes substituted with tubers and coconuts respectively in ritual action (including sacrifice). This is presumably ritual substitution of the sort mentioned by Barraud and Platenkamp (see previous chapter), not a substitution on grounds of cost.

Among the things that threaten this order is *hala*, glossed by Geirnaert as 'transgression; to go in the wrong way; wrong; mistake; incest' (ibid.: 402). This is specifically related to the idea of primordial chaos, a time of no distinctions among humans, when they were ignorant of affinal exchange and therefore presumably prone to incest, a time too of a lack of distinction between sky and earth, or between wet and dry seasons. Padu in particular is concerned with the renewal of the sociocosmic order, a ritual process which must begin with the effacing of all distinctions, thus temporarily recreating the primordial chaos, before order is restored by re-establishing social and other distinctions through hunting. The similarity with van Gennep's model is obvious, except that his period of 'liminality' in the rite can be seen here as a time of unity, chaos and transcendence. In the course of the rite, *hala* is re-expelled into the wild, where it belongs, and weaving as a metaphor for order is also present, though the ritual hunt ensures the association of Padu also with violence. Here, unlike among the Nyamwezi, for instance (see Chapter 4), primordial unity would seem to be regarded not as a desirable goal, given the chaos that is also associated with it, but as a necessary stage in the process of renewal.

The rite of Nyale, conversely, is connected with Laboya society as much as with its relations to the outside, which are important to the society's mythical origins. For reasons given above, the reference to origins may actually be more significant than what the author chooses to stress, namely its reaching out to the whole of humanity. In that it relates to 'the wish for the continuity of society and for the well-being of mankind at large' (ibid.: 407), she herself suggests that Nyale (i.e. the blessed time of unity) 'is an encompassing idea and value', expressing the Laboya's own view of themselves as 'primordial life-givers' (ibid.: 407). The exterior dimension has also been found elsewhere in the area, as is shown by Barraud's work on the Kei Islands (especially 1985), Platenkamp's in Halmahera, and Valeri's among the Hualu (see below). Padu, being informed by violence and concerned with the internal order of Laboya society, represents another, presumably subordinate level of Laboya ideology.

Geirnaert's own reluctance to follow the logic of an analysis involving levels further, on grounds of the need for more data, is signalled on a number of occasions (e.g. 1992: xxxiv, 405, 410). Her declared goals are anyway somewhat different: 'I have not followed the concept of hierarchization, or of encompassment, to the end. In this book, my goal is not primarily to establish the hierarchy of Laboya ideology but to identify the occurrence of certain ideas and values that are expressed by the "participant's models" in certain contexts.' (ibid.: xxxi-xxxii). This agnosticism regarding hierarchy deprives her analyses of what is distinctive in the Dumontian approach and renders them more conventional. She is nonetheless willing to 'make the assumption that Padu and Nyale express Laboya ideas and values' (ibid.: xxxii). And although she often uses 'value' normatively (e.g. ibid.: 6, 14, 287), she is happy to recognize encompassments where they are especially apparent. Thus while men's cloths represent 'all the basic relationships and activities that are essential for the whole of society' (ibid.: 132) and thus encompass female cloths on that ideological level, reversals take place in some myths and in affinal exchange that cause female cloths to become predominant (ibid.: 112).

We saw too in the previous chapter that Barraud and Platenkamp present the Dumontian-derived approach as an alternative to van Wouden's earlier model, which was developed specifically for, and in, Indonesia. However, Geirnaert links the former instead to the original Dutch model behind van Wouden's work, namely the idea of the Field of Ethnological Study (FES) as adumbrated by J.P.B. de Josselin de Jong in 1935 and developed by Dutch anthropologists since, especially under the impulse of his nephew, P.E. de Josselin de Jong. In Geirnaert's words (ibid.: xxvii), the Field of Ethnological Study was originally conceived 'as a reaction to random world-wide comparisons and to avoid single-culture specialisms'. She continues to regard this approach as valid, despite its restriction to a particular culture area which is to some extent defined linguistically (although non-Austronesian-speaking societies in Indonesia are also likely to be implicated in the comparisons involved). Nonetheless, she feels that the idea of the FAS 'may benefit from a different approach within a holistic perspective, the study of systems of "ideas and values" for comparative purposes' (ibid.: 408-9). Yet the perspective chosen continues to depend on the anthropological tradition of the researcher. Geirnaert is more interested in holism and Indonesia-wide comparison than in hierarchical opposition as a generator of ideological levels as expressed in ritual action. Barraud, on the other hand, holds Dumontian hierarchy dear and wants to go beyond the narrowness (both areally and heuristically) of the approach based on the Field of Ethnological Study idea.

Platenkamp is, on the face of it, better placed to unite the two perspectives. In him are united experience in Paris with ERASME and an explicit devotion to the development of the Field of Ethnological Study into a series of transformations of common themes across a number of societies being compared cross-culturally, as advocated by P.E. de Josselin de Jong (1984: 6-8).

In an article in a Festschrift for the latter, Platenkamp has sought to apply both perspectives to that classic Lévi-Straussian subject, the analysis of myth (1988). The study concerns four societies in northern Halmahera, Indonesia, which 'share the ideologeme *ma dutu*, which stipulates that man must be subject to ancestors in their different manifestations in order to acquire "life" and "image"' (1988: 163). *Ma dutu* 'signifies a hierarchical relationship between a superior entity and an inferior entity' (ibid.: 149), including kinship relationships. *Ma dutu* relationships are 'intrinsically hierarchical', and it is through them that one acquires the 'image and body' that are essential for life (ibid.). These concepts, body, image and life, 'not only refer to ideas about the human person, but also to the values which guide the maintenance of relations of *ma dutu* without which the person would not be complete' (ibid.: 150). Image (or reputation) and life are also necessary 'to maintain the society as a whole' (ibid.: 163). They are distinguished from one another in terms of their ritual sequences and symbolic associations:

> For example, the contexts in which the transfer of life is the dominant concern, such as the cultivation of rice, the harvest of the sago palm, and also pregnancy and birth, are marked by the cycle of the moon as a timing device, by cool, dark, and quiet circumstances, and by the contrast between woman and man as the basic form of kin classification. On the other hand, contexts in which reputation is the dominant value, such as in hunting, fishing and warfare, are marked by the heat of the sun and the contrast between elder brother and younger brother as the basic form of kin classification. (Ibid.: 150)

Ma dutu relationships also concern the ancestors, contact with whom evidently entails access to the sacred.

Sherry Ortner (1981) and Bruce Kapferer (1988) have worked along similar lines. Ortner, writing on gender relations in Polynesia and their connection with what she calls the 'prestige system', argues that there exists the type of situation we have already encountered (see Chapter 4), in which 'kinship', that is, consanguineal relations, especially bilateral ones, encompass marriage:

> most people marry kin; marriage performs few functions and establishes few relations not already performed or established by kinship; and it is kinship (specifically, descent) rather than marriage that generates rank and prestige. [...] The high culturally assigned status of women as kin thus encompasses their lower status as wives, and produces an overall *cultural* respect, or at least lack of disrespect, for women in general. Sisters are more respected than wives, *and* women in general appear to be seen more. (1981: 394, original emphasis)

Although no doubt appreciating this use of a Dumontian idea, Tcherkézoff (1993a; also 1994) points out that the prestige system is not necessarily male-oriented. In Samoa, for instance, it would be truer to see it oriented towards 'sisters', who encompass 'brothers' in a hierarchical relation. This interpretation is based partly on linguistic evidence, the term for 'sister' also being that for the brother–sister relationship, partly on the life-giving powers of the sister, and partly on the ritual device of wrapping the brother's exchange goods (meat etc.) in the sister's (mats). Most significantly, titles can be transmitted through women (sisters) alone, but not through men alone. The value of men becomes apparent on a secondary level, one of power, where the brother can chastise his sister for adultery or marriage within the village. Similarly, wives are designated according to their husbands' statuses. Thus one can identify hierarchical oppositions here between sisters and wives, and between sisters and brothers (male and female), both, contrary to Tcherkézoff's preferences, apparently existing entirely within the ideology.

Tcherkézoff also dismisses Shore's ambitious Needhamite analysis with respect to Samoan material (Shore 1981), which he bases on two global Yin-Yang type categories that Tcherkézoff sees as wholly misconceived both ethnographically and theoretically. Entering pairs like male/female and sister/wife in the same columns of the Needhamite table makes only wives seem female. Conversely, sisters are opposed to wives as culture is to nature. At times, Shore's analysis has some tantalizing glimpses of a recognition of hierarchical opposition, as in this statement of the obvious: 'In our own culture, at least, "man" or "the male" is linguistically and genetically implied to be generic to gender itself, with "woman" or "the female" as a second sex, an afterthought in creation, a derivative class ...' (1981: 192). However, most of his analysis is more conventional, and more in the manner of Lévi-Strauss than Needham, let alone Tcherkézoff or Barraud. For Shore, the distinction between male and female is also one between promiscuity (a male prerogative) and chastity (a female requirement), the former having more importance for gender definition than the latter. 'For females ... public control is over her sexuality. For males, public control is over his gender definition' (*sic*; ibid.: 211). Failure in the first produces the whore, failure in the second the male transvestite or *fa'afafine*, whom Shore explicitly sees as a third sex (ibid.: 209).

For Tcherkézoff, however, representations of the third sex are transcendent figures who overcome distinctions (1994: II, and n.15). The sister on Samoa, who encompasses her male brother, would thus appear to have a rival for this transcendental role. Schöeffel also comes in for Tcherkézoff's criticism (1979, 1987; cf. Tcherkézoff 1994: II), despite using something akin to hierarchical opposition for the *mana/pule* or sacred power/secular power distinction. The problem again comes from trying to match this analogously with the gender distinction, reintroducing Needham by the back door, so to speak, and with him a substantialism in that the respective powers are seen to be transmitted by the two genders separately. In fact, says Tcherkézoff, it is the brother–sister relationship that is the 'agent' of both, just as the titles themselves express relationships between holder and group, group and ancestors, etc.

Like Geirnaert, Valeri, who worked among the Huaulu, a tiny society of fewer than two hundred persons in northern Seram, Indonesia (1989, 1990), recognizes the implications of Dumont's work and, like her, he resists applying it to his own. Here, there is 'a permanent tension' between two 'images of social relations', which Valeri distinguishes as 'autonomy and heteronomy' (1990: 61, 59). The image of heteronomy concerns the four clans, one of which, also called Huaulu, stands for the society as a whole, although the other clans are equally essential. The society is bounded and segmented, its internal order fixed. In the image of autonomy, the four clans are equal in status and self-sufficient, their relationships being unfixed and negotiable. Which image is appealed to depends on circumstance as much as context, that is, specific incidents involving resistance to authority and threats to secede as much as ritual occasions or myth (the latter nonetheless enshrines the contrast). Valeri does not think Dumont's ideas are applicable here:

> I must emphasize that we have here a contrast between two images of social relations, not merely a contrast between structural levels or between an 'empirical' level of forces that tend to be divisive and a properly cultural, normative counterpart predicated on ideas of hierarchy. The tension to which I am referring would not be adequately described by such canonical anthropological contrasts as that of 'interest' and 'value' [Sahlins], or that of 'instrumental' and 'expressive', 'power' and 'ritual' [Geertz], nor even by something akin to Dumont's encompassing subordination of *artha* by *dharma*. (Ibid.: 61, references omitted)

And further: 'In sum, while the relationship of the two values is asymmetric, it is not one of unproblematic "encompassment": it defies the socio-logical [*sic*] totalitarianism of Chinese boxes or of Russian matrioshkas.' Instead, there is 'an ever-recurring and never resolved tension' (ibid.: 61-2).

The main *kahua* feast of the Huaulu shows how the dichotomy works itself out. The pressures not just to attend but to take part are considerable, and in this respect *kahua* is a ritual of heteronomy. But while some of its parts express this, others are representations of extreme violence, that is, of male autonomy, and furthermore it is not the 'structural chief' but the big man, whose achievement is personal, who has the best chance of persuading people to attend. Perhaps the impossibility of resolving the tension by reducing one image to the other means that equality (i.e. the equality of the images) is again the encompassing value in this case. For Barraud and Platenkamp, however (commenting on this paper, 1990: 114-15, 118), Huaulu individualism culminates in the taking of non-Huaulu heads. Since the strength to do this comes from the ancestors, and since the strength thus acquired is dedicated to them in the *kahua* ritual, which at the same time renews society, this individualism is ultimately subordinated to the society as a whole. 'The reproduction of Huaulu society requires the subordination of the relationship between non-Huaulu and Huaulu to the relationship between the Huaulu and their ancestors' (ibid.: 116). In Valeri's terms, by contrast, the former relationship stresses autonomy, the latter heteronomy.

In another paper (1989), on the dichotomy between moieties designated Siwa and Lima in certain Indonesian societies, including Huaulu, Valeri can again be seen teetering on the brink of a Dumontian approach to his material but hesitating to jump over the precipice. Some key oppositions in Huaulu cosmology are male/female, inside/outside, and social order/wilderness. However, the first pair are associated differentially with the second and third. Men are variously associated with the wild and thus the outside through head-hunting, and also with social order and thus with the inside. Women are associated more with the wild and with the outside (of the village), which is where they go to menstruate and to give birth. The outside is also the place of maximum gender separation in that male head-hunting and female menstruation and birth-giving endanger each other. The inside (of the village) is the arena of gender compatibility and of their cooperation in productive tasks (especially the engendering of children). Valeri is explicit (ibid.: 124, 125) that the village and its communal house represent 'the global society' and that, being male-dominated, this means that 'the mediation of male and female is associated with the male category'. In his words, here it is the male category that is 'unmarked', in the wild the female category. However, he is equally clear that what he calls 'mediation' takes place inside the village only, in male-dominated space.

This explains his explicit reluctance (ibid.: 125) to follow Dumont and Tcherkézoff to the limit. This reluctance is actually expressed in relation to another opposition, that between the veranda and the kitchen of the house. The former is male space, though also on the outside, while the latter is female space, though also representing the interior of the house. As such, the latter is 'where the heirlooms representing the identity of a lineage and *even the trophies of male hunting* are preserved' (ibid.). The words I have emphasised carry the key to the conundrum. Masculinity pervades the whole house, even though the 'female' kitchen is also located there, while conversely there is nothing female about the male veranda. Having got so far, Valeri's reluctance to go the whole hog is surprising. The further example he gives, when affinal alliance groups are called 'verandas', that of the wife-givers being 'male', that of the wife-takers 'female', may be seen as a different ideological level, one bearing on the relations of the house with the outside. It is anyway dependent on the role of the house as wife-giver or wife-taker in any particular alliance.

Valeri mentions other examples in this essentially comparative article. 'In much of central Seram the undivided Lima moiety, identified with maleness and center, is opposed to a female and outer Siwa moiety, which consists of two opposite sections, one called "black", the other "white"' (ibid.: 126), colours that are themselves associated with the two sexes. Again, mediation is a male, not a female phenomenon:

> The crucial fact is that the male Lima, in its unity, may be viewed as neutralizing the contrast of male and female that seems to define the female Siwa. There is thus an analogy between the local level (where the male inside, which socially mediates the opposition of male and female, is opposed to the female outside, which does not) and the global level (where the male moiety, Lima, fully mediates the opposition of male and female by neutralizing it, while the Siwa moiety does not, because it is divided into a male and a female section). (Ibid.: 127)

In the community of Maraina, similarly, there are two moieties, Ilela Potoa and Ilela Kiita, related to each other as senior and junior. Each moiety is divided into four units. The highest-ranking unit of the senior moiety provides the Lord of the Land, who represents the entire community. Thus this moiety and unit can be seen to stand for the whole, as well as being a part of that whole. By adding the whole to the four units, one reaches the number five, i.e. Lima, which is associated with the centre all over this region, while Siwa, nine, through its duplication of the number four, represents the differentiation and greater disorder associated with the outside (Valeri draws on the general ethnography of the area in making this statement rather than on Maraina as such).

There is plenty of evidence of an opposite Siwa view, based on the sterility of the male domain represented by the number five (Lima) and the inside: the domain of Siwa, being divided between male and female, is self-reproducing in a way that the domain of Lima can never be. Male mediation therefore equals sterility and incompleteness. However, this tends to become a female-centred model in which female fertility becomes mediating, with symbolically female rulers at the centre. At root, each moiety regards itself as superior and encompassing in respect of the other, as the Durkheimians basically believed (see

Hertz 1973: 8). Valeri himself stresses that there is no question here of complementary opposites:

> These opposites are already present in each moiety; they need not be exchanged. But each moiety is dependent on the inverted image of the hierarchy of these elements (an image realized by the opposite moiety) to produce its own hierarchy. [...] Each moiety needs an Other to which it can attach the negative terms of its own system of oppositions; the reciprocal relation between moieties consists in each moiety being the Other of its own Other, although it refuses to acknowledge the fact. (Ibid.: 135, 136)

One way in which this relation is expressed is by head-hunting: the head represents the opposite moiety, and its capture represents incorporation into the centre of one's own. Since it takes place on the outside, it also represents the inferior values of disorder, and of disunity between both the moieties themselves and between male and female. Once transferred to the inside, however, where it becomes the centrepiece in a ritual dance involving the whole village, it brings about mediation between male and female, as well as overcoming the disorder of the outside and fusing one's own moiety with the opposite one.

Valeri's earlier work on Hawaii (1985), which is largely historical, can also be shown to demonstrate the applicability of Dumont's model, though again Valeri's own views range from the diffident to the dismissive. It is somewhat ironic, therefore, to find that he has been subjected to criticism from Mosko (1994b: 51 ff.) on the basis of his alleged adoption of precisely this model. In fact, although in his major statement on this theme (1985) Valeri does talk of hierarchy and use the term 'encompassment' in relation to it, in citing Dumont he does not so much as mention hierarchical opposition, but instead criticizes Dumont for the inaccuracy of his account of Polynesia, as well as drawing distinctions between this area and India (see above, Chapter 6). Mosko's criticisms therefore do not seem to match Valeri's intentions entirely.

The other irony is that there is actually no shortage of hierarchical oppositions in Valeri's material on Hawaii. Major oppositions dealt with are male/female, gods/men and sacrifice/genealogy, which can be taken together (Valeri 1985: 110-14). Both gods and humans are hierarchically ranked, and one must sacrifice to a god that corresponds to one's own status. Moreover, while the major gods are the gods of all Hawaiians, the minor ones are the gods of different social groups (some of them occupational); Valeri explicitly refers to their relationship as one of encompassment. Purity also pervades the hierarchy as a value. Men of higher rank are purer than their social inferiors, a relationship that Valeri calls metonymic (indicating a part–whole relationship), through which 'inferiors can benefit from a complete relationship with the divine without having to realize it themselves' (ibid.: 110). Men are also purer than women, as are their sacrifices: here too, 'women have only a marginal relation to the sacrificial system; hence male sacrifice makes the absence, or the limited extent, of female sacrifice possible' (ibid.). In effect, superiors are sacrificed for inferiors and men for women, the second of each pair being dependent on the first.

In addition, it seems that women are not ordinarily allowed to perform sacrifices themselves, though they can supply a sacrifice to female gods (they can be a sacrifier but not a sacrificer, in Valeri's words). Even in rituals of concern to women, the sacrificer is a man, and in any ritual where male and female sacrifices are both made, it appears that female sacrifices come after male ones. Only in sorcery can women sacrifice: and this is explicitly a marginal domain dominated by individual interests rather than social ones. And even where a woman's social rank can overcome her gender and allow her a male role, she is still restricted in a way that men are not by not being able to eat the sacrifice herself. Goddesses, finally, are fewer than the gods and less hierarchized. We can therefore hardly agree with Mosko (1994b: 73-4) when he suggests that women played an equal role here with men in the sacrifice. That women are represented should occasion no surprise: their co-presence with men is of a piece with their encompassment by them. It is not their presence or absence that is significant, but the quality of their presence in comparison with that of the men. Valeri produces ample evidence that it is less.

Valeri goes on to say that women nonetheless achieve equality with men in 'the genealogically determined hierarchy', which relates principally to birth and is contrasted with the 'sacrificial hierarchy' (1985: 113). In his criticism, Mosko seizes on this as an example of mere antithesis without encompassment (1994b: 73). However, what is certainly a level of distinction is clearly subordinate to the encompassing level of male sacrifice, which is explicitly said to be 'superior to genealogy' (Valeri 1985: 114). That the two are related is shown by the statement that 'it is possible to represent childbearing as woman's sacrifice and sacrifice as men's childbearing', to which Valeri immediately adds, 'only the second metaphor is strongly emphasized' (ibid.). This is because it expresses the transcendental conversion of biological reproduction by women into social reproduction by men. Thus although this situation is clearly one of distinction between childbearing and sacrifice—'women's exclusion from sacrificial reproduction is symmetrical to men's exclusion from childbearing' (ibid.)—this distinction disappears in passing between levels to a situation in which only sacrifice is represented (and therefore encompasses genealogy). And not only is this a hierarchical opposition, it also implicates another, that between the genders. Other details confirm the encompassment here:

first, 'sacrifice implies a *direct* relationship with the gods, in contrast to the indirect relationship involved in genealogy' (ibid., original emphasis); secondly, because eating was associated with sacrifice, women could never eat with men or eat the foods reserved for the sacrifice, such as pig and coconut; and thirdly, 'women's role in reproduction involves the shedding of blood and therefore impurity, which ... disqualifies them from a direct relationship with the gods' (ibid.).

In another of his criticisms, Mosko focuses on this last point, suggesting that menstruation and parturition 'constitute no less a disjunction of the sexes in the genealogical system than women's participation with men in the *hale o Papa* rites represents their conjunction' (1994b: 74). Actually, given the evidence above—and provided one treats the conjunction as encompassing—this is a fairly precise description of a hierarchical opposition. Mosko's concentration on this ritual is precisely due to the prominent place of women in it, since it is principally connected with fertility. From Valeri's description (1985: 330 ff.), however, it would seem to be designed to ensure women's suitability for reproduction by assimilating their impure, actual childbirth to the pure, non-sexual reproduction through sacrifice of the men. In Valeri's words (ibid.: 331): 'It is precisely in this way that the ideal reproduction of the species by men translates into its empirical reproduction by women ... .' Again, therefore, we have a hierarchical opposition in which not only do male, social forms of reproduction encompass female, physical forms, but the ideal encompasses the actual, as Dumont so often suggested.

Another objection raised by Mosko is that male blood may also be spilled in the shrines to the gods: why is this not polluting? Valeri makes it clear (1985: 337-8) that this was connected with the taming of initially violent gods, who were offered a blood sacrifice first, followed by a bloodless one, as part of this ritual process. This can be interpreted as an attempt to make the gods accessible by humans by satisfying them as much as to make humans acceptable to the gods through the purity of their sacrifice.

One other encompassing opposition is worth discussing, since it too enters into Mosko's criticism (1994b: 65-6). This relates to the distinction between the kings and the prophets or *kaula*. Mosko focuses on the fact that the latter, although they can be male, are mainly associated with women and goddesses, again allegedly proving equality between the genders. Though marginal like sorcerers and associated with the lower ranks in society, prophets also differ from sorcerers, who are thought 'to pursue individual desires that are irreducible to social norms' (Valeri 1985: 138). Instead, the prophet 'transcends society, because he is free from all desire, or rather, because his desire has only the deity as its object' (ibid.: 139). Moreover, 'having reached the deity, [prophets] become consubstantial with him' (ibid.), and do so directly: 'The king, on the other hand, coincides with the god only to the extent that he coincides with society ... .' And while the king is 'the sacrifier par excellence', as such acting for the whole society, the prophet 'has no need to sacrifice', given his 'direct relationship with the god' (ibid.). There are obvious similarities here with the situation of the renouncer in India. Of greater immediate significance, in view of Mosko's criticism, is the distinction in terms of ideological dependence: while the king, like society, depends on the sacrifice to attain the divine, the non-social prophet does not. Moreover, the latter stands for values that transcend society, while the king's ritual actions simply reproduce society.

An article by Traube on the Mambai of East Timor (1989) combines a similar recognition of Dumont's perspective with a reluctance to accept it entirely. This is despite the fact that she starts out by posing the question 'of how dual categories may be socially realized as hierarchical relationships' (1989: 321). The idea of a primordial past is also present: 'Ritual exchange obligations project the narrativized past on to the present in the form of a primordial whole that both opposes and includes its parts' (ibid.). This is linked to different sorts of knowledge. 'Knowledge that refers only to existing conditions is defined as partial and incomplete and is opposed to an encompassing form of knowledge that comprehends the present as the outcome of temporal processes' (ibid.).

This temporality is Traube's basic reason for not wanting to adopt Dumont's approach entirely, for she sees in it a devotion to synchrony that is not entirely apt in the present case. This neglects the prominence Tcherkézoff gives to the idea of origins (see previous chapter). There is the familiar superiority of wife-givers, which is based on their status as the original sources of women and is associated with maleness. This, of course, concerns the relations of the group with the outside, in order to obtain women. Internally, conversely, it is femaleness which is associated with origins, being both the inside and the original source from which the male rulers of the outside obtained their right to rule. A part–whole relation of encompassment can be identified in both cases, in which the past is also implicated as encompassing the present. That past was also a time of unity, now dissolved into 'complementary but unequal parts' (ibid.: 325) whose obligations to one another express their inequality (as wife-givers and wife-takers, for instance). Periodical rituals seek to recreate this past, represented variously by the metaphor of the single trunk, in opposition to several 'tips' (to use a favourite botanical metaphor in eastern Indonesia); by the cult house, in opposition to the various dwellings into which each group is divided; by the elder brother who guards that house, in opposition to the many younger brothers who have parted from him and formed branches of their own; and by wife-givers as the original source of women, in opposition to the consecutive row of wife-takers, wife-takers' wife-takers, etc., who all depend on them ultimately for wives. The cult house is the site of these periodical rituals of unity, which, however, according to the author, do not represent a return to the past. Rather, the house itself simultaneously represents a past, a wholeness 'that remains lost' (ibid.: 328), and the origins of separation. It would therefore seem to be concerned as much with the renewal of society as with the temporary reconstruction of the original unity (cf. Geirnaert, above).

This overall view contrasts to some extent with the concerns of Tcherkézoff, de Coppet, Barraud etc. with particular rites and ritual stages. Traube concentrates on the part–whole, encompassing relation between primordial unity and present division, a relation which must take place in a temporal frame. It is, however, still linked to ultimate authority, since it is privileged access to knowledge about the past that gives the ritual elders their power. She ends by affirming that 'categorical asymmetry rests on the capacity of certain terms to both include and oppose their complements' (ibid.: 341), and even opposes this to the conventional structuralist notion of a whole being a union of two equal parts (as exemplified by Lévi-Strauss 1956).

Fox's paper in the same volume (1989) begins with a similar desire to modify the Lévi-Straussian approach on grounds of its excessive simplicity. He too relates dichotomies between moieties to a stage following the initial period of unity, stressing that they themselves do not represent primordial time. His concern is to challenge the idea of dual organization in ritual and kinship as heuristically useful and to replace it with abstract features of a sort that reminds one of some of Needham's work and may indeed have been inspired by it originally. His overall goal is actually to take the treatment of dual symbolic classification beyond Needham, but in a direction diametrically opposed to the path taken by the Dumontians in wishing to erect a coherent structure of oppositions based on analogy. According to him, 'a dual cosmology ... is characterized not by a simple pairing of elements but by the analogical concordance of elements within pairs according to some criterion of asymmetry' (1989: 43). At the same time, there is a recognition of the possibility of part–whole relations and of encompassment.

The features he refers to are parallelism, recursive complementarity, categorical asymmetry, category reversal and analogical crossover. Parallelism, as found within ritual language all over eastern Indonesia, takes the form of a simple linguistic dualism without reference to any asymmetry. Recursive complementarity refers to little more than the propensity for certain key oppositions, such as male/

female or left/right, to appear in a variety of situations, with the proviso that 'anything that is categorized according to one component of a complementary pair can *potentially* contain elements of its complement' (ibid.: 46, original emphasis). Categorical asymmetry refers not simply to the difference of value of each of the poles of an opposition, but to the encompassing quality of the superior pole when it stands for the whole domain of discourse. The asymmetry can be reversed, but for Fox this signifies contexts of disorder and subversion, not the emergence of the less valued pole from its encompassment at an inferior level of the ideology. In reversal, the values of the poles are altered, which is not the case for Dumont (see above, Chapter 3). But values need not be altered for Fox either: the more valued pole of one opposition may be associated with the less valued pole of another. This Fox calls analogical cross-over, and is his solution to the conundrum presented by bicolumnar tables, where the poles of particular oppositions are not regularly associated with one another (see above, Chapter 2). He remarks:

> The discrepancies between different sets of complementary categories, extended too far for coherence's sake, can only lead to evident contradictions. In eastern Indonesian societies, evident contradiction is often avoided by a continual process of mixing metaphors. Instead of allowing any set of complements to be extended to the point of contradiction, other complements are introduced to develop the system. (1989: 50)

In the end, Fox declines to go all the way with Dumont because of the absence in Indonesia of any overarching hierarchical opposition to resemble purity/impurity, which Dumont had uncovered in India. [1] Instead there are many oppositions, all of which may contribute to the structure. 'In these terms, hierarchy is not a principle but an outcome, the result of the application of several principles' (ibid.: 51-2).

But in any case, encompassment is not the only determinant of hierarchy for Fox. He prefers the idea of an 'order of precedence', a phrase also drawn from Dumont, though Fox applies it sequentially to different stages of a taxonomic hierarchy rather than to an opposition involving encompassment. Thus the segmentation of a clan into lineages can be seen as a sequential series in which younger branches split off from the original clan, which is elder to them, but in which these branches are themselves elder in relation to their segments. The relation involved in cycles of affinal groups exchanging women through asymmetric alliance, in which each group is male as wife-giver but female as wife-taker, is another example. Of course, as with the *varna* scheme or the three ends of life, these apparently multi-polar examples can, and for the Dumontian should, be seen as a series of oppositions which have to be taken separately. In fact, no particular advantage seems to have been gained over Dumont's model, which would express these facts much more simply in terms of elder encompassing younger, wife-givers encompassing wife-takers, or pure encompassing impure.

A more decisive attitude is displayed by Evens (1993), who has recently suggested that the dichotomy between mythical and rational forms of thought can be seen as a hierarchical opposition. Mythical thought is itself a form of rationality encompassing what Evens calls instrumental rationality, from which it is distinguished by being unconcerned with the law of non-contradiction, and more concerned with ends than with means. Because of the latter, mythical rationality is also directed towards ethics and involves the subject in a choice. It is therefore concerned with value, whereas instrumental rationality is involved with fact. However, while instrumental rationality, with its concern for logic, never makes use of myth, mythical rationality may and does make use of instrumental logic. Hence the latter is less bounded, in accordance with its encompassing nature. Instrumental rationality only emerges at all because of its own exclusion of the mythical, of value.

Evens calls on the Dinka for ethnographic support here (after Lienhardt 1961). Although prepared to recognize ailments as 'natural' up to a point, if these become too severe they invoke Divinity or Deng (i.e. the supernatural) as the cause. This involves Dinka in contradiction, in that causes that are radically different in kind are seen as underlying the same phenomenon. However, the contradiction involved is that of a hierarchical opposition: 'By apprehending the natural as also supernatural, the Dinka projects reality in terms of encompassment by the divine' (Evens 1993: 115). Further, 'while the Dinka draws a distinction between afflictions as material or spiritual, he finds that all afflictions are, if not especially, at least finally, spiritual' (ibid.: 116). Thus although Dinka are faced with a choice as regards proximate causes, it is divine solutions involving mythical rationality that they ultimately seek, since it is only through them that the removal of both types of cause becomes possible.

Innocence

It will be seen from the discussion above (this chapter and Chapter 5) that Dumont's notion of hierarchical opposition is far from having received universal acceptance, some commentators rejecting it outright, others regarding it as merely one possible form of opposition among several, not only logically but also ethnographically, while yet others have been prepared to accept it up to a point but no further. Yet that it deserves a place in our concepts is assured not only by Dumont's own work but by the fact that it has sometimes been identified in apparent ignorance of what he has written.

This is perhaps true of Gell's work on Polynesia, discussed in the previous chapter. Another example is Mimica's description of Oma-lyce, the primordial human being among the Iqwaye of New Guinea (1988: 84-5). He is represented as being dichotomized so that the front of his head, hand or whole body is male, their backs female: but this is duality within unity, for the body as a whole is always male. Gillison (1980) describes the gendering of space in Gimi society, where the village centre, which is dominated by the men's house, is surrounded by individual family houses which are principally the domain of the women, while the village as a whole is surrounded by the forest, another male space that is also linked to the wider cosmos and transcendent values. Like most of the authors in the same volume *Nature, Culture and Gender*, MacCormack and Strathern 1980), Gillison is mostly concerned to use her material as a counter-example to the Lévi-Straussian association of men with culture and women in nature. However, the hierarchization of space is also apparent, women being confined (a Gimi notion, apparently) between collective, transcendent male spaces in the centre of the village and around it. In South America too, Crocker distinguishes oppositions among the Bororo of Brazil that are associated with what is 'transcendent, complete, and timeless' from those between right and left, male and female, etc. which also exist in the society (and which Crocker actually associates theoretically with Needham's ideas; see 1977: 143-4). Whether he would be prepared to identify either sort of opposition as hierarchical is unclear (cf. Dumont 1979: 817: 19; also Lévi-Strauss 1944: 267-8, discussed above, Chapter 3).

Apart from Tcherkézoff's early work on the Nyamwezi, the conscious application of Dumont's ideas to material from Africa is rare. Yet examples can be drawn from the innocent examples presented by many authors, some well known. Giles mentions what is clearly a hierarchical opposition involving different sorts of spirits on the Swahili coast (1987: 240, n.22). The familiar term *jini* may mean 'spirit' in general, but it also stands for sea-dwelling spirits, then being opposed to *shaitani* or *pepo*, synonyms referring to land-dwelling spirits. In addition, *jini* in this sense are said to 'have religion', that is, they are associated with Islam and Christianity, which are prestige religions here.

Willis's article in a collection of essays concerning ideas of evil (*The Anthropology of Evil*, David Parkin 1985), especially in relation to good (which, as we have seen, sometimes subsumes evil, sometimes not), moves closer to Dumont in this respect. He comments:

Many cultures have been and are aware of dualism as a cognitive fact and see it as a problem to be transcended through various techniques and practices. Such doctrines are to be found not only in the sophisticated philosophies of the East or in the esoteric traditions of European mysticism and magic, but also in many a small-scale, non-literate society. Victor Turner has richly described Ndembu ritual aimed at resolving clusters of perceived oppositions in a moment of spiritual wholeness. (1985: 211)

Willis points out that this 'wholeness' may come about through what Dumont would call encompassment: 'For instance, the Nuer of the southern Sudan are aware of a basic duality opposing Spirit and Creation, but they are also aware, perhaps in moments of heightened understanding, that Creation is a part of Spirit in unitary wholeness' (ibid.: 212, after Evans-Pritchard). He relates this to Evans-Pritchard's 'context of situation' in a Nuer's definition of where he stands in his social structure, which influenced Dumont too (see above, Chapter 4). Among the neighbouring and closely related Dinka too, although Nhialic or Divinity is the source of all things, another supernatural being, Macardit, appears as the source of disasters (drought, sterility etc.; Lienhardt 1961). Although Lienhardt recognizes Macardit's ultimate lack of independence with regard to Nhialic, he regards him as an aspect and not as the subordinate pole of a hierarchical opposition.

As regards Willis's own work among the Fipa of Tanzania, this sort of hierarchy seems at first sight to be absent. Ordinarily, there is 'little emphasis on classificatory distinctions in Fipa society, including the anthropologically classic symbolic oppositions of "right" and "left", [and] males and females, contrary to the segregationist norm prevailing over most of Africa, sit down together to eat meals' (ibid.: 214). Elsewhere (1989: 142), he says that the distinctions between men and women are merged in the concept of the person: every Fipa 'participates symbolically and equally in the complementarity of male and female attributes which is part of the cosmological dualism that unites bodily "head" and "loins" in dynamic and reciprocal opposition.' However, the village women are dominant at childbirth, to the extent of treating the pregnant woman's husband as a servant (1985: 218 n.11). Similarly, 'the Us/Them opposition ... which Fipa perceive as one between Settlers and Strangers, is culturally "played down" in favour of the continuing process, by which as a deliberate matter of social and State policy, outsiders are incorporated into the society' (Howell and Willis 1989: 23; also Willis 1989: 140). Thus one might say that the Settlers ultimately encompass the Strangers who become assimilated to them.

Fipa colour symbolism, of red, white and black, also suggests hierarchy within unity (1985: 218-20). Red has contrasting positive and negative values, as has black, but white is unitary. Red and black are never opposed to each other in the same ritual context because the former is identified with the public domain, the latter with the occult. They are only opposed to white, and separately. Willis gives this structure the form of an isosceles triangle divided down the middle between red and black, with white at its apex. He remarks that this is very similar to the Ndembu colour system which Victor Turner made so famous (e.g. 1966). Given the relation between black and red, Dumont would probably prefer a segmented, hierarchical image like that for the *varna* scheme instead. Tcherkézoff, on the other hand, regards red among the Nyamwezi (also of Tanzania), as a 'ritual operator', not as a separate pole (1987: 51ff., especially p. 56).

Another body of work with evident potential in this context is Bloch's studies of the Merina of Madagascar. Bloch is generally aware of Dumont's work, which he often cites approvingly. Nonetheless, in discussing the relationship between hierarchy and equality, and between status and power, on Madagascar he prefers a neo-Marxist, dialectical approach to Dumont's concentration on ideology. For Bloch, who is careful to avoid the 'vulgar Marxist' reduction of ideology to the ethnocentric concepts of class, what he calls 'the economic and political base' (1989a: 47) can still influence the ideology as well as vice versa. On the whole Bloch's Marxism is less concerned with materialist explanations than with the use of ideology to mystify power in societies like the Merina, which were kingdoms in pre-French days.

Despite this, there are clearly areas where, although Bloch does not mention Dumont, his material practically invites a Dumontian rather than Marxist approach. One example is the opposition he describes between the values of ancestry and the potentialities of the life of individuals (see especially 1985; 1989b). There are many other contrasts linked to this basic pair. The ancestors are represented by massive tombs that ideally unite all members of the deme (cognatic descent group) upon death in such a manner that their individual identities are lost. Land is also associated with the ancestors, as is the rice grown upon it, and neither should be alienated outside the deme; as a result, there is an ideal of endogamy. In addition, rice must be consumed in any proper meal, and it is associated with being human (one dehumanizing objection raised to the French colonizers, Bloch tells us, was their preference for bread over rice).

Opposed to this set of values is another set denoted by the term *harena* and focusing on the individual. *Harena* is connected with the enjoyment of life and with the differentiation of individual members of the deme. In this domain it is accepted that individuals may become more or less wealthy on their own initiative. This wealth is expressed primarily in cattle, which are also linked to the virility of their (apparently generally male) owners. It is also alienable, and flows especially between affines, who are the antithesis of the ideal consanguineal unity of the deme. However, such property must be dispersed before its owner's death, since, once one has become an ancestor, such markers of differentiation are no longer appropriate (for a similar reason, says Bloch, there is a prohibition on individuals planting trees that are likely to outlive themselves). Thus whereas ancestry is linked to the moral, *harena* denotes what is amoral at best, though it is still necessary to humans' physical reproduction in this world.

Another basic opposition is that between wet and dry. Both are linked to the ancestors, but in different ways. Blessings from the ancestors, which provide life, are conveyed by water being blown on to junior members of the deme by the elders acting on behalf of the ancestors. Wet is also linked to the process of the putrefaction of bodies after death, which is clearly a dangerous, liminal period. However, putrefaction also diminishes this wetness, and the ancestors themselves are dry in their permanent state, represented by the bones that are ultimately placed in the tomb. Wet is also linked to nature and the vitality of life, to cattle and to the Vazimba, mythical creatures who originally possessed the land but were subdued by the Merina in the primordial time as part of their own process of becoming human. Another link concerns kinship, which in this context is seen as matrilineal and matrilateral rather than cognatic (the Vazimba stressed female links). At birth, children are seen as being physically linked to their mothers alone, only becoming cognatically related later in life, especially after initiation, which separates boys from the world of the women.

Here is one indication that the values of ancestry encompass those of *harena*: as one grows older, one becomes more like an ancestor in becoming cognatically linked. Ancestry, we can take it, is linked with transcendent values: here eternity, which transcends the temporary nature of both worldly and individual lives; and unity, which transcends the 'anti-descent' nature of the 'individuation' of worldly existences (Bloch 1989b: 179). And although the ancestors convey life through their blessings, the wetness that symbolizes this is converted into dryness in the tomb. Another way in which this transcendence is marked is by the massive payments made by sons-in-law to their wives' fathers. This is linked to the ideological opposition to the movement of people away from ancestral land. In the main, two categories of people are associated with such moves. The first is traders, who are associated anyway professionally with *halena*. The second are women marrying virilocally outside the deme. The payments from their husbands are compensation for this violation of the ideal. In the case of men moving away from the deme to marry uxorilocally, they themselves become responsible for such payments.

But the ultimate symbol of this reduction of *harena* to ancestry is the violence with which cattle are killed at rites of passage. The consumption of cattle on these occasions is assimilated with consumption of the deceased, and therefore with union with the ancestors. Before this union can take place, however, the vitality associated with individuation, which is represented by the cattle, must be overcome. The cattle are therefore provoked and attacked viciously before being tied up and despatched with little ceremony, except that they are laid down to the north-east, the direction of the ancestors.

As Bloch himself sums up matters (1985: 644): 'The living may have vitality but it must be conquered by descent. The vital element must be subordinated and consumed by the descent element in order to be strong and moral.' In other words, both vitality and descent are necessary to Merina existence. However, it is the values that are associated with the latter that are clearly transcendent and which, in Dumontian language, encompass the former. In effect, life in this world is pregnant with distinctions between these two levels, but it is also a voyage towards a situation in which the distinction is overcome in favour of the encompassment of vitality by ancestry. [2]

Another example of particular interest is the work of an Indian anthropologist who is especially concerned to 'defy the European monopoly of scientific method' (Uberoi 1984: 9). This is almost a hymn to the ideological form that underlies Dumont's ideas, though there is no reference to them, nor to him, as such. What strikes Uberoi is evidently the similarity of the 'non-official' science of Europe represented by Paracelsus, Goethe and Rudolf Steiner to the science of traditional India, both of which have been driven underground, but not eradicated, by the 'official' science of Copernicus, Galileo, Newton and Heisenberg. As well as Goethe's attempts to unify man and nature instead of separating them, with nature subordinate, we have the unity of fact and value (ibid.: 19). 'Goethe's scientific method ... is that of the unity in the duality', i.e. of the individual in the whole (ibid.: 32), and macrocosm and microcosm are related 'by difference as well as similarity' (ibid.: 66). Uberoi even traces the origins of 'official' science, which is what Dumont identifies as 'modern', back to virtually the same time and place, though he chooses Zwingli, not Calvin, as the 'prototype of modern man', to use Dumont's phrase (Uberoi 1984: 52; cf. Dumont 1982: 234).

The relevance of myth has already been discussed from time to time in this and the previous chapter, but there the association with hierarchical opposition was made explicitly by either authors or editors. There are other examples, however, where the association is concealed by the author's innocence. Among those who come close at times to hierarchical opposition without ever quite getting there must be numbered Lévi-Strauss. Given the importance to him of binary opposition in the analysis of myth especially, it is reasonable to pose the question whether the substitution of hierarchical opposition would produce results of a different nature (cf. Platenkamp 1988). Lévi-Strauss often represents oppositions as if they are irresolvable (for example, in his well-known analysis of the Asdiwal myth; 1967: 15), and he often seems puzzled, even disappointed, to find that certain oppositions seem not to be symmetric. We have already noted (Chapter 3, above) his reluctance to accept a hierarchical opposition when faced with one between Bororo moieties, and in his famous article 'Les organisations dualistes existent-elles?' (1956) he expresses further surprise over instances of obvious moiety inequality. And as we have seen (Chapter 3, above), it was left to Tcherkézoff (1987: 98-112) to show how his treatment of Osage classification in Chapter 5 of *The Savage Mind* (1966) could be taken further in the direction of hierarchical opposition.

However, a re-examination of his discussion of the Murngin creation myth (1966: 91-6, after Warner 1958) shows how contradictions can be resolved using hierarchical opposition. The following précis is my modification of Lévi-Strauss's own account (ibid.: 91):

> At the beginning of time, the Wawilak sisters set off on foot towards the sea. One was pregnant and the other carried her child with her. After the younger sister's child was born, they continued their journey and one day stopped near a water hole, the dwelling of the snake Yurlunggur. The older sister polluted the water with menstrual blood. This angered the snake, who brought the rains and caused a flood, afterwards swallowing the women and their children. When the snake raised himself, the waters covered the entire earth; when he lay down, the flood receded.

Lévi-Strauss connects this myth with the dramatic change in the seasons in this part of northern Australia, where the seven dry months rapidly change into five wet months, which, although necessary in ensuring vegetation for the succeeding dry season, are themselves a time of scarcity, difficulty of movement and low levels of social activity. The mythical associations with the different seasons yield a set of dichotomies such that the snake, maleness, the ability to fertilize and being initiated are all associated with the wet season and with flooding, while the sisters, femaleness, being fertilized and being uninitiated are all associated with the dry season and with dry land. Of the two sets of associations, the former is superior to the latter in each case, but for Lévi-Strauss there is a contradiction in that the superior rainy season is life-threatening, the inferior dry season that of collective life (this is also, of course, a dichotomy between nature and society). Taking each of the above oppositions separately, it is clear that the superior regularly encompasses the inferior: thus the snake swallows the sisters, which also indicates the initiated absorbing the uninitiated (sc. unclean; cf. Warner 1958: 387, quoted by Lévi-Strauss 1966: 93), the fertile fertilize the barren (i.e. the men possess the women), and famine eats up plenty.

In other words, what Lévi-Strauss calls 'two degrees of culture' (ibid.: 94) are for a Dumontian two differently valued ideological levels. Lévi-Strauss himself indicates the direction the resolution of this apparent contradiction might take, though he still leaves it in the end as a conundrum. As he points out (ibid.), 'on the natural plane ... the good season is subordinate to the bad, while on the social plane the relation between the corresponding terms is reversed.' Actually, the social plane and the good season must ultimately encompass the natural plane and the bad season: otherwise, neither social life nor natural life could continue. Thus although the earlier encompassments are valid, they relate to an ideological level that is subordinate overall. Not only might other myths be treated in the same way, so too might other instances where seasonal variation entails a dichotomy between social life and its relative absence, for example, the Eskimo (Mauss and Beuchat 1906) and the Nuer (Evans-Pritchard 1940: Ch. 2).

Other possible hierarchical oppositions occur in *The Savage Mind*. Lévi-Strauss notes (1966: 170) that among the Sauk Indians of North America, whereas 'members of the Oskush moiety ("the Blacks") had to complete all their enterprises, those of the Kishko moiety ("the Whites") might give up or turn back'. There is little more detail, but it is at least evident that one moiety has greater responsibilities, the other lesser ones. A footnote on different sorts of history (ibid.: 261-2) remarks that contradictions on one plane may be eliminated on another: it is tempting to replace 'plane' here with 'level'. Another example is Lévi-Strauss's distinction between cold and hot societies (ibid.: 233-42; cf. above, Chapter 1): in cold societies, which as far as possible suppress history, synchrony encompasses diachrony, whereas in hot societies, which recognize the past as something distinct, the reverse obtains. Finally, in his reply to Sartre (ibid.: Ch. 9) Lévi-Strauss refuses to follow his antagonist in seeing dialectical reason as separate from analytical reason and reduces the former to the latter. This amounts to a declaration that analytical reason encompasses dialectical reason (see above, Chapter 5).

Ethnic Relations: Another Application?

Among other possible applications of hierarchical opposition is the analysis of ethnic relations, or rather, perhaps, relations between ethnicities or ethnic identities. This, by definition, has a relational aspect and would seem to be a clear candidate for consideration in this context, though in fact studies on this topic from a Dumontian perspective are lacking. This is less the case with nationalism, which Dumont himself treated in terms of hierarchical oppositions (see above, Chapter 4), though in discussing the German situation it is noticeable that he used the more Durkheimain term 'ideology' than the now more common Anglo-Saxon term 'identity'. One other example is Kapferer who, in comparing Sri Lankan nationalism with that of his native Australia, shadows Dumont's whole development in taking seriously the precept that fieldwork in a different society can tell you a lot about your own. The hierarchical opposition in Sinhalese Buddhism between the values of the Buddha and the demonic, between reason and non-reason, are said to disappear in Australia, where it is rather manifestations of hierarchy that are seen as the embodiment of evil (1988: 11, 14). Of course, this simply means that the values of egalitarianism encompass those of hierarchy, not that Australians lack any sense of value, and therefore of hierarchy, in Dumontian terms. As Kapferer realizes (ibid.: 220 n. 3; cf. above, Chapter 5), one cannot escape from Dumont by simply postulating equality as a value.

That ethnicity has not attracted similar treatment so far may be due to the French flavour of hierarchical opposition, combined with the fact that ethnicity is hardly dealt with in French anthropology, whereas the Anglo-Saxon tradition, which has dealt with it extensively, is much more sceptical with regard to hierarchical opposition. But also, this tradition took a long time to see ethnicity as a matter of relations. For many decades after the Chicago school of sociologists virtually invented ethnicity as an academic topic in the 1920s and 1930s, [3] definitions of it were generally based on substantive traits, even where, as in Barth's studies of Pathan identity (1969a, 1969b), ethnic group organization was seen as being more constant. Culture then tended to become reduced to the adoption of behaviour appropriate to particular situations: as Benjamin remarks of the Temiar of West Malaysia, 'the particular cultural system borne by the individual at any one time is determined by the particular aboriginal territory in which he finds himself' (1967: 11; also Eriksen 1993: 65-6, on Mauritius). However, even Barth recognized a basic cultural inventory upon which ethnic group identity could focus. It was precisely the failure to maintain these minimal traits which led to the abandonment of Pathan identity in favour of Kohistani or Baluchi identities by particular individuals.

In the 1970s, the school of Edwin Ardener at Oxford, observing that ethnicities often define themselves in opposition to one another, developed a more relational approach. This tendency is perhaps best exemplified by the title of McDonald's work on the Breton movement: *We are not French!* (1990). This sort of relation may lend itself to encompassment: ethnic relations are frequently hierarchized, as with relations between minorities and the majority in a nation state. For example, although a large part of the Breton movement rejects a French identity for itself, it nonetheless has to put up with encompassment in many relations with the outside, as when the French government speaks for the whole country, or in passport and other official matters.

Similarly in the United States, a land primarily of immigrants of different origins, one's American identity mostly occupies the public sphere, while in private or on informal occasions one can assume an ethnic label indicating, if only vicariously through descent, one's origin outside the United States; there is then at least an implicit dichotomy between the hyphenated identity and being American. This also stresses the fact that Americanism is a creation of the New World, in opposition to the mostly Old World ethnicities with which immigrants arrived and which they frequently continue to claim. This origin does not make them any less created, but their creation has nothing to do with America, which on the contrary seeks to keep them within bounds. Thus the person who on one, especially formal and public level is purely American is on another, often more private level identifiable with an often older yet minority ethnicity to which Americanism is opposed in a hierarchical opposition. [4] A similar situation prevails in the case of the more assimilated Sami of Norway, who demonstrate an exclusive Norwegianness in the public sphere but allow some discreet expressions of Saminess at home which are opposed to it (language, for example; Eidheim 1969, 1971). Other Sami, however, resist assimilation and stress a separate identity through, for instance, a Sami parliament.

Indeed, the issue here and in many similar cases is whether to assimilate or whether to claim a distinct identity. One risk for a group seeking to assimilate is that they will merely be accorded a low status by the group they are assimilating to, so long as their origins in a different identity are remembered. This clearly seems to be the case for the assimilated Sami, and Eidheim uses the term 'stigma' frequently to describe their situation. There is thus a contrary incentive to remain separate, which motivates other Sami. In effect, assimilation and separation form a hierarchical opposition, though which pole will be seen as the encompassing one will depend on one's goals and perspectives. Indeed, one might say that, as with hierarchy and equality on occasions, here encompassment and distinction are themselves contrasted as values, and not just essential elements of the structural model called hierarchical opposition. For assimilating Sami, being Norwegian is the supreme value, Saminess being discarded ideologically as backward, divisive etc., although it may be privately recalled in certain situations. For Sami seeking to keep their identity, cultivating Saminess is the key value, and it encompasses assimilation as something that occurs on occasion but is demeaning, encourages discrimination, and is destructive of a primordial identity. Similar remarks might apply to Basques or Catalans in Spain or France, Bretons in Brittany, or Corse on Corsica, all of which are examples where both tendencies occur [5], or to the contrast between assimilating Juang and separatist Santal, two tribes of Bihar and Orissa who are responding differently to the dominance of the caste society (see Parkin 2000).

What of regional identities, which are achieving an increasing salience in Europe especially, as part of the rush to European integration (Parkin 1999)? If the key encompassment in the case of ethnicity concerns assimilation and separation as values, a preference for (i.e. valuing of) the latter being the supposedly 'modern' case of ethnic identity, with regionalism it is rather segmentation between region and nation that is involved. In France, for instance, while some Bretons, Basques, Catalans or Corse may claim a separate identity from the dominant French, Normans or Gascons, and even Alsatians and Lorrainers, despite their German speech, do not. The latter identities do not rule out their bearers being French also, in different contexts, and legitimately so, whereas the Breton etc./French distinction is seen by the militants as mutually exclusive.

The same may be said of other prominent regional identities in Europe, such as Bavaria or the Rhineland in Germany or Yorkshire or 'Geordieland' in England. MacClancy mentions a similar situation regarding Navarre identity within Spain, which is segmented with the national identity in a way that being Basque or Catalan is not (1993). Conversely, regional identities of this sort may become ethnicized, as with the Northern League in Italy, in its opposition to Rome and to the supposedly parasitic south. [6] This kind of separatism may even demolish once multi-ethnic states, as has happened in Czechoslovakia and Yugoslavia. This is also threatening British identity, through devolution: the subtraction of Scottish, Welsh and Irish identities from it leaves England, not Britain.

The connection between ethnicity and class is another issue potentially involving hierarchy. Ethnic identity can enter into the criteria for class, though it will rarely do so exclusively, because of competition from other criteria such as income and life-style (see Eriksen 1993: 7, 50-4). Also, in principle the ethnic group is shaped differently than a class structure, being a vertically not horizontally demarcated structure. Ethnicity is perhaps ultimately more restrictive than class, the boundaries being firmer. Despite cultural convergence and ethnic switching by individuals, and the possibility of claiming more than one ethnic identity in different situations, it is classes that tend to merge into one another at the margins rather than ethnicities—hence the proliferation of sub- and sub-sub-classes (upper middle, lower middle, etc.). On the other hand, an ethnic group may either become a class or dissolve itself into different classes, primary contacts then being with similar classes in the mass society. Of course, the marginality of ethnic minorities, especially if immigrants, is often exploited to keep them out of the majority class system, perhaps weakening lower-class solidarity through, for example, the threat of an alternative labour source that these minorities provide—minorities do not always occupy distinct economic niches.

As we have seen, however (Chapter 5; cf. Tambiah 1989), the trend has been more away from class struggle and towards ethnic conflict in much political activity today and in the recent past. This may be partly because the class struggles of the nineteenth and early twentieth centuries have evaporated in a welter of compromise, extensive upward class mobility and improved living conditions, coupled with the complete failure of the most extreme anti-class movement to provide either economic or social-status satisfactions. In Europe, the collapse of communism has frequently left ethnicity or nationalism rather than democracy as the mainspring of political activity. [7] But even before this, the prime political concern of many ethnic groups within polyethnic states was not secession, but simply to ensure that they obtained their fair share of the national economic cake. Tambiah argues (ibid.) that this has replaced democracy, reward according to merit and other modern liberal values as political goals in many Third-World states.

As Glazer and Moynihan point out (1975: 16), such claims amount to a shift away from achievement and back to ascription (cf. Dahrendorf's 'refeudalization') in the distribution of wealth and influence. Parsons (1975: 71) expresses this as a shift from the equality of the individual to the equality of the ethnic group, Bell (1975: 147) as a shift from equality of opportunity to equality of results. Bell also sees this process as an extension of the shift from nineteenth-century campaigns for uniform political rights (universal suffrage and so forth) to twentieth-century campaigns for uniform social rights (full employment, health care, social security etc.). As with all economic collectivism, there is therefore a tendency for the open competition of the market to be reduced in favour of monopoly organization (ibid.: 144-5). Such expectations may be considered modern, in the sense that their mainspring is equal treatment for all groups. Claims for equal treatment may, however, produce resentment in other groups, who feel themselves suddenly disadvantaged or who lose out in the competition for economic benefits. India and Malaysia are examples where this has led to popular unrest. These are also, in a sense, examples of hierarchy reasserting itself: in India, Brahmans and other high castes may react with hostility to the extension of Untouchable rights, as may Hindus generally in relation to Moslem assertiveness.

Nonetheless, it is not difficult to identify ethnic divisions of labour. One or more ethnic groups may monopolize management positions, others being manual workers, perhaps with further ethnic distinctions as regards artisanal specializations (Eriksen 1993: 47, 51). Also, immigrants, who are usually different ethnically from the host population, usually receive the most menial jobs, unless they enter trade. Alternatively, as in Guyana (ibid.: 47-8), different ethnic groups may occupy different sectors of the economy. Occupying an economic niche may bring with it a measure of economic security, but may also entail having to accept an inferior status. This may lead to position as a lower class being masked by assertion of an ethnic identity, as with Indians in Guyana (Jayawardene 1980). Also, if a high-status ethnic identity can be adopted, low status jobs can be avoided.

This is the case with some Poles in the city of Berlin, whose escape from the stereotypes of building worker, cleaner and minor smuggler depends on a sufficient degree of assimilation to Germanness. Polish–German relations, officially egalitarian, cease to be so at a popular level, with both sides holding similar stereotypes about the other, for example as dirty, dishonest, inefficient, stupid etc. So far, this is reciprocal denunciation, not hierarchy. In Berlin, however, to which many Polish citizens have immigrated and assimilated, and where there is a history of working on the margins of the law, a distinct hierarchization is discernible. This becomes especially evident when established migrants employ black Polish labour (building workers, cleaning women etc.) or conduct business with acknowledged Poles from across the border (which may well involve smuggling). Assimilated as far as possible to Germanness, the migrants exploit and therefore must acknowledge their Polishness in negotiations with such contacts. These negotiations are always set against the background of a very German cultural and legal environment, including the possibility of penalties if the authorities discover what is going on. For the established migrants, therefore, Polishness is encompassed by Germanness in most everyday situations, but the two become implicitly dichotomized when informal Polish labour is being recruited or deals being made. This is also a contrast between an ideal Germanness and an actual revealing of Polishness for a subordinate and temporary purpose. [8]

However, there are many cases in which encompassment seems scarcely conceivable at first, largely because it is difficult to see the

ethnicities concerned as being hierarchized. This is perhaps especially
the case where they are in conflict. Prime examples are Serb–Croat
and Serb–Bosnian relations since the collapse of Yugoslavia, which
are primarily antagonistic, neither side being willing to acknowledge
the least inferiority to the other in either case. We might therefore say
that these conflicts are modern and egalitarian in Dumont's terms,
characterized by mutual exclusion rather than the accommodation
afforded by a true hierarchy. Perhaps we should say that for a Dumontian the exclusiveness of ethnicity, like the notion of ethnicity itself, is
essentially a modern phenomenon, characterized by disjunctiveness,
boundedness and substantialist definitions. On the other hand, it is
evident that the purely political dominance of the Yugoslav federation
by Serbs, especially after the death of the Croat Tito, has been translated into an ideological association of Serb identity with the notion of
Yugoslavia in the Milosevic period, which builds on the memory of
the growth of Yugoslavia out of the Kingdom of Serbia after the First
World War. Indeed, the Federal Republic that remains is a Serb polity
simultaneously encompassing remaining non-Serb ethnicities (principally Albanians) and excluding independence for the separate but
still Serb republic of Montenegro (cf. Denich 1994). Holy (1996)
describes the similar identification of the Czechs with the whole of
Czechoslovakia, to the exclusion on the subordinate ideological level,
but encompassment on the superior level, of their Slovak national
partners (or, to paraphrase Holy's title, 'the little Czech nation and the
Great Czech nation').

The idea of the essential modernity of ethnicity also has a bearing
on forms of oppression. Formerly, conflict between groups was often
solved through the assimilation of one to another (for example,
through religious conversion, change of feudal or other allegiance): in
other words, group boundaries were adjusted to let in newcomers of
less pure origins who nonetheless became part of the group (Nuer of
Dinka slave origin in the Sudan are another example; see Evans-
Pritchard 1940). In the modern period, expulsion or outright extermination appear to be the preferred options in many cases. Yet
encompassment does appear to survive even in supposedly 'modern'
situations. Although in the Yugoslav conflict of the 1990s expulsion
achieved notoriety as 'ethnic cleansing', not all manifestations of the
non-modern absorption of opponents were absent. One example was
the mass rape of Bosnian women by Serb men, the issue of which were
to be claimed as Serbs for Serbia. Symbolically, this was justified as a
way of Serbianizing (or de-Bosnianizing) the population of Bosnia for
the future, an operation that entailed forgetting the 'Bosnian' side of
the descent of such children and only remembering the 'Serb' side.
Similarly, Anderson quotes a Colombian liberal of the early indepen-

dence period advocating the eradication of the Indian population through 'miscegenation' with whites, who would obviously claim the issue as their own (1991: 13-14).

Thus there are actually probably as many situations in which ethnicities are hierarchized as those where they are not. In the Dumontian perspective, the latter situation might be deemed more typical of the modern period, which is also indicated by the relative boundedness of ethnic groups, despite ethnic switching in some cases: boundedness encourages definitions in terms of intrinsic qualities, which a segmented hierarchy eschews. This corresponds with the essential modernity which is often attributed to ethnic group organization and to ethnicity in general. Yet there are also situations in which hierarchical encompassment is not too difficult to discern—another example of the contradictions of modernity, which hierarchy is able to avoid, though modernity cannot avoid hierarchy. Dumont's model sheds light both on the hierarchization of ethnicities and on those cases where hierarchy fails and conflict results.

Notes

1. Cf. Barnes (1985a: 88): 'Maritime Southeast Asia still lacks and undoubtedly will never have its own *Homo Hierarchicus*.'
2. That this direction of encompassment is not uniform on Madagascar when it comes to kinship is shown by Astuti's work on the Vezo (1995), where cognatic kinship in life becomes patrilineal in the tomb. For a brief discussion of Bloch's neo-Marxist alternative to Dumont, see Parkin 1989.
3. The term itself only dates from the 1950s, when it was coined by the American sociologist David Riesman (see Glazer and Moynihan 1975: 1).
4. On the other hand, members of minorities whose origin is obvious through their physical appearance, their limited knowledge of English, etc. (e.g. Blacks and Hispanics respectively), find it almost impossible to leave their minority ethnic identity at home.
5. The divisions among Bretons between separatist activists and sceptical farmers tending towards a degree of assimilation to the dominant French society is especially well documented by McDonald (1987).
6. Actually the two are connected in northern minds, because of the alleged southern dominance of the national bureaucracy (Farrell and Levy 1996; Cento Bull 1996). The movement may now (2001) have peaked, despite its leader's inclusion in the new Berlusconi government.
7. In effect, this is another example of nationalism as a post-colonial phenomenon, which seems to me to be implicit in Anderson's oft-cited account of the rise of nationalism (1991). In the case of eastern Europe in the 1990s and since, it is of

course independence from the Soviet Union, the institutional expression of the last great colonial empire to break up, namely the Russian, that is involved.

8. M. Irek, personal communication; also Irek (1998); Angenendt (1997: 49-50). On immigration into Germany more generally, see Otto (1990); on its earlier history, see Herbert (1986); on German communities in Poland, many of whom have now left, seen Urban (1994). A similar hiding of origins went on among refugees in Germany from the lost territories after 1945; see Lehmann (1991).

Chapter 9

LEGACIES AND LESSONS

The Legacy of Hertz

It can be seen that something of a contest has arisen over the custody of Hertz's work on right and left, between Dumont and Tcherkézoff on the one hand and Needham on the other, and also between Tcherkézoff on the one hand and de Coppet and Barraud on the other, regarding Dumont's own orientation in respect of the phenomenon of opposition. Despite this later fragmentation, something of both the spirit and the method of the *Année sociologique* school clearly survives in all of Dumont's followers with regard of the particular ideas they draw on and are seeking to develop further. This even extends to co-operative publishing on occasion (e.g. Barraud et al. 1994), in the tradition of Mauss's activities in particular. There is also a direct intellectual lineage here, of course: given that Durkheim taught Mauss, and Mauss Dumont, these are mostly followers of a student of a student of the great master, Durkheim. The Dumontian version of hierarchy may have been contested outside France, and it may no longer be even a Parisian preoccupation. Nonetheless there are signs that the language of encompassment and levels is entering some of the general discourse on ritual without any need being felt to explain it or reference it. This indicates that it is gaining some of the currency of old favourites like totemism, exogamy and, of course, sacred and profane.

What of the specific legacy of Hertz, with whom our story started? There is, of course, a direct connection thematically, through Needham, then, in an adversarial sense, through Dumont, to the latter's followers. But there are other contrasts one might make than simply the obvious one between the Needhamite and Dumontian perspectives, one of which even manages to draw them briefly together.

Notes for this section can be found on page 220.

In writing his paper on right and left, Hertz was, of course, very much influenced by Durkheim's dichotomy between sacred and profane. However, he not only modified it in the way described earlier (Chapter 1), he also shifted its focus in such a way as to bring it closer to ethnographic realities. While sacred and profane basically formed an analytical pair of categories to which all human dichotomizing was supposedly reducible, right and left formed just one pair among many, though emblematic and representative of it. Despite such indigenous dichotomies as those between God and the devil, or good and evil spirits, sacred/profane as such is much less likely to arise explicitly in people's consciousness than right/left, which indeed seems to be a universally acknowledged dichotomy, if not as important everywhere as others. This means that Hertz's account gives no ammunition to the relativists, but at the same time it has not been dismissed as unworkable or irrelevant like sacred/profane.

Secondly, there is a contrast in how the basic idea of such dichotomies has been handled analytically. Hertz tends to treat them as an example of symbolic classification, and he regards them simply as distinctive oppositions. It was Lévi-Strauss's contribution to turn the distinctive opposition into something more dynamic in his very dialectical analyses of myth (of course others, like Jakobson and Saussure, rather than Hertz, were the main inspiration here). It was Dumont's contribution to generate the hierarchical opposition out of the distinctive opposition, but he remained on the whole in the domain of classification—of the *varna* scheme, of the Hindu *trivarga* or ends of life, of the elements of German ideology, etc. It has been left to his followers to make hierarchical opposition in its turn a dynamic force in analysis, this time of ritual, but also of myth, and through them, whole cosmologies. Thus where Hertz and Dumont have each defined a model, Lévi-Strauss and Dumont's followers have, in their different ways, developed them. This is what one might expect: Radcliffe-Brown once remarked that classification comes early in the history of any science (1952 [1940]: 191, 195), and much of his own work was concerned with establishing models and definitions.

This was also largely true of the *Année sociologique* school, for whom sociology was an infant science, battling not only to establish itself academically and institutionally against the hostility of longer-standing subjects like philosophy, psychology and law, but also to get its own terms straight. This was done in relation to carefully chosen topics, which were examined as they occurred in single societies or in a range of closely related ones, the ultimate aim being to produce a perspective that was universally applicable based on an examination of the most highly developed examples (see Evans-Pritchard 1960: 14-15; Needham 1972: 209-10). Ritual was, of course, important in the overall theory of the *Année sociologique* school, and many of their studies deal with it. In being defined as the occasions when the social was at its height, in effect actually produced through the imparting of social knowledge and values to the crowd taking part in it, it provided Durkheimian sociology with a sense of process. But these studies were generally interpretative in a comparative rather than strictly ethnographic sense, despite the frequent focus on single societies. Again, the ultimate concern was with definition—what the global nature of sacrifice was, for example, or of exchange, or of sin—rather than with analysing it for a specific society. And it was left to Arnold van Gennep—an outsider to the school whom it mostly derided as a folklorist—to give the first comprehensive account of the general dynamics of ritual process, rather than simply the different circumstances in which and for which it was performed.

And what of Needham? If there is one word that characterizes his work more than any other, it is again classification, or rather, perhaps, the problems of classification, both ethnographically and comparatively. In respect of the first, the analyst's task is to attempt to grasp the categories of an alien culture. In respect of the second, it is to establish the underlying principles of order through which alone different societies might be truly comparable. In these as in other respects, he too is consciously adhering, in broad terms, to the Durkheimian tradition, though the solutions he proposes are all his own: the polythetic idea, in regard to the witch, for example, or the unilateral figure; the final choice of terminology—itself a classification—as the most useful means of classifying kinship systems; the debunking of categories like belief and inner states as cross-cultural phenomena, and so on. Even when the result is negative, the focus has remained in the last resort comparative, referring social phenomena ultimately to standard properties of the human brain or at least mind, and dealing ultimately in abstract categories, such as symmetry, asymmetry, reversal or opposition, which a society might not explicitly recognize.

Such categories are themselves often seen as a polythetic class, though Tcherkézoff specifically resists hierarchical opposition being added to their number (see above, Chapter 4). What Needham has been less concerned with on the whole is the analysis of myth or ritual, that is, with dynamic processes, however they be conceived. This emphasis is equally true of his work on what he calls dual symbolic classification, so that, whatever his differences with Dumont, in this respect they can be bracketed together as direct intellectual descendants of Durkheim, Mauss and Hertz.

However, it may be this very concern for classification that underlies Needham's relative indifference to, or frustration with, the objections raised by Dumont and others to the form of presentation he has chosen for his own analyses of dual symbolic classification. For him, the two-column table of binary pairs is simply a record, a list, an *aide-mémoire* of what the ethnography has thrown up: it is explicitly *not* a method, nor—unless the ethnography gives clear indications to the contrary—is it to be seen as representing a structure of any sort. As a result, the attempts of Dumont and Tcherkézoff in particular to discern what Needham considers a false structure in such tables, simply to satisfy their own predispositions towards a spurious notion of hierarchy, are not simply wrong, they are completely misguided. For Needham, there is no common structure to systems of dual symbolic classification that is applicable cross-culturally. This partly reflects ethnographic facts, but it is also because oppositions themselves are logically of different sorts. For Needham, if hierarchical opposition belonged anywhere it would surely belong here; but in fact it seems to have no validity for him, whether ethnographically, theoretically or methodologically. In any event—at least to judge from his more programmatic statements—for him only the faculty of opposing is at all constant cross-culturally, not any one sort of opposition in particular.

And here lies the crux of the matter for any anthropologist. One might accept that some oppositions are conceived of hierarchically in some situations and in some societies in the way Dumont intends; or else one might regard them as very generally but not universally applicable. The determination of Dumont and his followers to see them everywhere is bound to attract criticism based on the existence of supposedly countervailing examples—the fate of practically every other universal that has been claimed in the history of anthropology. Certainly there is sometimes a simple worry about plausibility: for example, we have come quite a long way from Hertz's initial observations concerning simple and very generally recognized oppositions such as right/left, life/death, white/black etc., if Iteanu can oppose initiation ritual to kinship and claim to explain all Orokaiva ideology as a result.

However, as we have seen many times in the foregoing pages, even examples supposedly contradicting Dumont's model actually turn out to confirm the validity of his overall approach. Either further examination of the data uncovers the order of levels that at first sight appeared to be lacking; or else the opposition appears to be a symmetric one that is characteristic of modern modes of thought that separate fact and value. Even in the latter case, a different perspective may still reveal hierarchy in the end. So long as human beings continue to distinguish and to value, and to classify, oppositions will continue to manifest hierarchy between the poles and between the two sorts of relation that link them.

The Legacy of Dumont:
Hierarchical Opposition Summed Up

As for Dumont's legacy specifically, the first lesson to be drawn from his work, I would argue, is his claim that no distinction is neutral in value, since, as an operation, distinguishing two things is simultaneous with stating a preference for one over the other. To the extent that this is debatable, it would appear to relate to the level of consciousness with which such operations are carried out. They may take place unreflectively, in which case Dumont's claim is most likely to be fulfilled. Alternatively they may take place consciously, in which case any differentiation in terms of value is going to be explicit; we have encountered many examples of this in the foregoing pages. On the other hand, indigenous statements accompanying the operation may stress the equality of the terms; we have seen this on occasion too. This recalls the Durkheimian dictum that, when people become conscious of their categories (and only when), they may challenge, alter or manipulate them. However, there is another aspect to these statements than that suggested by their face value. We may call the present case one of equality as a value not only being consciously preferred in explicit statements, but also unreflectively encompassing inequality as the opposite preference, in which case hierarchy still results between the two terms. In other words, hierarchy and equality are candidates as superordinate values in their own right.

The second lesson of Dumont's writings is that distinctions are not only asymmetric, they are the only situation in which the subordinate pole ever manifests itself. Conversely, when there is no distinction, this pole is encompassed by the superordinate one, which represents the transcendent value. This difference of situation is what produces the two levels and is also what constitutes the hierarchical opposition. In this sense, however—and it is this that has been the source of much confusion and controversy—hierarchy is not just one of many possible superordinate values encompassing its opposite, but the essential basis of the structural model itself. This is why hierarchy is unavoidable, even where equality appears as the transcendent value. In yet other words, to proclaim equality is to express a preference for it, and therefore to value it, to *hierarchize* it, over its opposites (say, inequality or hierarchy as subordinate values). This is also separate, of course, from the proposition that hierarchy is present in these cases in the subordinate domain. One familiar example in western societies is the world of work, which is hierarchical in practice even in societies that see themselves as ideologically, or transcendentally, composed of individuals who are equal. There may be attempts to obscure this by symbolically asserting the equal importance of all employees to the company and so forth, but ultimately orders are given by some and received by others, workers hired and fired by management, and management approved and censured by shareholders.

For a similar reason, the distinction between modern and non-modern thought, much exploited by Dumont, also needs to be qualified. If modern thought involves the separation of fact and value, here too it is because it is *preferred* to the non-modern alternative in which the two are fused together. As Kluckhohn pointed out even before Dumont (see above, Chapter 4), for the scientist objectivity is a value with respect to subjectivity because it is the only way to arrive at scientific truth. It is therefore a transcendent value for science that encompasses its contrary, which is only made manifest in order to criticize it—a clear indication of its ideological subordination.

It is because hierarchy *in the sense of a structure* is not just unavoidable but invariant that Dumont and supporters have proclaimed it as an effective tool for the comparison of whole societies. Increasingly, this has come to be seen as a matter of treating societies as (co-ordinate with their) cosmologies, through which key 'mother' values—superordinate values—may be identified and compared. This specific development post-dates Dumont, though it is firmly grounded in his model. For anthropology too, this model has given a new lease of life to structuralism, which, both in its Lévi-Straussian version and its combination with Marxism, had run out of steam by about 1980.

In this context, we should not forget that structuralism pre-dates both of these trends and cannot be associated exclusively with either of them (Allen 1990); by the same token, therefore, it is capable of development. Dumont and his followers have assured its continued applicability even in an anthropology seemingly dominated by action-based approaches to social life; they have done this precisely by incorporating pragmatics into their model. The focus for Dumont may still be ideology, which is seen as subordinating the level of pragmatics, but the latter is still represented, and more so than in either Lévi-Strauss or Durkheim. No wonder that Dumont has been aligned with Bourdieu in some more recent work. [1]

As well as its nature and its applicability in academic analysis, I have argued that Dumont's model also has wider significance in coming to terms with the nature of the typical western, modern society. This is especially relevant with respect to the latter's inability as yet to overcome the contradictions that tarnish its own view of itself as fundamentally egalitarian. Enough has been said here on the nature of these contradictions, which show hardly any sign of being resolved. This in itself, of course, is a challenge to at any rate some versions of the liberal conscience, which Durkheimian sociology has often been accused of opposing. One of the reasons for the disquiet in Dumont's case is the concern that, in talking so benignly about hierarchy, his work may be undermining the goal many social scientists have set themselves in exposing the contingent and political bases of inequalities of power and its links to ideology.

In part, this may reflect the fear that, in seeking to understand hierarchy, one is according it validity. This impression too may have been reinforced by Dumont's neutral language. But Dumont always took the view that understanding something did not imply approval of it. This objection is not generally made in other cases where the exercise of stripping away ideological mystifications of actual power relations is undertaken more explicitly, nor in the increasingly copious discussions of racism or ethnic conflict, and it hardly seems any more justified in Dumont's case. In any case, it should be obvious that Dumont's insistence on the necessity of hierarchy is purely intellectual and relates to the invariant structure of his chosen model; it is in this sense that he thinks that hierarchy is unavoidable. His critics notwithstanding, nowhere to my knowledge does he put forward hierarchy as a prescription for the organization of society, express a personal preference for it, or advocate the perpetuation of social inequalities.

In any case, intellectual projects seeking to deconstruct egalitarianism are inherently no more objectionable than those that focus on another cherished western ideal, namely individualism, which anthropologists have repeatedly unpacked. [2] By using hierarchy as a tool in understanding these notions, Dumont is not preferring the former to the latter but finding a new and, I would argue, more precise way of laying bare their variety and implications, as well as producing a fresh understanding of hierarchy and inequality. Dumont's originality in these respects in no way distances him from the deconstructionist project that, in a broad sense, has always been at the heart of the social sciences.

Notes

1. Cf. Alvi (1999), a recently completed doctorate on exchange in a village in the Pakistani Punjab, which seeks theoretically to combine Dumont's models with Bourdieu's version of pragmatics. In a more recent article, Alvi seeks to relate Punjabi notions of the self and the person as a hierarchical opposition in which the latter encompasses the former: 'the concept of the self cannot be formed without the general expectations of the society about what a person should be' (2001: 61).
2. For example, André Celtel has recently completed a doctorate on individualism at Oxford, in which Dumont is prominently discussed (Celtel 2002).

BIBLIOGRAPHY

Ajawaila, J.W. 1990. Marriage Rituals of the Galela People, *Bijdragen tot de Taal-, Land- en Volkenkunde* 146/1, 93-102.

Allen, N.J. 1982. A Dance of Relatives, Journal of the Anthropological Society of Oxford 13/2, 139-46.

_____ 1985. Hierarchical Opposition and Some Other Types of Relation, in Barnes et al. (eds) 1985.

_____ 1986. Tetradic Theory: An Approach to Kinship, Journal of the Anthropological Society of Oxford 17/2, 87-109.

_____ 1990. On the Notion of Structure, , Journal of the Anthropological Society of Oxford 21/3, 279-82.

_____ 1994. Primitive Classification: The Argument and its Validity, in W.S.F. Pickering and Herminio Martins (eds), Debating Durkheim, London and New York: Routledge.

_____ 1998. Obituary: Louis Dumont (1911-1998), Journal of the Anthropological Society of Oxford 29/1, 1-4.

Alvi, Anjum 1999. Bearers of Grief: Death, Women, Gifts and Kinship in Muslim Punjab, Berlin: Free University (doctoral thesis).

_____ 2001. The Category of the Person in the Rural Punjab, Social Anthropology 9/1, 45-63.

Anderson, Benedict 1991. Imagined Communities: Reflections on the Origin and Spread of Nationalism, London and New York: Verso.

Angenendt, Steffan 1997. Deutsche Migrationspolitik im neuen Europa, Opladen: Leske und Budrich.

Apthorpe, Raymond 1961. Foreword, in C.M.N. White 1961.

_____ 1984. Hierarchy and Other Social Relations: Some Categorical Logic, in Jean-Claude Galey (ed.), Différences, valeurs, hiérarchie: textes offerts à Louis Dumont, Paris: Editions de l'Ecole des Hautes Etudes en Sciences Sociales.

Ardener, Edwin 1975. The 'Problem' Revisited, in Shirley Ardener (ed.), Perceiving Women, London: Malaby Press.

_____ 1982. Social Anthropology, Language and Reality, in David Parkin (ed.), Semantic Anthropology, London: Tavistock (ASA Monographs 22).

_____ 1987. 'Remote Areas': Some Theoretical Considerations, in Anthony Jackson (ed.), Anthropology at Home, London and New York: Tavistock Publications. (ASA Monographs 25)

_____ 1989. The Voice of Prophecy and Other Essays, Oxford: Basil Blackwell.

Astuti, Rita 1995. People of the Sea: Identity and Descent among the Vezo of Madagascar, Cambridge: Cambridge University Press.

Bailey, F.G. 1961. 'Tribe' and 'Caste' in India, Contributions to Indian Sociology 5, 7-19.

_____ 1991. Religion and Religiosity: Ideas and their Use, Contributions to Indian Sociology (n.s.) 25/2, 211-31.

Barley, Nigel 1983. Symbolic Structures: An Exploration of the Culture of the Dowayos, Cambridge: Cambridge University Press, and Paris: Maison des Sciences de l'Homme.

Barnes, R.H. 1974. Kédang: The Collective Thought of an Eastern Indonesian People, Oxford: Clarendon Press.

_____ 1984. Two Crows Denies It: A History of Controversy in Omaha Sociology, Lincoln and London: University of Nebraska Press.

_____ 1985a. The Leiden Version of the Comparative Method in Southeast Asia, Journal of the Anthropological Society of Oxford 16/2, 87-110.

_____ 1985b. Hierarchy Without Caste, in Barnes et al. (eds) 1985.

_____ and Daniel de Coppet 1985. Introduction, in Barnes et al. (eds) 1985.

Barnes, R.H., Daniel de Coppet and R.J. Parkin (eds) 1985. Contexts and Levels: Anthropological Essays on Hierarchy, Oxford: JASO (JASO Occasional Papers 4).

Barraud, Cécile 1972. De la chasse aux têtes à la pêche de la bonite: essai sur la chefferie à Eddystone, L'Homme 12/1, 67-104.

_____ 1981. Tanebar-Evav: une société de maisons tournée vers le large, Cambridge and Paris; Cambridge University Press and Maison des Sciences de l'Homme.

_____ 1984. Comments on J.D.M. Platenkamp's Paper, in P.E. de Josselin de Jong (ed.), Unity in Diversity: Indonesia as a Field of Anthropological Study, Dordrecht and Cinnaminson: Foris Publications.

_____ 1985. The Sailing-Boat: Circulation and Values in the Kei Islands, Indonesia, in Barnes et al. (eds) 1985.

_____ 1990a. A Turtle Turned on the Sand in the Kei Islands, Bijdragen tot de Taal-, Land- en Volkenkunde 146/1, 35-55.

_____ 1990b. Wife-givers as Ancestors and Ultimate Values in the Kei Islands, Bijdragen tot de Taal-, Land- en Volkenkunde 146/2-3, 193-225.

_____ 1990c. Kei Society and the Person: An Approach through Childbirth and Funerary Rituals, Ethnos 1990/3-4, 214-31.

_____ and J.D.M. Platenkamp 1990. Rituals and the Comparison of Societies, Bijdragen tot de Taal-, Land- en Volkenkunde 146/1, 103-23.

Barraud, Cécile, Daniel de Coppet, André Iteanu and Raymond Jamous 1994 [1984]. Of Relations and the Dead: Four Societies Viewed from the Angle of Their Exchanges, Oxford and Providence, R.I.: Berg.

Barth, Frederik 1969a. Pathan Identity and its Maintenance, in Barth (ed.) 1969b.

_____ (ed.) 1969b. Ethnic Groups and Boundaries: The Social Organization of Culture Difference, London: George Allen & Unwin.

Basso, Ellen B. 1970. Xingi Carib Kinship Terminology and Marriage: Another View, Southwestern Journal of Anthropology 26, 402-16.

Bataille, George 1988 [1938]. Attraction and Repulsion, I and II, in Denis Hollier (ed.), The College of Sociology (1937-39), Minneapolis: University of Minnesota Press.

Beattie, John 1968. Aspects of Nyoro Symbolism, Africa 38/4, 413-42.

_____ 1976. Right, Left and the Bunyoro, Africa 46/3, 217-35.

_____ 1978. Nyoro Symbolism and Nyoro Ethnography: A Rejoinder, Africa 48/3, 278-95.

Beck, Brenda 1973. The Right-Left Division of South Indian Society, in Needham (ed.) 1973d.

Beidelman, T.O. 1973. Kaguru Symbolic Classification, in Needham (ed.) 1973d.

_____ 1989. Review of Tcherkézoff 1987, American Ethnologist 61/1, 173-4.

Bell, Daniel 1975. Ethnicity and Social Change, in Glazer and Moynihan (eds) 1975.

Benjamin, Geoffrey 1967. Temiar Kinship, Federated Museums Journal 12, 1-25.

Bernardi, B. 1959. The Mugwe: A Failing Prophet, London: Oxford University Press.

Berreman, Gerard 1971. The Brahmanical View of Caste, Contributions to Indian Sociology n.s. 5, 16-23.

Beteille, André 1986. Individualism and Equality, Current Anthropology 27/2, 121-34.

_____ 1987. Reply to Dumont 1987, Current Anthropology 28/5, 672-7.

Bloch, Maurice 1985. Almost Eating the Ancestors, Man 20/4, 631-46.

_____ 1989a. Ritual, History and Power: Selected Papers in Anthropology, London: The Athlone Press.

_____ 1989b. The Symbolism of Money in Imerina, in Parry and Bloch (eds) 1989.

_____ and Jonathan Parry (eds) 1982. Death and the Regeneration of Life, Cambridge etc.: Cambridge University Press.

_____ and Jonathan Parry 1989. Introduction: Money and the Morality of Exchange, in Parry and Bloch (eds) 1989.

Bouez, Serge 1985. Réciprocité et hiérarchie: l'alliance chez les Hos et les Santal de l'Inde, Paris: Société de l'Ethnographie.

Bouglé, Célestin 1899. Les idées égalitaires: étude sociologique, Paris: Félix Alcan.

_____ 1908. Essais sur le régime des castes, Paris: Félix Alcan.

Boulay, Juliet du 1982. The Greek Vampire: A Study of Cyclic Symbolism in Marriage and Death, Man 17/2, 219-38.

Bourdieu, Pierre 1977. Outline of a Theory of Practice, Cambridge: Cambridge University Press.

Brown, Cecil 1984. Language and Living Things: Uniformities in Folk Classification and Naming, New Brunswick, N.J.: Rutgers University Press.

Burghart, Richard 1978. Hierarchical Models of the Hindu Social System, Man 13/4, 519-36.

_____ 1983. Renunciation in the Religious Traditions of South Asia, Man 18/4, 635-53.

Cahnman, Werner J. 1977. Toennies in America, History and Theory 16, 147-67.

Carsten, Janet 1989. Cooking Money: Gender and the Symbolic Transformation of Means of Exchange in a Malay Fishing Community, in Parry and Bloch (eds) 1989.

Casajus, Dominique 1984. L'énigme de la troisième personne, in Jean-Claude Galey (ed.) Différences, valeurs, hiérarchie: textes offerts à Louis Dumont, Paris: Editions de l'Ecole des Hautes Etudes en Sciences Sociales.

_____ 1985. Why Do the Tuareg Veil Their Faces?, in Barnes et al. (eds) 1985.

Celtel, André 2002. Louis Dumont and the 'Category of the Individual': A Study in Anthropological Theory, Oxford: Oxford University (doctoral thesis).

Cento Bull, Anna 1996. Ethnicity, Racism and the Northern League, in Carl Levy (ed.), Italian Regionalism: History, Identity and Politics, Oxford and Washington: Berg.

Collingwood, R.G. 1933. An Essay on Philosophical Method, Oxford: Clarendon Press.

Crocker, J.C. 1977. The Mirrored Self: Identity and Ritual Inversion Among the Eastern Bororo, Ethnology 16/2, 129-45.

Culshaw, W.G. 1949. Tribal Heritage: A Study of the Santals, London: Butterworth.

Czeglédy, André P. 1999. Corporate Identities and the Continuity of Power in an International Joint Venture in Hungary, in Birgit Müller (ed.), Power and Institutional Change in Post-Communist Easter Europe, Canterbury: Centre for Social Anthropology and Computing..

Das, Veena 1976. Masks and Faces: An Essay on Punjabi Kinship, Contributions to Indian Sociology n.s. 10/1, 1-30.

_____ 1977a. On the Categorization of Space in Hindu Ritual, in Ravindra K. Jain (ed.), Text and Context: The Social Anthropology of Tradition, Philadelphia: Institute for the Study of Human Issues (ASA Essays in Social Anthropology, 2).

_____ 1977b. Structure and Cognition, Delhi: Oxford University Press.

_____ 1982. Kama in the Scheme of Purusarthas: The Story of Rama, in T.N. Madan (ed.), Way of Life - King, Householder, Renouncer: Essays in Honour of Louis Dumont, Delhi: Vikas, and Paris: Editions de la Maison des Sciences de l'Homme.

_____ and Jit Singh Uberoi 1971. The Elementary Structure of Caste, Contributions to Indian Sociology n.s. 5, 33-43.

de Coppet, Daniel, 1968. Pour une étude des échanges cérémoniels en Mélanésie, L'Homme 8/4, 45-57.

_____ 1970a. 1, 4, 8; 9, 7 - La monnaie: présence des morts et mesure du temps, L'Homme 10/1, 17-39.

_____ 1970b. Cycles de meurtres et cycles fun,raires: esquisse de deux structures d'échange, in J. Pouillon and P. Maranda (eds), Echanges et communications: mélanges offerts à Claude Lévi-Strauss, Paris and The Hague: Mouton.

_____ 1976. Jardins de vie, jardins de mort en Mélanesie, Traverses 5-6, 166-77.

_____ 1977. Des porcs et des hommes, Traverses 8, 60-70.

_____ 1981. The Life-giving Death, in S.C. Humphreys and Helen King (eds), Mortality and Immortality: The Anthropology and Archaeology of Death, London etc.: Academic Press.

_____ 1990. The Society as an Ultimate Value and the Socio-Cosmic Configuration, Ethnos 1990/3-4, 140-50.

_____ 1992a. Introduction, in Daniel de Coppet (ed.), Understanding Rituals, London and New York: Routledge.

_____ 1992b. Comparison, a Universal for Anthropology: From 'Representation' to the Comparison of Hierarchies of Value, in Kuper (ed.) 1992.

_____ 1995. 'Are'are Society: A Melanesian Point of View. How are Bigmen the Servants of Society and Cosmos?, in Daniel de Coppet and André Iteanu (eds), Cosmos and Society in Oceania, Oxford and Washington: Berg.

De Coppet, Daniel, and Hugo Zemp 1978. 'Ar é'are, un peuple mélanésien et sa musique, Paris: Seuil.

De Coppet, Daniel, and André Iteanu 1995. Introduction, in Daniel de Coppet and André Iteanu (eds), Cosmos and Society in Oceania, Oxford and Washington: Berg.

Deliège, Robert 1992. Brahmanes et possédés: deux modèles de pratique dans la société indienne, Recherches Sociologiques 23/2, 91-114.

Denich, Bette 1994. Dismembering Yugoslavia: Nationalist Ideologies and the Symbolic Revival of Genocide, American Ethnologist 21/2, 367-90.

Dieterlin, Germaine 1968. Norme et lateralité en Afrique occidentale, in Raoul Kourilsky and Pierre Grapin (eds), Main droite et main gauche: norme et lateralité, Paris: Presses Universitaires Françaises.

Dilley, Roy (ed.) 1999. The Problem of Context, New York and Oxford: Berghahn.

Dirks, Nicholas 1987. The Hollow Crown: Ethnohistory of an Indian Kingdom, Cambridge: Cambridge University Press.

_____ 1989. The Original Caste: Power, History and Hierarchy in South Asia, Contributions to Indian Sociology 23/1, 59-77.

Duff-Cooper, Andrew 1985. Hierarchy, Purity and Equality Among a Community of Balinese on Lombok, in Barnes et al. (eds) 1985.

_____ ms. A Balinese Conception for Attaining the 'Full Life' from Western Lombok.

Dumézil, Georges 1948. Mitra-Varuna: essai sur deux représentations indo-européenes de la souveraineté, Paris: Gallimard (2nd edition).

Dumont, Louis 1957a. For a Sociology of India, Contributions to Indian Sociology 1, 7-22.

_____ 1957b. Une sous-caste de l'Inde du sud: organisation sociale et religion des Pramalai Kallar, Paris: Mouton.

_____ 1959. Pure and Impure, Contributions to Indian Sociology 3, 9-39.

_____ 1960. World Renunciation in Indian Religions, Contributions to Indian Sociology 4, 33-62.

_____ 1962a. The Concept of Kingship in Ancient India, Contributions to Indian Sociology 6, 48-77.

_____ 1962b. 'Tribe' and 'Caste' in India, Contributions to Indian Sociology 6, 120-2.

_____ 1966. A Fundamental Problem in the Sociology of Caste, Contributions to Indian Sociology 9, 17-32.

_____ 1970. The Individual as an Impediment to Sociological Comparison and Indian History, in L. Dumont, Religion/Politics and History in India: Collected Papers in Indian Sociology, Paris and The Hague: Mouton.

_____ 1971a. Putative Hierarchy and Some Allergies To It, Contributions to Indian Sociology n.s. 5, 58-78.

_____ 1971b. Introduction à deux théories d'anthropologie sociale, Paris: Ecole Pratique des Hautes Etudes and Mouton.

_____ 1972 [1966]. Homo Hierarchicus: The Caste System and its Implications, London: Paladin.

_____ 1977. From Mandeville to Marx: The Genesis and Triumph of Economic Ideology, Chicago: The University of Chicago Press (main title in French, Homo Aequalis I, Paris: Gallimard 1977).

_____ 1979. The Anthropological Community and Ideology, Social Science Information 18, 785-817.

_____ 1980 [1966]. Homo Hierarchicus: The Caste System and its Implications (2nd revised English edition), Chicago: The University of Chicago Press.

_____ 1982. On Value [Radcliffe-Brown Lecture 1980], Proceedings of the British Academy 66, 207-41.

_____ 1983. Affinity as a Value: Marriage Alliance in South India, with Comparative Essays on Australia, Chicago: The University of Chicago Press.

_____ 1984. Interview with Jean-Claude Galey, in Jean-Claude Galey (ed.), Différences, valeurs, hiérarchie: textes offerts à Louis Dumont, Paris: Editions de l'Ecole des Hautes Etudes en Sciences Sociales.

_____ 1986a. Essays on Individualism: Modern Ideology in Anthropological Perspective, Chicago and London: The University of Chicago Press.

_____ 1986b. Are Cultures Living Beings? German Identity in Interaction, Man 21/4, 587-604.

_____ 1987a. On Individualism and Equality, Current Anthropology 28/5, 669-72.

_____ 1987b. Reply to Hart 1987, Man (n.s.) 22/4, 747-8.

_____ 1991. Homo Aequalis II: l'idéologie allemande, France-Allemagne et retour, Paris: Gallimard.

_____ 1992. Left versus Right in French Political Ideology: A Comparative Approach, in John A. Hall and I.C. Jarvie (eds), Transition to Modernity: Essays on Power, Wealth and Belief, Cambridge etc.: Cambridge University Press.

_____ and David Pocock 1958. A.M. Hocart on Caste, Contributions to Indian Sociology 2, 45-63.

Durkheim, Emile 1898. L'individualisme et les intellectuals, Revue Bleue (4ième Serie) 10, 7-13.

_____ 1899. De la définition des phénomènes religieux, Année Sociologique 2, 1-28.

_____ 1915 [1912]. The Elementary forms of the Religious Life: A Study in Religious Sociology (transl. J.W. Swain), London: George Allen & Unwin.

_____ 1984 [1893]. The Division of Labour in Society, London: Macmillan.

_____ and Marcel Mauss 1963 [1903]. Primitive Classification (transl. Rodney Needham), London: Cohen & West.

Eliade, Mircea 1974 [1949]. The Myth of the Eternal Return (Cosmos and History), Princeton: Princeton University Press.

Eidheim, Harald 1969. When Ethnic Identity is a Social Stigma, in Barth ed. 1969b.

_____ 1971. Aspects of the Lappish Minority Situation, Oslo: Universitetsforlaget.

Eriksen, Thomas Hylland 1993. Ethnicity and Nationalism, London and Boulder: Pluto Press.

Evans-Pritchard, E.E. 1940. The Nuer: A Description of the Modes of Livelihood and Political Institutions of a Nilotic People, Oxford: Clarendon Press.

_____ 1960. Introduction, in Hertz 1960.

_____ 1965. Theories of Primitive Religion, Oxford: Clarendon Press.

_____ 1973 [1953]. Nuer Spear Symbolism, in Needham (ed.) 1973d.

Evens, T.M.S. 1982. Two Concepts of `Society as Moral System': Evans-Pritchard's Heterodoxy, Man 17/2, 205-18.

_____ 1993. Rationality, Hierarchy and Practice: Contradiction as Choice, Social Anthropology 1/1b, 101-18.

Fardon, Richard 1987. African Ethnogenesis: Limits to the Comparability of Ethnic Phenomena, in Ladislav Holy (ed.), Comparative Anthropology, Oxford: Blackwell.

Farrell, Joseph, and Carl Levy 1996. The Northern League: Conservative Revolution?, in Carl Levy (ed.), Italian Regionalism: History, Identity and Politics, Oxford and Washington: Berg.

Forth, Gregory 1985. Right and Left as a Hierarchical Opposition: Reflections on Eastern Sumbanese Hairstyles, in Barnes et al. (eds) 1985.

Foster, George M. 1965. Peasant Society and the Image of Limited Good, Americxan Anthropologist 67/2, 293-315.

Fox, James J. 1988. Introduction, in James J. Fox (ed.), To Speak in Pairs: Essays on the Ritual Languages of Eastern Indonesia, Cambridge etc.: Cambridge University Press.

_____ 1989. Category and Complement: Binary Ideologies and the Organization of Dualism in Eastern Indonesia, in Maybury-Lewis and Almagor (eds) 1989.

Fox, James J. (ed.) 1980. The Flow of Life: Essays on Eastern Indonesia, Cambridge, Mass.: Harvard University Press.

Fuchs, Martin 1992. Le paradoxe comme méthode? La structure antithétique de la théorie sociale de Louis Dumont, Recherches Sociologiques 23/2, 19-42.

Fürer-Haimendorf, Christoph von 1967. Morals and Merit: A Study of Values and Social Controls in South Asian Societies, London: Weidenfeld & Nicolson.

Fuller, C. 1984. Servants of the Goddess, Cambridge: Cambridge University Press.

_____ 1988. The Hindu Pantheon and the Legitimation of Hierarchy, Man 23/1, 19-39.

GDAT (Group for Debates in Anthropological Theory) 1990. The Concept of Society is Theoretically Obsolete, Manchester: GDAT.

Geirnaert, Danielle 1987. Hunt Wild Pig and Grow Rice: On Food Exchanges and Values in Laboya, West Sumba (Eastern

Indonesia), in R. de Ridder and J.A.J. Karremans (eds), The Leiden
    Tradition in Structural Anthropology: Essays in Honour of P.E. de
    Josselin de Jong, Leiden etc.: E.J. Brill.
Geirnaert-Martin, Danielle C. 1992. The Woven Land of Laboya:
    Sociocosmic Ideas and Values in West Sumba, Eastern Indonesia,
    Leiden: Centre of Non-Western Studies (CNWS Publications no.
    11).
Gell, Alfred 1995. Closure and Multiplication: An Essay on
    Polynesian Cosmology and Ritual, in Daniel de Coppet and André
    Iteanu (eds), Cosmos and Society in Oceania, Oxford and
    Washington: Berg.
Gennep, Arnold van, 1960 [1909]. The Rites of Passage, London
    and Henley: Routledge and Kegan Paul.
Giles, Linda 1987. Possession Cults on the Swahili Coast: A Re-
    examination of Theories of Marginality, Africa 57/2, 234-57.
Gillison, Gillian 1980. Images of Nature in Gimi Thought, in Carol
    MacCormack and Marilyn Strathern (eds), Nature, Culture and
    Gender, Cambridge: Cambridge University Press.
Glazer, Nathan, and Daniel P. Moynihan (eds) 1975. Ethnicity:
    Theory and Experience, Cambridge, Mass., and London: Harvard
    University Press.
Good, Anthony 1987. Review of Barnes et al. (eds) 1985, Man 22/3,
    570.
Good, Anthony 1993. Review of Quigley 1993, Current
    Anthropology 34/5, 797-8.
Goody, Jack 1977. The Domestication of the Savage Mind,
    Cambridge: Cambridge University Press.
_____ 1990. The Oriental, the Ancient and the Primitive: Systems of
    Marriage and the Family in the Pre-industrial Societies of
    Eurasia, Cambridge: Cambridge University Press.
Granet, Marcel 1973 [1933, 1953]. Right and Left in China, in
    Needham (ed.) 1973d.
Guermonprez, Jean-François 1987. Les Pandé de Bali: la formation
    d'une 'caste' et la valeur d'un titre, Paris: Ecole Française
    d'Extrême-Orient (Publications, Vol. CXLII).
Hage, Per, Frank Harary and Bojka Milicic 1995. Hierarchical
    Opposition, Oceania 65, 347-54.
Hallpike, C.R. 1979. The Foundations of Primitive Thought, Oxford:
    Clarendon Press.
Hart, Keith 1987. L'Allemagne au dessus de tout?, Man (n.s.), 746-7.
Heesterman, J.C. 1971. Priesthood and the Brahman, Contributions
    to Indian Sociology n.s. 5, 43-7.
_____ 1985. The Inner Conflict of Tradition: Essays in Indian Ritual,
    Kingship, and Society, Chicago: The University of Chicago Press.
Herbert, Ulrich 1986. Geschichte der Ausländerbeschäftigung in
    Deutschland 1880 bis 1980, Bonn: J.H.W. Dietz.
Hertz, Alice 1928. Préface, in Robert Hertz, Mélanges de sociologie
    religieuse et de folklore, Paris: Presses Universitaires Françaises.

Hertz, Robert 1907. Contribution à une étude sur la représentation collective de la mort, Année Sociologique 10, 48-137.

_____ 1909. La prééminence de la main droite: étude sur la polarité religieuse, Revue Philosophique 68, 553-80.

_____ 1910. Socialisme et dépopulation, Paris: Librairie du Parti Socialiste (Cahiers du Socialiste, 10).

_____ 1911. Le socialisme en Angleterre: la société fabienne. Unpublished manuscript of talk presented to Ecole Socialiste, 13/1/1911. Paris: Fonds Robert Hertz, Laboratoire d'Anthropologie Sociale.

_____ 1960. Death and the Right Hand (translations of Hertz 1907 and 1909 by Rodney and Claudia Needham), London: Cohen & West. With an Introduction by E. E. Evans-Pritchard.

_____ 1973. The Pre-eminence of the Right Hand: A Study in Religious Polarity, in Needham (ed.) 1973d (slightly revised translation of Hertz 1909 by Rodney Needham).

_____ 1994. Sin and Expiation in Primitive Societies (transl. Robert Parkin), Oxford: British Centre for Durkheimian Studies, Occasional Papers no. 2.

Herzfeld, Michael 1992. Segmentation and Politics in the European Nation-state: Making Sense of Political Events, in Kirsten Hastrup (ed.), Other Histories, London and New York: Routledge.

Hicks, David 1976. Tetum Ghosts and Kin: Fieldwork in an Indonesian Community, Palo Alto, CA: Mayfield.

Hirsch, Eric 1995. The 'Holding Together' of Ritual: Ancestrality and Achievement in the Papuan Highlands, in Daniel de Coppet and André Iteanu (eds), Cosmos and Society in Oceania, Oxford and Washington: Berg.

Hobart, Mark 1985. Texte est un Con, in Barnes et al. (eds) 1985.

Hocart, A.M. 1937. Kinship Systems, Anthropos 32/3-4, 345-51.

_____ 1938. Les Castes, Paris: Geuthner.

_____ 1954. Social Origins, London: Watts & Co.

_____ 1970 [1936]. Kings and Councillors: An Essay in the Comparative Anatomy of Human Society, Chicago: The University of Chicago Press.

Holy, Ladislaw 1996. The Little Czech and the Great Czech Nation: National Identity and the Post-communist Social Transformation, Cambridge: Cambridge University Press.

Houseman, Michael 1984. La relation hiérarchique: idéologie particulière ou modèle général?, in Jean-Claude Galey (ed.), Différences, valeurs, hiérarchie: textes offerts à Louis Dumont, Paris: Editions de l'Ecole des Hautes Etudes en Sciences Sociales.

Howe, L.E.A. 1989. Hierarchy and Equality: Variations in Balinese Social Organization, Bijdragen tot de Taal-, Land- en Volkenkunde 145/1, 47-71.

Howell, Signe 1985. Equality and Hierarchy in Chewong Classification, in Barnes et al. (eds) 1985.

_____ 1990a. Hierarchy and Value: An Introduction, Ethnos 1990/3-4, 137-9.

_____ 1990b. Husband/Wife or Brother/Sister as the Key Relationship in Lio Kinship and Sociosymbolic Relations, Ethnos 1990/3-4, 248-59.

_____ and Roy Willis 1989. Introduction, in Signe Howell and Roy Willis (eds), Societies at Peace: Anthropological Perspectives, London and New York: Routledge.

Hubert, Henri 1905. Etude sommaire de la représentation du temps dans la religion et la magie, Annuaire de l'Ecole Pratique des Hautes Etudes, section des sciences religieuses 1905, 1-39.

_____ and Marcel Mauss 1899. Essai sur la nature et la fonction sociale du sacrifice, Année Sociologique 2, 29-138.

Hughes, Austin L. 1988. Evolution and Human Kinship, New York and Oxford: Oxford University Press.

Ingold, Tim 1986. Comment on Beteille 1986, Current Anthropology 27/2, 129-30.

Irek, M. 1998. Der Schmugglerzug: Warschau—Berlin—Warschau. Materialien einer Feldforschung, Berlin: Das Arabische Buch.

Isambert, François-André, 1982. Le sens du sacré: fête et religion populaire, Paris: Les Editions de Minuit.

Iteanu, André 1980. Qui as tu tué pour demander la main de ma fille? Violence et mariage chez les Ossetes, in R. Verdier (ed.), La Vengeance, Vol. 2, Paris: Cujas.

_____ 1983a. La ronde des échanges: de la circulation aux valeurs chez les Orokaiva, Cambridge and Paris: Cambridge University Press and Editions de la Musée des Sciences de l'Homme.

_____ 1983b. Idéologie patrilinéaire ou idéologie de l'anthropologue?, L'Homme 23/2, 37-55.

_____ 1985. Levels and Convertibility, in Barnes et al. (eds) 1985.

_____ 1990a. The Concept of the Person and the Ritual System: An Orokaiva View, Man 25/1, 35-53.

_____ 1990b. Sacred and Profane Revisited: Durkheim and Dumont Considered in the Orokaiva Context, Ethnos 1990/3-4, 169-83.

_____ 1991. Person, Society and the Ritual System among the Orokaiva [Correspondence with John Barker and William H. McKellin], Man (n.s.) 26/2, 345-8.

_____ 1995. Rituals and Ancestors, in Daniel de Coppet and André Iteanu (eds), Cosmos and Society in Oceania, Oxford and Washington: Berg.

Izikowitz, Karl Gustav 1951. Lamet: Peasants of French Indo-China, Goteborg: Etnologiska Studier 17.

Jamous, Raymond 1981. Honneur et Baraka: les structures sociales traditionelles dans le Rif, Cambridge and Paris; Cambridge University Press and Maison des Sciences de l'Homme.

_____ 1991. La relation frère-soeur: parenté et rites chez les Meo de l'Inde du Nord, Paris: Editions de l'Ecole des Hautes Etudes en Sciences Sociales.

Jayawardene, Chandra 1980. Culture and Etthnicity in Guyana and Fiji, Man 15/4, 430-50.

Jennings, Ivor 1959. Cabinet Government, Cambridge: Cambridge University Press.

Jones, Robert Alun 1986. Emile Durkheim: An Introduction to Four Major Works, Beverly Hills etc.: Sage Publications.

Josephides, Lisette 1995. Replacing Cultural Markers: Symbolic Analysis and Political Action in Melanesia, in Daniel de Coppet and André Iteanu (eds), Cosmos and Society in Oceania, Oxford and Washington: Berg.

Josselin de Jong, J.P.B. de, 1935. De Maleische Archipel als Ethnologisch Studieveld, Leiden: J. Ginsberg.

Josselin de Jong, P.E. de, 1972. Marcel Mauss et les origines de l'anthropologie structurelle hollandaise, L'Homme 12/4, 62-84.

_____ 1976. Review of Needham (ed.) 1973d, Bijdragen tot de Taal-, Land- en Volkenkunde 132/1, 171-4.

_____ 1984. A Field of Anthropological Study in Transformation, in P.E. de Josselin de Jong (ed.), Unity in Diversity: Indonesia as a Field of Anthropological Study, Dordrecht and Cinnaminson: Foris Publications.

Kantorowicz, E.H. 1957. The King's Two Bodies: A Study in Mediaeval Political Theology, Princeton: Princeton University Press.

Kapferer, Bruce 1988. Legends of People, Myths of State: Violence, Intolerance and Political Culture in Sri Lanka and Australia, Washington and London: Smithsonian Institution Press.

Keeler, Ward 1987. Review of Barnes et al. (eds) 1985, American Ethnologist 14/3, 571-2.

Kensinger, Kenneth M. 1984. An Emic Model of Cashinahua Marriage, in Kenneth M. Kensinger (ed.), Marriage Practices in Lowland South America, Urbana and Chicago: University of Illinois Press.

King, Victor 1977. Unity, Formalism and Structure: Comments on Iban Augury and Related Problems, Bijdragen tot de Taal-, Land- en Volkenkunde 133/1, 63-87.

_____ 1980. Structural Analysis and Cognatic Societies: Some Borneo Examples, Sociologus 30/1, 1-28.

Kluckhohn, Clyde 1951. Value and Value-orientation in the Theory of Action: An Exploration in Definition and Classification, in Parsons and Shils (eds) 1951.

Krauskopff, Gisèle 1987. Review of Barnes et al. (eds) 1985, L'Homme 27/1, 162-4.

Kruyt, Alb. C. 1973 [1941]. Right and Left in Central Celebes, in Needham (ed.) 1973d.

Kuper, Adam (ed.) 1992. Conceptualizing Society, London and New York: Routledge.

Kurzweil, Edith 1980. The Age of Structuralism: Lévi-Strauss to Foucault, New York: Columbia University Press.

Leach, E.R. 1954. Political Systems of Highland Burma: A Study of Kachin Social Structure, London: Bell.

Leeuwen-Turnovcova, Girina van 1990. Rechts und Links in Europa: ein Beitrag zur Semantik und Symbolik der Geschlechterpolarität, Wiesbaden: Otto Harrassowitz.

Lehmann, Albrecht 1991. Im Fremden ungewollt zuhaus: Flüchtlinge und Vertriebene in Westdeutschland 1945-1990, Munich: C.H. Beck.

Lévi-Strauss, Claude 1944. Reciprocity and Hierarchy, American Anthropologist 46/2, 266-8.

_____ 1956. Les organisations dualistes existent-elles?, Bijdragen tot de Taal-, Land- en Volkenkunde 112/2, 99-128.

_____ 1963. The Bear and the Barber [Henry Myers Lecture 1962], Journal of the Royal Anthropological Institute 1963, 1-11.

_____ 1966. The Savage Mind, London: Weidenfeld and Nicholson.

_____ 1967. The Myth of Asdiwal, in Edmund Leach (ed.), The Structural Study of Myth and Totemism, London: Tavistock.

_____ 1969 [1949]. The Elementary Structures of Kinship: London: Eyre & Spottiswoode.

_____ 1987. Anthropology and Myth: Lectures 1951-1982, Oxford: Basil Blackwell.

Lévy-Bruhl, Lucien 1985. How Natives Think, Princeton: Princeton University Press (translation of Les fonctions mentales dans les sociétés inférieures, Paris: Alcan 1910).

Lewis, Gilbert 1980. Day of Shining Red: An Essay on Understanding Ritual, Cambridge: Cambridge University Press.

Lienhardt, R.G. 1954. Forms of Thought, in E.E. Evans-Pritchard et al., The Institutions of Primitive Society: A Series of Broadcast Talks, Oxford: Basil Blackwell and Mott.

_____ 1961. Divinity and Experience: The Religion of the Dinka, Oxford: Clarendon Press.

Llobera, Josep R. 1996. The French Ideology? Louis Dumont and the German Conception of the Nation, Nations and Nationalism 2/2, 193-211.

Lloyd, G.E.R. 1966. Polarity and Analogy: Two Types of Argumentation in Early Greek Thought, Cambridge: Cambridge University Press.

Lutkehaus, N. 1990. Hierarchy and 'Heroic Society': Manam Variations in Sepik Social Structure, Oceania 60, 179-97.

Lynch, Owen 1977. Method and Theory in the Sociology of Louis Dumont: A Reply, in Kenneth David (ed.), The New Wind: Changing Identities in South Asia, The Hague and Paris: Mouton.

MacClancy, Jeremy 1993. At Play with Identity in the Basque Arena, in Sharon MacDonald (ed.), Inside European Identities, Providence, R.I. and Oxford: Berg.

Madan, T.N. 1982. For a Sociology of India, in T.N. Madan (ed.), Way of Life—King, Householder, Renouncer: Essays in Honour of

Louis Dumont, Delhi: Vikas, and Paris: Editions de la Maison des Sciences de l'Homme.

Makarius, R., and L. Makarius 1973. Structuralisme ou ethnologie: pour une critique radicale de l'anthropologie de Lévi-Strauss, Paris: Editions Anthropos.

Malamoud, Charles 1982. On the Rhetoric and Semantics of Purusartha, in T.N. Madan (ed.), Way of Life—King, Householder, Renouncer: Essays in Honour of Louis Dumont, Delhi: Vikas, and Paris: Editions de la Maison des Sciences de l'Homme.

Marcus, Julie 1984. Islam, Women and Pollution in Turkey, Journal of the Anthropological Society of Oxford 15/3, 204-18.

Marriott, McKim 1959. Interactional and Attributional Theories of Caste Rank, Man in India 39/2, 92-107.

_____ 1976. Hindu Transactions: Diversity without Dualism, in Bruce Kapferer (ed.) Transactions and Meaning, Philadelphia: Institute for the Study of Human Issues.

Matsunaga, Kazuto 1986. The Importance of the Left Hand in Two Types of Ritual Activity in a Japanese Village, in Joy Hendry and Jonathan Webber (eds), Interpreting Japanese Society: Anthropological Approaches, Oxford: JASO (JASO Occasional Papers 5).

Mauss, Marcel 1920. La notion de nation et d'internationalisme, Proceedings of the Aristotelian Society (n.s.) 20, 242-52.

_____ 1938. Une catégorie de l'esprit humain: la notion de personne, celle de 'moi' [Huxley Memorial Lecture 1938], Journal of the Royal Anthropological Institute 68, 263-81 (reprinted in Mauss 1950).

_____ 1950. Sociologie et anthropologie, Paris: Presses Universitaires Franṭaises.

_____ 1954 [1925]. The Gift: Forms and Functions of Exchange in Archaic Societies, London: Cohen & West (reprinted in Mauss 1950).

_____ 1968, 1969. Oeuvres, Paris: Editions de Minuit (3 vols.).

_____ and Henri Beuchat 1906. Essai sur les variations saisonnières des sociétés eskimos: étude de morphologie sociale, Année Sociologique 9, 39-132 (reprinted in Mauss 1950).

Maybury-Lewis, David 1989. The Quest of Harmony, in Maybury-Lewis and Almagor (eds) 1989.

Maybury-Lewis, David, and Uri Almagor (eds) 1989. The Attraction of Opposites: Thought and Society in the Dualistic Mode, Ann Arbor: The University of Michigan Press.

Mayer, Adrian C. (ed.) 1981. Culture and Morality: Essays in Honour of Christoph von Fürer-Haimendorf, Delhi etc.: Oxford University Press.

McDonald, Maryon 1987. The Politics of Fieldwork in Brittany, in Andrew Jackson (ed.), Anthropology at Home, London and New York: Tavistock (ASA Monographs 25).

_____ 1990. We are not French! Language, Culture, and Identity in
      Brittany, London: Routledge.
McDonaugh, C.E. 1985. The Tharu House: Oppositions and
      Hierarchy, in Barnes et al. (eds) 1985.
_____ 1987. The Tharu House: Deities and Ritual, Etudes
      Himalayennes 1, 261-73.
Middleton, J. 1973. Some Categories of Dual Classification among
      the Lugbara of Uganda, in Needham (ed.) 1973d.
Miller, Jay 1972. Priority of the Left, Man (n.s.) 7/4, 646-7.
Mimica, Jadran 1988. Intimations of Infinity: the Cultural Meaning
      of the Iqwaye Counting System and Number, Oxford etc.: Berg.
Moffat, Michael 1979. An Untouchable Community in South India:
      Structures and Consensus, New Jersey: Princeton University
      Press.
Monnerie, Denis 1995. On 'Grandmothers', 'Grandfathers' and
      Ancestors: Conceptualizing the Universe in Mono-Alu: Solomon
      Islands, in Daniel de Coppet and André Iteanu (eds), Cosmos and
      Society in Oceania, Oxford and Washington: Berg.
Morris, Brian 1987. Anthropological Studies of Religion: An
      Introductory Text, Cambridge: Cambridge University Press.
Mosko, Mark S. 1985. Quadripartite Structures: Categories,
      Relations and Homologies in Bush Mekeo Culture, Cambridge:
      Cambridge University Press.
_____ 1992a. Other Messages, Other Missions; or, Sahlins among the
      Melanesians, Oceania 63/2, 97-113.
_____ 1992b. Motherless Sons: 'Divine Kings' and 'Partible Persons'
      in Melanesia and Polynesia, Man 27/4, 697-717.
_____ 1994a. Transformations of Dumont: The Hierarchical, the
      Sacred and the Profane in India and Ancient Hawaii, History and
      Anthropology 7/1-4, 19-86.
_____ 1994b. Junior Chiefs and Senior Sorcerers: The Contradictions
      and Inversions of Mekeo Hierarchy, History and Anthropology
      7/1-4, 195-222.
Mosse, David 1994. Replication and Consensus among Indian
      Untouchable (Harijan) Castes, Man 29/2, 457-60.
Mousalimas, S.A. 1990. The Concept of Participation in Lévy-
      Bruhl's 'Primitive Mentality', Journal of the Anthropological
      Society of Oxford 21/1, 33-46.
Müller, Jean-Claude 1986. Complementarité, symétrie et hiérarchie:
      les organisations dualistes irigwe et rukuba (Nigéria central),
      Culture 6/2, 33-48.
Nagengast, Carole 1991. Reluctant Socialists, Rural Entrepreneurs:
      Class, Culture, and the Polish State, Boulder, CO: Westview Press.
Needham, Rodney 1958. A Structural Analysis of Purum Society,
      American Anthropologist 60/1, 75-101.
_____ 1959. An Analytical Note on the Kom of Manipur, Ethnos
      24/3-4, 121-35.

_____ 1960a. Alliance and Classification among the Lamet, Sociologus 10/2, 97-119.

_____ 1960b. A Structural Analysis of Aimol Society, Bijdragen tot de Taal-, Land- en Volkenkunde 116/1, 81-108.

_____ 1962a. Structure and Sentiment: A Test Case in Social Anthropology, Chicago and London: The University of Chicago Press.

_____ 1962b. Genealogy and Category in Wikmunkan Society, Ethnology 1/2, 223-64.

_____ 1963. Introduction to Durkheim and Mauss 1963 [1903].

_____ 1966. Terminology and Alliance: 1, Garo, Manggarai, Sociologus 16/2, 141-57.

_____ 1967. Terminology and Alliance: 2, Mapuche, Conclusions, Sociologus 17/1, 39-53.

_____ 1970. Introduction to Hocart 1970.

_____ 1971. Remarks on the Analysis of Kinship and Marriage, in Rodney Needham (ed.), Rethinking Kinship and Marriage, London etc.: Tavistock Publications (ASA Monographs, 11).

_____ 1972. Belief, Language, and Experience, Oxford: Basil Blackwell and Chicago: The University of Chicago Press.

_____ 1973a. Introduction, in Needham (ed.) 1973d.

_____ 1973b [1960]. The Left Hand of the Mugwe: An Analytical Note on the Structure of Meru Symbolism, in Needham (ed.) 1973d.

_____ 1973c [1967]. Right and Left in Nyoro Symbolic Classification, in Needham (ed.) 1973d.

Needham, Rodney 1973d. Right & Left: Essays on Dual Symbolic Classification, Chicago and London: The University of Chicago Press.

_____ 1975. Polythetic Classification: Convergence and Consequences, Man 10, 349-69.

_____ 1976. Nyoro Symbolism: The Ethnographic Record, Africa 46/3, 236-46.

_____ 1978. Primordial Characters, Charlottesville, VA: University of Virginia Press.

_____ 1979a. Symbolic Classification, Santa Monica, CA: Goodyear.

_____ 1979b. Hertz, Robert, International Encyclopedia of the Social Sciences, New York: The Free Press/London: Collier Macmillan (Bibliographical Supplement, Vol. 18, 295-7).

_____ 1980a. Reconnaissances, Toronto: The University of Toronto Press.

_____ 1980b. Diversity, Structure, and Aspect in Manggarai Social Classification, in R. Schefold, J.W. Schoorl and J. Tennekes (eds), Man, Meaning and History: Essays in Honour of H.G. Schulte Nordholt, The Hague: Martinus Nijhoff.

_____ 1981. Circumstantial Deliveries, Berkeley etc.: University of California Press.

_____ 1983. Against the Tranquility of Axioms, Berkeley etc.:
University of California Press.
_____ 1985. Exemplars, Berkeley etc.: University of California Press.
_____ 1987. Counterpoints, Berkeley etc.: University of California
Press.
Ogden, C.K. 1932. Opposition: A Linguistic and Psychological
Analysis, London: Kegan Paul, Trench, Trubner.
Ortner, S.B. 1978. Sherpas through their Rituals, Cambridge:
Cambridge University Press.
_____ 1981. Gender and Sexuality in Hierarchical Societies: The Case
of Polynesia and some Comparative Implications, in Sherry
Ortner and Harriet Whitehead (eds), Sexual Meanings: The
Cultural Construction of Gender and Sexuality, Cambridge:
Cambridge University Press.
Ostor, Akos, and Liza Fruzzetti 1991. For an Ethnosociology of
India?, Contributions to Indian Sociology (new series), 25/2,
309-20.
Otto, Karl A. (ed.) 1990. Westwärts—Heimwärts? Aussiedlerpolitik
zwishen 'Deutschtümelei' und Verfassungsauftrag', Bielefeld:
ArbeiterInnen Jugendzentrum.
Parkin, David 1985. Introduction, in Parkin (ed.) 1985
_____ (ed.) 1985. The Anthropology of Evil, Oxford: Basil Blackwell.
Parkin, Robert 1989. Review of Maurice Bloch, Ritual, History and
Power: Selected Papers in Anthropology, Sociologus 39/2, 187-9.
_____ 1992a. Asymétrie dualiste ou opposition hiérarchique? Le legs
de Robert Hertz dans l'oeuvre de Rodney Needham et de Louis
Dumont, Recherches Sociologiques 23/2, 43-68.
_____ 1992b. The Munda of Central India: An Account of their
Social Organization, Delhi: Oxford University Press.
_____ 1994. Equality, Hierarchy and Temperament, Journal of the
Anthropological Society of Oxford 25/1 (Andrew Duff-Cooper
Memorial Issue), 69-76.
_____ 1995a. The Dark Side of Humanity: The Work of Robert Hertz
and its Legacy, Reading: Harwood Academic Publishers.
_____ 1995b. Review of Quigley 1993, Journal of the
Anthropological Society of Oxford 26/3, 318-19.
_____ 1999 Regional Identities and Alliances in an Integrating
Europe: A Challenge to the Nation State? Oxford: ESRC
Transnational Communities Programme, Working Papers Series.
_____ 2000. Proving 'Indigenity', Exploiting Modernity: Modalities of
Identity Construction in Middle India, Anthropos 95/1, 49-63.
_____ 2002. Perilous Transactions and Other Papers in General and
Indian Anthropology, Bhubaneswar: Institute of Tribal Studies.
Parry, Jonathan 1979, Caste and Kinship in Kangra, London:
Routledge & Kegan Paul.
_____ 1980. Ghosts, Greed and Sin: The Occupational Identity of the
Benares Funeral Priests, Man 15/1, 88-111.

_____ 1985. The Brahmanical Tradition and the Technology of the Intellect, in Joanna Overing (ed.), Reason and Morality, London: Tavistock Press (ASA Monographs 24).

_____ 1989. On the Moral Perils of Exchange, in Parry and Bloch (eds) 1989.

_____ 1991. The Hindu Lexicographer? A Note on Auspiciousness and Purity, Contributions to Indian Sociology (new series), 25/2, 267-85.

_____ 1994. Death in Banares, Cambridge: Cambridge University Press.

_____ and Maurice Bloch (eds) 1989. Money and the Morality of Exchange, Cambridge: Cambridge University Press.

Parsons, Talcott 1975. Some Theoretical Considerations on the Nature and Trends of Change of Ethnicity, in Nathan Glazer and Daniel P. Moynihan (eds), Ethnicity: Theory and Experience, Cambridge, Mass., and London: Harvard University Press.

_____ and Edward A. Shils (eds) 1951. Towards a General Theory of Action, Cambridge, Mass.: Harvard University Press.

Pickering, W.S.F. 1984. Durkheim's Sociology of Religion, London etc.: Routledge & Kegan Paul.

Platenkamp, J.D.M. 1984. The Tobelo of Eastern Halmahera in the Context of the Field of Anthropological Study in P.E. de Josselin de Jong (ed.), Unity in Diversity: Indonesia as a Field of Anthropological Study, Dordrecht and Cinnaminson: Foris Publications.

_____ 1988. Myth of Life and Image in Northern Halmahera, in David S. Moyer and Henri J.M. Claessen (eds), Time Past, Time Present, Time Future: Essays in Honour of P.E. de Josselin de Jong, Dordrecht and Providence (USA): Foris Publications 1988.

_____ 1992. Transforming Tobelo Ritual, in Daniel de Coppet (ed.), Understanding Rituals, London and New York: Routledge.

Pocock, David 1962. Notes on jajmani Relationships, Contributions to Indian Sociology 6, 48-77.

Prince, Ruth, and David Riches 1999. The Holistic Individual: Context as Political Process in the New Age Movement, in Roy Dilley (ed.), The Problem of Context, New York and London: Berghahn.

Quigley, Declan 1992. Le Brahmane pur et le prêtre impur, Recherches Sociologiques 23/2, 69-89.

_____ 1993. The Interpretation of Caste, Oxford: Clarendon Press.

Radcliffe-Brown, A.R. 1950. Introduction, in A.R. Radcliffe-Brown and Daryll Forde (eds), African Systems of Kinship and Marriage, London: Oxford University Press for the International African Institute.

_____ 1952 [1940]. On Social Structure, in A.R. Radcliffe-Brown, Structure and Function in Primitive Society, London: Cohen & West.

Radtke, Frank-Olaf 1990. Reaktiver Nationalismus oder
    Verfassungschauvinismus? Zur Entstehung aversiven Verhaltens
    gegen Zuwanderer im Sozialstaat, in Otto ed. 1990.
Raheja, Gloria Goodwin 1988a. The Poison in the Gift: Ritual,
    Prestation, and the Dominant Caste in a North Indian Village,
    Chicago: The University of Chicago Press.
_____ 1988b. India: Caste, Kingship, and Dominance Reconsidered,
    Annual Review of Anthropology 17, 497-522.
_____ 1989. Centrality, Mutuality and Hierarchy: Shifting Aspects of
    Inter-caste Relationships in North India, Contributions to Indian
    Sociology n.s. 23/1, 79-101.
Rigby, Peter 1973 [1966]. Dual Symbolic Classification among the
    Gogo of Central Tanzania, in Needham (ed.) 1973d.
Sahlins, Marshall 1963. Poor Man, Rich Man, Big-man, Chief:
    Political Types in Melanesia and Polynesia, Comparative Studies
    in Society and History 5, 285-303.
_____ 1985. Islands of History, Chicago: The University of Chicago
    Press.
Salzman, Philip Carl 1978. Does Complementary Opposition Exist?,
    American Anthropologist 80/1, 53-70.
Schärer, H. 1963 [1946]. Ngaju Religion: The Conception of God
    Among a South Borneo People (transl. Rodney Needham), The
    Hague: Martinus Nijhoff.
Scheffler, Harold 1984. Markedness and Extensions: The Tamil Case,
    Man 19/4, 557-74.
Schöeffel, Penelope 1979. Daughters of Sina: A Study of Gender,
    Status and Power in Samoa, Canberra: Australian National
    University (doctoral thesis).
_____ 1987. Rank, Gender and Politics in Ancient Samoa: The
    Genealogy of Salamasina O le Tafa'ifa, Journal of Pacific History
    22/3-4, 174-94.
Schoffeleers, Matthew 1991. Twins and Unilateral Figures in Central
    and Southern Africa: Symmetry and Asymmetry in the
    Symbolization of the Sacred, Journal of Religion in Africa 21/4,
    345-72.
Shore, Bradd 1981. Sexuality and Gender in Samoa: Conceptions
    and Missed Conceptions, in Sherry Ortner and Harriet
    Whitehead (eds), Sexual Meanings: The Cultural Construction of
    Gender and Sexuality, Cambridge: Cambridge University Press.
Sitwell, Osbert 1945, 1946. Left Hand, Right Hand! An
    Autobiography, London: World Books.
Sperber, Dan 1975. Rethinking Symbolism, Cambridge: Cambridge
    University Press.
Srinivas, M.N. 1952. Religion and Society among the Coorgs of
    South India, Oxford: Clarendon Press.
Stanner, W.E.H. 1985. Radcliffe-Brown's Ideas on 'Social Value',
    Social Analysis 17, 113-25.

Stewart, Charles 1994. Honour and Sanctity: Two Levels of Ideology in Greece, Social Anthropology 2/3, 205-28.

Stirrat, R.L. 1989. Money, Men and Women, in Parry and Bloch (eds) 1989.

Strathern, Marilyn 1988. The Gender of the Gift: Problems with Women and Problems with Society in Melanesia, Berkeley etc.: The University of California Press.

_____ 1992. Parts and Wholes: Refiguring Relationships in a Post-plural World, in Kuper (ed.) 1992.

Tambiah, Stanley J. 1989. Ethnic Conflict in the World Today, American Ethnologist 16/2, 335-49.

Tcherkézoff, Serge 1977. Rites et classification nyamwezi, Paris: Diplome d'études approfondies.

_____ 1980. Vengeance et hiérarchie, ou comment un roi doit être nourri, in R. Verdier (ed.), La Vengeance, Volume 2, Paris: Cujas.

_____ 1981. Le rituel dans l'ordre des valeurs: hiérarchie et sacrifice dans les royautés nyamwezi à la fin du XIXe siècle, Paris: Thèse de 3e cycle, Ecole des Hautes Etudes en Sciences Sociales.

_____ 1985a. Black and White Dual Classification: Hierarchy and Ritual Logic in Nyamwezi Ideology, in Barnes et al. (eds) 1985.

_____ 1985b. The Expulsion of Illness or the Domestication of the Dead: A Case Study of the Nyamwezi of Tanzania, History and Anthropology 2, 59-92 (Special Issue on `Interpretating Illness', ed. Marc Augé).

_____ 1986a. Les amendes du roi en pays Nyamwezi: la continuation du sacrifice par d'autres moyens, Droit et Cultures 11, 89-110.

_____ 1986b. Logique rituelle, logique du tout: l'exemple des jumeaux nyamwézi (Tanzanie), L'Homme 26/4, 91-117.

_____ 1987 [1983]. Dual Classification Reconsidered: Nyamwezi Sacred Kingship and Other Examples, Cambridge: Cambridge University Press.

_____ 1989. Rituel et royauté sacrée: la double figure du 'père', in A. Muxel and J.-M. Rennes (eds), Le père, métaphore paternelle et fonctions du père: L'interdit, la filiation, la transmission, Paris: Denoël.

_____ 1991a. Le serment individuelle chez les Nyamwezi: la mort réunit les ennemis jurés et sépare les amis fidèles, in R. Verdier (ed.), Le Serment, Paris: Editions du CNRS.

_____ 1991b. Review of Michel Carty (ed.), Sous le masque de l'animal: essais sur le sacrifice en Afrique noire, L'Homme 31/1, 180-3.

_____ 1993a. The Illusion of Dualism in Samoa: 'Brothers-and-sisters' are not 'Men-and-women', in Teresa del Valle (ed.), Gendered Anthropology, London: Routledge.

_____ 1993b. Une hypothèse sur la valeur du 'prix de la fiancée' nyamwézi, in Françoise Héritier-Augé and Elizabeth Copet-Rougier (eds), Les complexités d'alliance, Volume 3: Economie, politique et fondements symboliques de l'alliance (Afrique), Paris: Editions des Archives Contemporaines.

_____ 1993/94. L'''individualisme' chez Louis Dumont et l'anthropologie des idéologies globales: genèse du point de vue comparatif, Anthropologie et Sociétés 17/3, 141-58; 18/1, 203-22.

_____ 1994. On Hierarchical Reversals, Ten Years Later, Journal of the Anthropological Society of Oxford 25/2, 133-67; 25/3, 229-53.

_____ 1994/95. L'inclusion du contraire (L. Dumont), la hiérarchie enchevêtrée (J.P. Dupuy) et le rapport sacré/pouvoir: relectures et révision des modèles à propos de l'Inde, Culture 24/2, 113-34; 25/1, 33-47.

_____ 1995. La totalité durkheimienne (Emile Durkheim et Robert Hertz): un modèle holiste du rapport 'sacré/profane', L'Ethnographie 91/1, 53-69.

Toren, Christina 1989. Drinking Cash: The Purification of Money through Ceremonial Exchange in Fiji, in Parry and Bloch (eds) 1989.

_____ 1990. Making Sense of History: Cognition as Social Process in Fiji, London: Athlone Press.

_____ 1994a. All things go in Pairs, or the Sharks will bite: The Antithetical Nature of Fijian Chiefship, Oceania 64/3, 197-216.

_____ 1994b. Transforming Love: Representing Fijian Hierarchy, in P. Gow and P. Harvey (eds), Sex and Violence: Issues in Representation and Experience, London and New York: Routledge.

_____ 1995. Cosmogonic Aspects of Desire and Compassion in Fiji, in Daniel de Coppet and André Iteanu (eds), Cosmos and Society in Oceania, Oxford and Washington: Berg.

Trager, George L. 1939. 'Cottonwood' = 'Tree': A Southwestern Linguistic Trait, International Journal of American Linguistics 9, 117-18.

Traube, Elizabeth G. 1980. Affines and the Dead: Mambai Rituals of Alliance, Bijdragen tot de Taal-, Land- en Volkenkunde 136/1, 90-115.

_____ 1989. Obligations to the Source: Complementarity and Hierarchy in an Eastern Indonesian Society, in Maybury-Lewis and Almagor (eds) 1989.

Trautmann, Thomas 1981. Dravidian Kinship, Cambridge: Cambridge University Press.

Turner, Terence 1984. Dual Opposition, Hierarchy, and Value: Moiety Structure and Symbolic Polarity in Central Brazil and Elsewhere, in Jean-Claude Galey (ed.) Différences, valeurs, hiérarchie: textes offerts à Louis Dumont, Paris: Editions de l'Ecole des Hautes Etudes en Sciences Sociales.

Turner, Victor 1966. Colour Classification in Ndembu Ritual, in Michael Banton (ed.), Anthropological Approaches to the Study of Religion, London: Tavistock Publications (ASA Monographs 3).

Uberoi, J.P.S. 1984. The Other Mind of Europe: Goethe as a Scientist, Delhi: Oxford University Press.

Urban, Thomas 1994. Deutsche in Polen: Geschichte und Gegenwart einer Minderheit, Munich: C.H. Beck.

Valeri, Valerio 1985. Kingship and Sacrifice: Ritual and Society in Ancient Hawaii, Chicago: The University of Chicago Press.

_____ 1989. Reciprocal Centers: The Siwa-Lima System in the Central Moluccas, in Maybury-Lewis and Almagor (eds) 1989.

_____ 1990. Autonomy and Heteronomy in the Kahua Ritual: A Short Meditation on Huaulu Society, Bijdragen tot de Taal-, Land-en Volkenkunde 146/1, 56-73.

van der Kroef, Justus M. 1954. Dualism and Symbolic Antithesis in Indonesian Society, American Anthropologist 56, 847-62.

Visser, Leontine E. 1988. The Elder and the Younger: Dual Opposition and a Hierarchy of Values, in David S. Moyer and Henri J.M. Claessen (eds), Time Past, Time Present, Time Future: Essays in Honour of P.E. de Josselin de Jong, Dordrecht and Providence (USA): Foris Publications 1988.

Vogt, W. Paul 1983. Durkheimian Sociology versus Philosophical Radicalism: The Case of Célestin Bouglé, in Philippe Besnard (ed.), The Sociological Domain: The Durkheimians and the Founding of French Sociology, Cambridge and Paris; Cambridge University Press and Maison des Sciences de l'Homme.

Warner, W. Lloyd 1958. A Black Civilization, New York: Harper and Brothers.

Watson, C.W. 2000. Multiculturalism, Buckingham and Philadelphia: Open University Press.

White, C.M.N. 1961. Elements in Luvale Belief and Rituals, Manchester: Manchester University Press (Rhodes-Livingstone Papers no. 32).

White, Jenny B. 2000. Kinship, Reciprocity and the World Market, in Peter P. Schweizer (ed.), Dividends of Kinship: Meanings and Uses of Social Relatedness, London and New York: Routledge.

White, John 1887-90. Ancient History of the Maori: His Mythology and Traditions, Wellington (6 vols.).

Willis, Roy 1975. Review of Needham (ed.) 1973d, Man 10/3, 489-90.

_____ 1985. Do the Fipa Have a Word For It?, in David Parkin (ed.) 1985.

_____ 1989. The 'Peace Puzzle' in Ufipa, in Signe Howell and Roy Willis (eds), Societies at Peace: Anthropological Perspectives, London and New York: Routledge.

Wouden, F.A.E. van, 1968 [1935]. Types of Social Structure in Eastern Indonesia (translated by Rodney Needham), The Hague: Martinus Nijhoff.

Zaehner, R.C. 1961. The Dawn and the Twilight of Zoroastrianism,
   London: Weidenfeld & Nicolson.
Zanen, Sj. M., and A.W. van den Hoek 1987. Dinka Dualism and the
Nilotic Hierarchy of Values, in R. de Ridder and J.A.J. Karremans
(eds), The Leiden Tradition in Structural Anthropology: Essays in
Honour of P.E. de Josselin de Jong, Leiden etc.: E.J. Brill.

INDEX

NAMES

SUBJECT